EMPOWERING

INTELLECTUAL PROPERTY

BEST PRACTICES FOR

INNOVATORS, MANAGERS,

AND INVESTORS

SECOND EDITION

MICHAEL N. HAYNES

Empowering Intellectual Property
Best Practices for Innovators, Managers, and Investors
Second Edition

ISBN-13: 978-0-9837619-1-4
Printed in U.S.A.
Published by Strategia Publishing
Design, Graphics, & Editorial Assistance: Kelly B. Smoker

To my clients, team, and family.

Jan. 11, 1927.

L. F. HERRESHOFF

1,613,890

SAIL BOAT

Filed Dec. 11, 1925

3 Sheets—Sheet 1

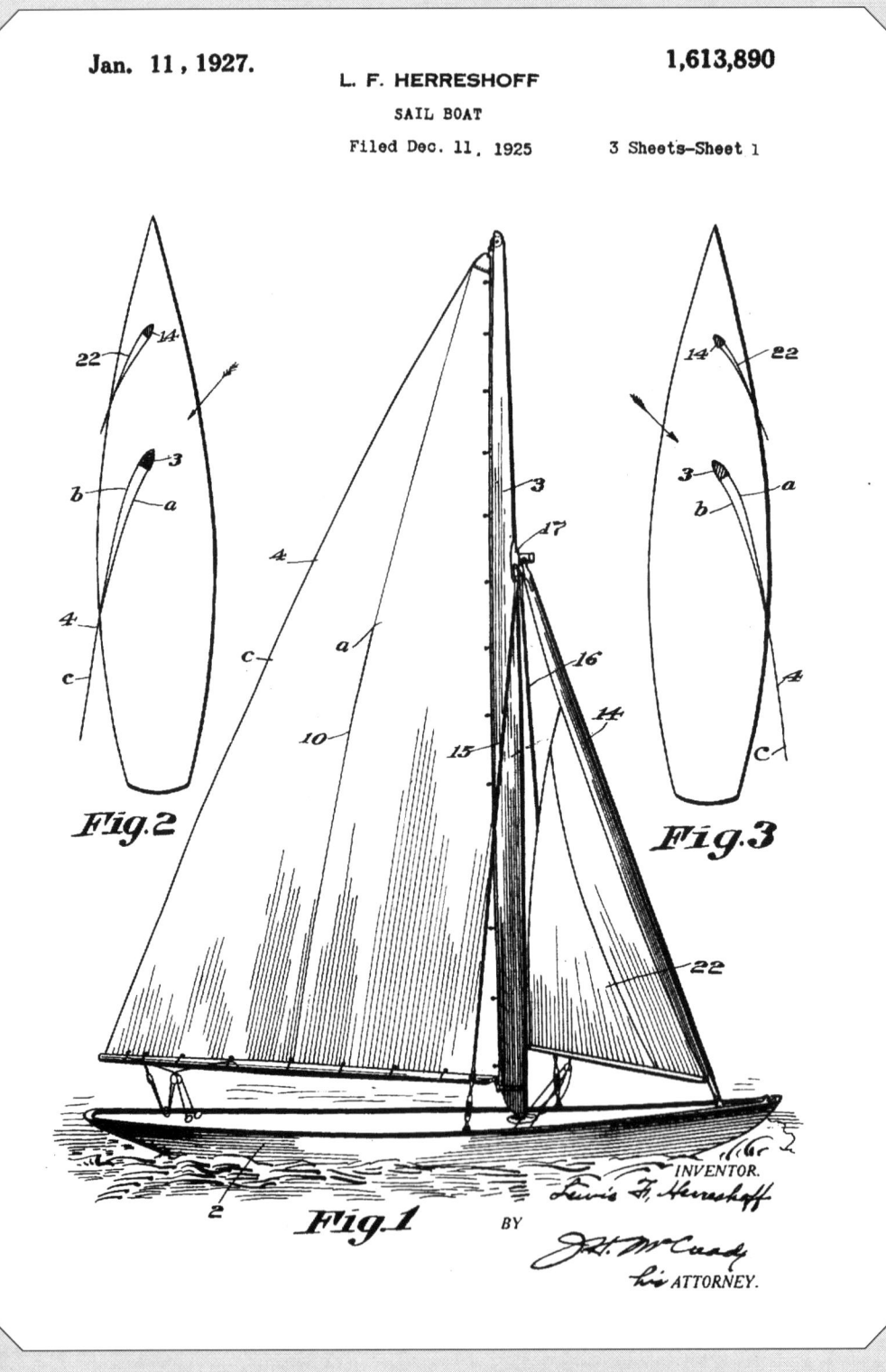

Fig.2

Fig.3

Fig.1

INVENTOR.

Lewis F. Herreshoff

BY

J.H. McCuadg

his ATTORNEY.

CONTENTS

CONTENTS

CONTENTS

Step 6 – Enhance 271

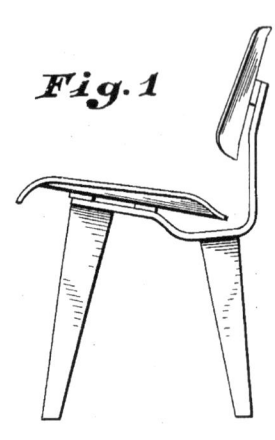

Fig.1

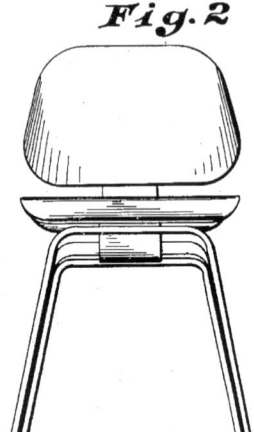

Fig.2

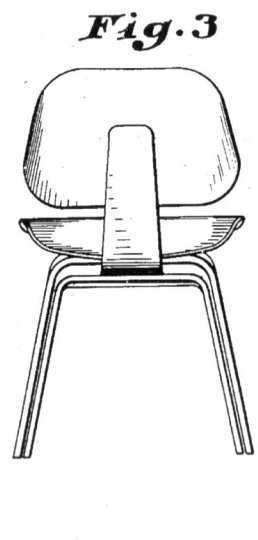

Fig.4

Fig.3

Inventor

Charles Eames

By Lyon & Lyon Attorneys

Acknowledgements

This book would not have been possible without the unwavering support of my family, who has graciously granted me the tremendous amount of time needed to research, write, and organize the content you hold in your hands.

I am also enormously appreciative of my team members at Michael Haynes PLC, who have edited my drafts, offered immeasurably helpful insights and feedback, and loyally served my firm for many years.

Finally, I thank my clients, who have presented me with innumerable challenges, real-world problems, and thought-provoking learning opportunities. Much of the wisdom that I've gained from those experiences is summarized in these pages.

W. PAINTER.
BOTTLE SEALING DEVICE.

No. 468,226.   Patented Feb. 2, 1892.

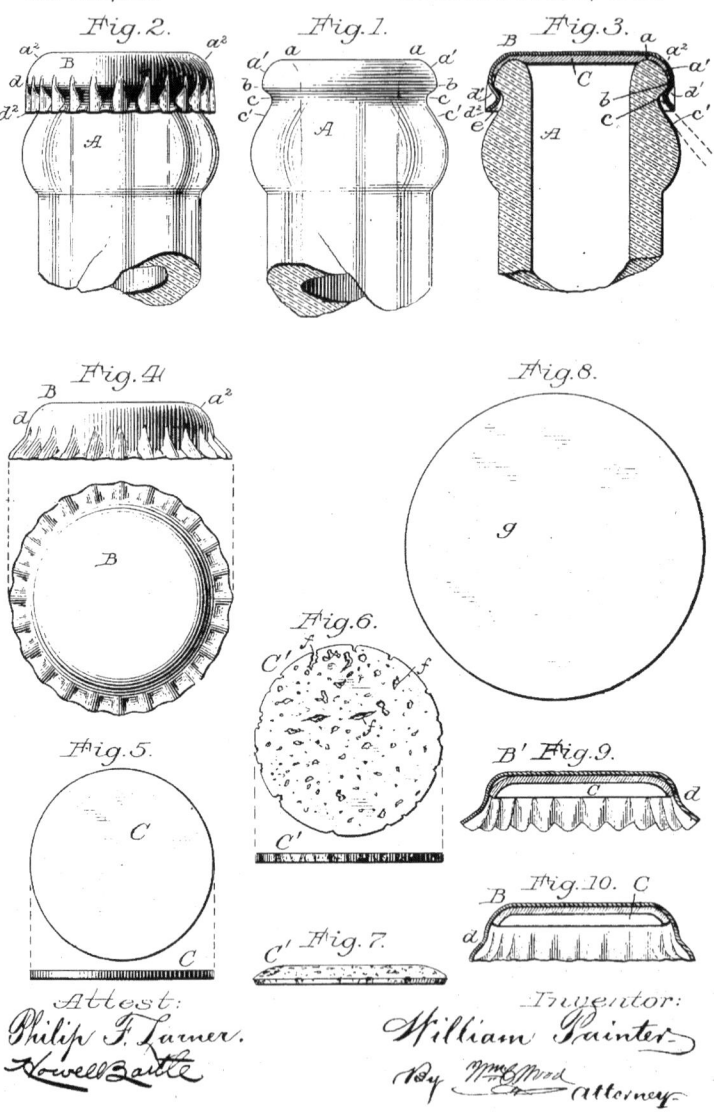

Fig. 2.   Fig. 1.   Fig. 3.

Fig. 4.   Fig. 8.

Fig. 6.

Fig. 5.   Fig. 9.

Fig. 7.   Fig. 10.

Attest:
Philip F. Larner.
Howell Bartle

Inventor:
William Painter
By Wm. C. Wood
Attorney

Forward

I started writing this book's content over a decade ago, as an intermittent series of messages that I sent via e-mail to myself, those messages containing tips, caselaw citations, and learning experiences regarding various intellectual property-related legal and business issues. From there, the information was compiled on my firm's website, and in various guidelines that I shared with my clients from time to time. As new situations have arisen, and as the legal and business climates have evolved, I have continually updated and organized this information, a sampling of which can be found on my website as a set of free Guides.

This book builds substantially on the content of those Guides. After looking it over, I hope you will agree that it provides a rather complete summary of best practices that can allow you to strongly position your company to extract the maximum value from its intellectual property portfolio, avoid wasting thousands of dollars and hundreds of hours, and bypass unnecessary risks that can destroy that value.

So with that background, let's get started.

(12) **United States Patent**

Trevino

(10) **Patent No.:** **US 6,655,077 B1**

(45) **Date of Patent:** **Dec. 2, 2003**

(54) **TRAP FOR A MOUSE**

(76) Inventor: **Jose Trevino**, 7556 Alameda Ave., El Paso, TX (US) 79915

(*) Notice: Subject to any disclaimer, the term of this patent is extended or adjusted under 35 U.S.C. 154(b) by 0 days.

(21) Appl. No.: **10/197,961**

(22) Filed: **Jul. 17, 2002**

(51) Int. Cl.⁷ **A01M 23/30**

(52) U.S. Cl. **43/81**; 43/81.5

(58) Field of Search 43/81, 81.5, 88, 43/92, 82, 83.5, 97, 58

(56) **References Cited**

U.S. PATENT DOCUMENTS

1,167,493 A	*	1/1916	Grubbs	43/81
1,223,271 A	*	4/1917	Grubbs	43/81
1,623,841 A	*	4/1927	King	43/81
1,799,323 A	*	4/1931	Ross et al.	43/81
2,188,297 A	*	1/1940	Graybill	43/81
2,216,529 A	*	10/1940	Brzykcy	43/81
2,231,984 A	*	2/1941	Anderson	43/81
2,581,628 A	*	1/1952	Burwell	43/81
2,616,211 A	*	11/1952	Johnson	43/81
3,968,589 A	*	7/1976	Basham	43/81
4,071,972 A	*	2/1978	Conibear	43/92
4,245,423 A		1/1981	Souza et al.	
4,574,519 A		3/1986	Eckebrecht	

4,592,162 A	*	6/1986	Hallback	43/81
4,711,049 A		12/1987	Kness	
5,001,857 A	*	3/1991	McDaniel et al.	43/81
5,148,624 A		9/1992	Schmidt	
6,119,391 A		9/2000	Maconga	
6,137,415 A	*	10/2000	Rast	43/81
6,199,314 B1		3/2001	Ballard	
6,282,832 B1		9/2001	Manno	

FOREIGN PATENT DOCUMENTS

GB	2209113 A	*	5/1989	A01M/23/24

* cited by examiner

Primary Examiner—Peter M. Poon
Assistant Examiner—Joan M. Olszewski
(74) *Attorney, Agent, or Firm*—Richard L. Miller

(57) **ABSTRACT**

An improved trap for a mouse of the type having a baseboard, a U-shaped jaw member that is pivotally mounted on the baseboard for pivotal movement from a cocked position to a sprung position, a bait pedal that is attached to the baseboard, and a trigger mechanism that has a longitudinal axis and which is operatively attached to the bait pedal and when the U-shaped jaw member is in the cocked position thereof the trigger mechanism is operatively connected to the U-shaped jaw member. The improvement includes the trigger mechanism allowing the U-shaped jaw member to achieve the sprung position thereof only when the trigger mechanism is rotated about the longitudinal axis thereof.

7 Claims, 1 Drawing Sheet

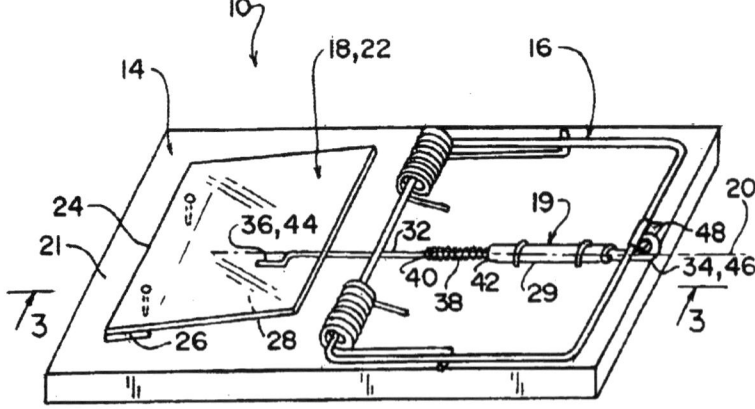

Overview

If you really want to strongly position your company* to extract the maximum value from its intellectual property portfolio, avoid wasting thousands of dollars and hundreds of hours, and bypass unnecessary risks that can destroy that value, this book describes best practices that can truly help you. Its content is divided into these **7** fundamental steps:

1. **Understand** why your company's sustained profitability almost inevitably depends on its successful exploitation of the intellectual properties that protect its most valuable innovations, know-how, and brands.

2. **Strategize** the best ways to align and manage your company's innovation process, intellectual assets, and IP, so that you can continually identify, enhance, and extract their full value.

3. **Survey** potential customer needs, market and technology trends, innovation opportunities, under-protected assets, threatening activities, infringements, and strategic relationships.

4. **Innovate** valuable solutions that can meaningfully differentiate your company from its competitors and lead to sustained profitability.

5. **Secure** your company's distinctive market position, such as by capturing and strongly protecting its intellectual assets, acquiring valuable intellectual properties, and avoiding infringements.

6. **Enhance** your company's intellectual assets, such as via careful analysis, valuation, and filtering, to optimize their value, and prepare your company to extract all of that value.

7. **Harness** the full value of each of your company's intellectual assets, by applying any of my **70+** tactics.

   ** Whether the company is your investment, employer, or client, **you** can make a big difference in how well its IP is managed.*

H. HOLLERITH.
ART OF COMPILING STATISTICS.

No. 395,782.　　　　　　　　　　Patented Jan. 8, 1889.

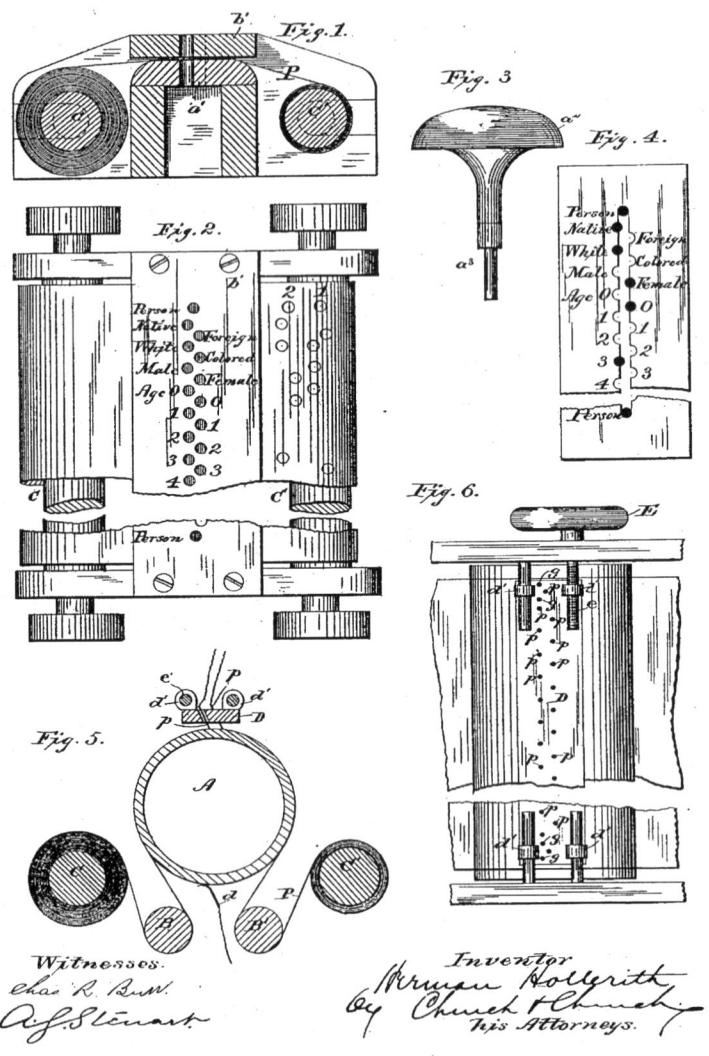

Witnesses.
Chas. R. Bull.
A. L. Stewart.

Inventor
Herman Hollerith
By Church & Church
his Attorneys.

STEP 1

UNDERSTAND

If you really want to **understand** why your company's sustained profitability almost inevitably depends on its successful exploitation of the intellectual properties that protect its most valuable innovations, know-how, and brands, then this section was written for you.

What you'll learn

- ▸ What really impacts profitability?
- ▸ What enables sustained profitability?
- ▸ How vital is intellectual property to sustaining profitability?
- ▸ What is the intellectual capital management model?
- ▸ What are the fundamental steps of the innovation process?
- ▸ How can IP protect innovations, know-how, and brands?
- ▸ In what basic ways can IP be exploited for profit?

1

Achieving Profitability – Innovate

When most business people talk about profitability, that is, the ability to earn financial profits, they tend to focus on the economic contributions of commonly-recognized components of operational effectiveness, such as product or service features, cost, price, sales volume, quality, service, and relationships. Certain measurements of these components can address how well a business has performed its chosen activities with respect to its rivals. Occasionally, business folks mention how profits are affected by strategic positioning, that is, what activities the business has chosen to perform, and in particular, how its selected activities differ from those of its rivals. Sometimes, the conversation turns to the impact of competitive forces, which includes the activities associated with the incessant jockeying for position among current competitors. Much less frequently discussed, competitive forces also include the threat of new market entrants, the leverage of suppliers, the threat of substitute products or services, and the bargaining power of customers.

Of course, merely *achieving* profitability is rarely the motivation for prolonged conversation. Instead, the supreme goal, the consuming desire, and the most intense craving is nearly always for _sustained profitability_, which is so richly rewarded, yet so difficult to obtain. Surprisingly however, when experts talk about sustained profitability and the challenges of obtaining it, they point out that *simply improving operational effectiveness alone is usually futile*. Yet that's the most commonly followed path among those striving for sustained profitability.

For example, one of the foremost authorities on strategy and competition, Dr. Michael Porter, who is a Professor of Business Administration at the Harvard Business School, wrote in his McKinsey Award-winning article that:

> *"**constant improvement in operational effectiveness**
> is necessary to achieve superior profitability. However, it*

is **not usually sufficient**. *Few companies have competed successfully on the basis of operational effectiveness over an extended period, and staying ahead of rivals gets harder every day. The most* **obvious reason** *for that* **is the rapid diffusion of best practices. Competitors can quickly imitate** *management techniques, new technologies, input improvements, and superior ways of meeting customers' needs."* [1]

Professor Porter also recognized that strategic positioning is insufficient to ensure sustained profitability, stating:

"Choosing a unique position... is not enough to guarantee a sustainable advantage. **A valuable position will attract imitation....**" [2]

So what *is* the answer? Is the quest for sustained profitability truly hopeless, and doomed to failure? Experience and casual observation teach us that the correct answer is an emphatic "NO!" Certainly a least a few companies have achieved sustained profitability, at least for a reasonably prolonged period of time (Apple, Google, GE, and lots of smaller companies quickly come to mind).

So what then, are the requirements for achieving sustained profitability?

In one of his earlier works on competitive forces, Professor Porter provides a few hints at the answer:

"The key to growth—even survival—is to stake out a position that is less vulnerable to attack from head-to-head opponents, whether established or new, and less vulnerable to erosion from the direction of buyers, suppliers, and substitute goods. Establishing such a position can take many forms – solidifying relationships with favorable customers, **differentiating the product** *either substantively or psychologically through marketing, integrating forward or backward, [or]*

3

establishing technological leadership." [3]

Professor Porter also suggests that:

> "**A company can outperform rivals only if it can establish a difference that it can preserve**. It must deliver greater value to customers or create comparable value at a lower cost, or do both. The arithmetic of superior profitability then follows: delivering greater value allows a company to charge higher average unit prices; greater efficiency results in lower average unit costs." [4]

Finally, Professor Porter gives us this vital clue:

> "**Innovation is the central issue** in economic prosperity."

But what does Porter mean by "central issue"? Is innovation the answer, or is it the problem? Is innovation both necessary, and *sufficient*, to achieve sustained profitability?

Sustaining Profitability – Own The Profits

Let's assume that Professor Porter is right, that innovation is *the* "central issue" in economic prosperity. What does that really tell us? Practically speaking, if best practices rapidly diffuse, competitors quickly imitate, and the key to survival is to stake out a less vulnerable position, exactly how does one do that?

To find the bottom line answer, we turn to some different experts, Mark Blaxill and Ralph Eckardt. Here's what they say:

> "the key to competitive advantage is to own the distinctive parts of your business that create value. And **the only way to truly own your distinction is through intellectual property**.... With the right IP, companies can command premium prices, increase market share, sustain lower costs, and even generate income directly. Without it, their

4

> products (and services) lack **differentiation**, and they can only compete on price. Businesses that have no IP are, by definition, "commodity" businesses that, no matter how well run, lack any sustainable edge, and are destined to limp along on razor-thin margins, subject to the vagaries of supply and demand." [5]

These guys should know what they're talking about. Blaxill is the former senior vice president of Boston Consulting Group, which trumpets itself as the "world's leading advisor on business strategy". Eckardt is the former head of the Boston Consulting Group's intellectual property strategy practice. In their excellent book, *"The Invisible Edge – Taking Your Strategy to the Next Level Using Intellectual Property"*, Blaxill and Eckardt provide plenty of compelling evidence and powerful arguments to support their views. For example, they explain that:

> "Any business strategy not built around intellectual property is no strategy at all. Why? Well, **without intellectual property protection a business can have no sustainable advantage over its competitors**. Without sustainable competitive advantage, the odds of developing and sustaining outstanding profit performance plummet. Without an expectation of outstanding profit performance, businesses have little incentive to invest in innovation. Without innovation, the opportunity for growth vanishes. And without growth opportunities, the potential for wealth creation and generating high returns for shareholders disappears. Just about any way you look at it, **a modern business needs to place intellectual property strategy close to the center of any strategic plan. Anything else amounts to negligence**." [6]

Wow. Strong words indeed. Here's a few more.

> "After years of experience in the strategy development

*process, we have become convinced that **intellectual property protection is the missing ingredient in most executives' strategy toolkit**. They don't talk about it much, they don't think about it enough, and they don't know how to manage it very well and as a result their business performance suffers. But **the evidence is clear** if you take a hard look at business performance: **highest business returns go to intellectual property-based businesses** and that outstanding profit performance results directly from the limited market power that valuable intellectual property provides. Indeed, these profit results are well deserved, for **it is the companies who innovate rapidly and compete aggressively that profit the most**. Yet as we know, when competitors smell profits they come running, so **without some form of protection, those competitors will quickly copy the innovations and drive the profits (for both the innovator and themselves) down to nothing**." [7]*

Finally, Blaxill and Eckardt reveal that:

"In hindsight it seems obvious – intellectual property is the indispensable but unheralded key to understanding businesses, markets, and economies in the modern era.... IP is rapidly becoming the central foundation of businesses and markets, the most precious resource in the world, and the most important source of newly minted wealth...." [8]

So perhaps it should come as no surprise that

"[c]onservative estimates say that annual intellectual capital investments have grown exponentially to more than $1 trillion in the United States". [9]

Of course, investors also have a nose for profits, and high expectations of achieving them. So with investments of that magnitude, it becomes clear why Blaxill and Eckardt loudly proclaim, and strongly justify, that "*whoever owns the IP owns the profits*". [10]

My decades of business and legal experiences suggest a very similar observation. ***You must own the IP to own the profits.***

For example, in the last few years, I have helped close several deals valued at over $10 million that revolved around patent portfolios that I built for my clients. Each of those clients was very pleased with the outcome, since they realized tremendous profits on their IP. Once again, the message is clear: ***You must own the IP to own the profits.***

Let's take a look at why that rule seems to be almost universally true.

Recognizing the Extent of IP's Impact

If you want a little more evidence of the importance of IP, not just to individual companies, but even to the entire U.S. economy, consider a few broad statistics:

- IP-intensive industries accounted for approximately 60 percent of total U.S. exports from 2000-07 – rising from $665 billion in 2000 to $910 billion in 2007. In that time period, American firms exported an annual average $405.5 billion of IP-intensive products versus $278.1 billion of non-IP-intensive products. [11]

- In 2010, intangible assets were responsible for 80% of the market value of the S&P 500 companies. [12]

- U.S. intellectual property is worth between $5.0 trillion and $5.5 trillion – roughly 45% of gross domestic product (GDP) and more than the GDP of any other country. [13]

- IP-intensive industries directly account for 27.1 million American jobs. That's 18.8 percent of all U.S. employment. These jobs also indirectly support an additional 12.9 million more supply chain jobs, such that every two jobs in IP-intensive industries supports an additional job somewhere else in the economy. [14]

- During 2000-07, the annual salary of all workers in IP-intensive industries averaged about 60 percent higher than the workers at similar levels in non-IP-intensive industries. Even annual salaries of low-skilled workers in IP-intensive industries averaged 40 percent higher than in non-IP-based industries. IP jobs include all educational levels, skills levels, demographics, and industrial sectors. [15]

- In 2010, the hourly wage of workers in patent-intensive industries was 73% higher than that of workers in non-IP intensive industries. [16]

Modeling Intellectual Capital Management

To better understand the relationships between knowledge, innovation, and intellectual property, and particularly how they are connected to sustained profitability, I have developed this pyramid-style model of Intellectual Capital Management:

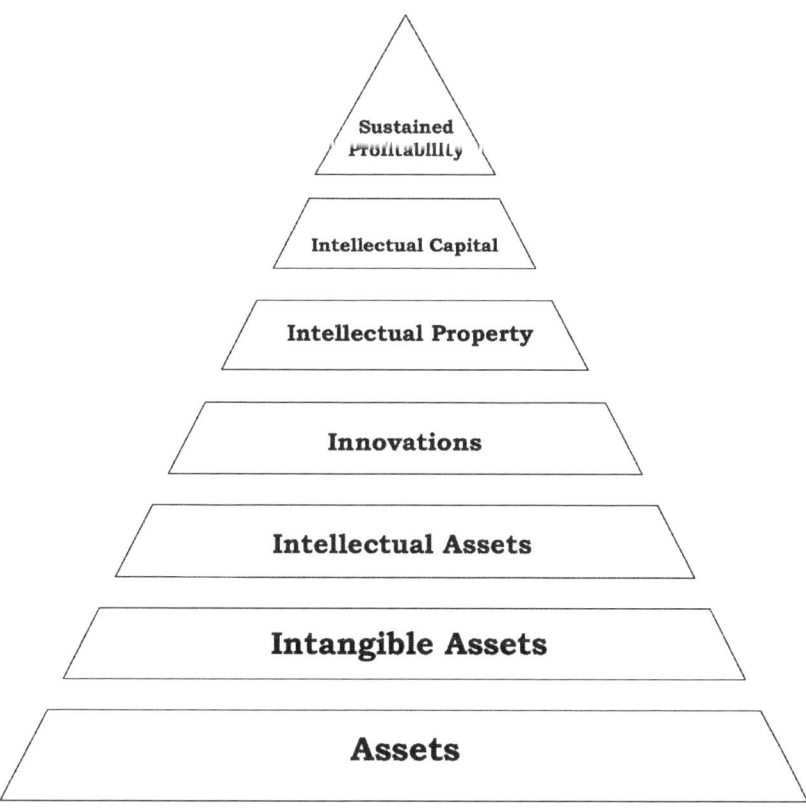

As shown, at the base or level 1 of this pyramid are **Assets,** which include tangible, monetary, and intangible assets. Nearly every business person is intimately familiar with tangible and monetary assets. Tangible assets include a company's land, buildings, equipment, inventory, and supplies. Monetary assets include the company's cash, accounts receivables, and bank balances.

But of the 3 types of assets, probably the most important to this model are **Intangible Assets,** which are shown on level 2. As a rough measure of their relative significance, consider that nearly a decade ago, the U.S. Federal Reserve Bank of Philadelphia estimated that annual U.S. investment in intangible assets had steadily increased to over $1 trillion dollars per year, and roughly 20 years ago overtook U.S. investment in tangible assets.

So what are intangible assets? Intangible assets are non-monetary things of potential value that typically are thought of as not requiring physical storage space. Examples include a company's knowledge, skills, data, software, organizational structure, employee motivation and flexibility, R&D, legal and marketing activities, brands, reputation, goodwill, agreements, and relationships, etc. I have identified over 40 such examples in 7 major categories, and I'm happy to share them on request.

One of the more notable and broad classes of intangible assets is "*knowledge*", which is the understanding of a topic obtained by education, experience, and/or insight. In recent years, many companies have discovered and harnessed substantial opportunities involving "*Knowledge Management*", which I define as the systematic and disciplined strategies and processes for proactively creating, gathering, filtering, organizing, representing, disseminating, leveraging, and using knowledge, potentially originating from any source, to make decisions, cause action, and generate value.

Moving up to level 3, some intangible assets can be codified, that is, recorded (via text, graphics, photo, audio, video, animation, etc.) so they can be perceived later in time. If they provide value to a company, such codified intangible assets are referred to as **Intellectual Assets**, and can include knowledge, brands, and agreements.

At level 4 are **Innovations**, which are new intellectual assets, associated with goods and/or services, that typically result from the Innovation Process. I define the "*Innovation Process*" as the act of introducing something new (such as a new or improved product or service) for economic benefit, based on the application and integration of existing intangible assets, such as knowledge, relationships, and/or attitudes to generate new intellectual assets ("innovations") that are associated with (embodied in, branded/labeled on, etc.) the newly introduced thing.

Rising higher up the model, we next come to level 5, **Intellectual Property**. Simply stated, intellectual properties are legally protected, or owned, intellectual assets. Such legal protection typically arises in the form of patents, marks, and copyrights. The owner of such protected intellectual assets holds legally enforceable property rights in those assets. That is, the owner can seek damages from infringers (which are analogous to "trespassers") of those property rights.

Nevertheless, only a minority of all intellectual properties have significant value, so at level 6 we find **Intellectual Capital**, which is significantly valuable intellectual property. On a closely related note, I refer to the systematic and disciplined strategies and processes for proactively extracting the value inherent in a company's valuable intellectual properties as "Intellectual Capital Management".

When performed well, I argue that Intellectual Capital Management (along with strong management of the Innovation Process, intellectual assets, and IP) can lead to golden level 7, **Sustained Profitability**. Expressed most optimistically, this level represents the state of continuously earning above-market net profits throughout the life of a company.

So finally, there it is... at the top of the pyramid... the holy grail of nearly every company... ***Sustained Profitability***... that state of continuously earning above-market net profits throughout the life of a company.

Wow. Sounds great... if you can get it!

But what specifically must a company do to achieve sustained profitability? To learn more about Intellectual Capital Management and how it can lead to Sustained Profitability, let's first take a closer look at level 4, Innovations, and the Innovation Process that facilitates them.

Managing the Innovation Process

Before describing the fundamental steps of the Innovation Process, let's consider what exactly IP protects, and answer a fundamental question: **What is innovation?**

Here's what a few experts say:

☛ *"Creativity is thinking up new things. Innovation is doing new things."*

> Theodore Levitt (1925-2006), marketing expert, Professor at Harvard Business School, and four-time winner of the McKinsey Awards competitions for best annual article in the Harvard Business Review.

☛ *"Innovation is the process of turning ideas into manufacturable and marketable form."*

> Watts Humphrey, Vice President of IBM, Professor at Carnegie Mellon, recipient of the National Medal of Technology, and sometimes called "the father of software quality".

☛ *"Usually, managers equate innovation with creativity. But innovation is not creativity. Creativity is about coming up with the big idea. Innovation is about executing the idea – converting the idea into a successful business."*

> Vijay Govindarajan, Chief Innovation Consultant to General Electric, Professor of International Business at Dartmouth College, and one of the world's leading experts on strategy and innovation.

☛ *"'Innovation' is not just inventions; it is a process of making changes by introducing valuable new methods, ideas, or products.... Innovations may of course be inventions, but they may also be beliefs, organizational methods, and discoveries. An innovation is a value-creation mechanism. It is the way we humans manage to extract more value".*

> Lawrence Husick, *From Stone to Silicon: A Brief Survey of Innovation*, Footnotes, The Newsletter of

the Foreign Policy Research Institute's Wachman Center, October 2008.

☛ *"Innovation [is] defined broadly as the application of knowledge in a novel way primarily for economic benefit".*
> Susan Rose, Stephanie Shipp, Bhavya Lal and Alexandra Stone of the Science and Technology Policy Institute, *Frameworks for Measuring Innovation: Initial Approaches*, March 2009.

☛ *"Innovation – the process by which individuals and organizations generate new ideas and put them into practice – is the foundation of American economic growth and national competitiveness".*
> National Economic Council, Council of Economic Advisers, and Office of Science and Technology Policy, *A Strategy for American Innovation: Securing our Economic Growth and Prosperity*, 2011.

☛ *"Innovation is the design, invention, development, and/or implementation of new or altered products, services, processes, systems, organizational structures, or business models for the propose of creating new value for customers and financial returns for the firm."*
> United States Department of Commerce (DOC), Advisory Committee on Measuring Innovation in the 21st Century Economy. *Innovation Measurement: Tracking the State of Innovation in the American Economy*. Report to the Secretary of Commerce, 2008.

These quotes should enrich your view of what innovation is, but to be complete, here's another fundamental and closely related question we ought to briefly investigate: **Why is innovation so important?**

Again we turn first to some experts for their insights:

☛ ***"Innovation distinguishes** between a leader and a follower."*
> Steve Jobs, Founder and CEO of Apple, Inc.

☞ **"Innovation** *is the specific instrument of entrepreneurship... the act that **endows** resources with **a new capacity to create wealth.**"*

> Peter Drucker (1909 - 2005), one of the best-known and most widely influential thinkers and writers on the subject of management theory and practice, *Innovation and Entrepreneurship*, 1985.

☞ *"We recognize that the American economy is changing in fundamental ways—and that **most** of this **change relates directly to innovation**".*

> United States Department of Commerce (DOC), Advisory Committee on Measuring Innovation in the 21st Century Economy. *Innovation Measurement: Tracking the State of Innovation in the American Economy.* Report to the Secretary of Commerce, 2008.

☞ **"Wealth flows directly from innovation...** *not optimization... wealth is not gained by perfecting the known."*

> Kevin Kelly, founder and editor of *Wired* magazine, publisher of *Whole Earth Review*, author of *What Technology Wants*, and publisher of the *Cool Tools* website.

☞ *"Somewhere out there is a bullet with your company's name on it. Somewhere out there is a competitor, unborn and unknown, that will render your strategy obsolete. You can't dodge the bullet – you're going to have to shoot first. **You're going to have to out-innovate the innovators.**"*

> Gary Hamel, bestselling author, Professor of Strategic Management at the London Business School, and proclaimed by Fortune magazine as the "world's leading expert on business strategy".

☞ *"Strong and sustained economic growth results from several factors, but among the most important is innovation..."*

> National Economic Council, Council of Economic Advisers, and Office of Science and Technology

Policy, *A Strategy for American Innovation: Securing our Economic Growth and Prosperity*, 2011.

Along with these expert views, let's turn again to the thoughts of one of the utmost strategy experts, Dr. Michael Porter, who tells us that:

> "**Companies achieve competitive advantage through acts of innovation**. *They approach innovation in its broadest sense, including both new technologies and new ways of doing things. They perceive a new basis for competing or find better means for competing in old ways. Innovation can be manifested in a new product design, a new production process, a new marketing approach, or a new way of conducting training. Much innovation is mundane and incremental, depending more on a cumulation of small insights and advances than on a single, major technological breakthrough. It often involves ideas that are not even "new"— ideas that have been around, but never vigorously pursued. It always involves investments in skill and knowledge....*" [17]

For example, at the time Apple introduced the iPod, the market was already well-familiar with portable MP3 music players. Yet Apple recognized that those devices had lousy user interfaces, and were either too bulky or underpowered. So Apple paired a much-improved user interface with the integration of a new and very small disk drive, and the rest is history.

Starting from the foundation that innovation is very important to wealth creation, I propose that, not only must the typical company own the IP to own the profits, but to succeed over the long term, that company must excel at fueling and exploiting its IP by intensively implementing a continuous and iterative **Innovation Process** that includes:

1. discovering the market's needs;

2. innovating to meet those needs;

3. identifying, proving, and analyzing its innovations;

4. determining the value of its innovations;

5. strongly protecting its most valuable innovations;

6. marketing its protected innovations; and

7. harnessing the power of its innovations.

Although we'll explore each of these components of this general Innovation Process in much greater depth throughout this book, let's very briefly touch on them now.

To get us started, let's consider the answers to another fundamental question: **What are some of the drivers of innovative ideas?**

You can probably think of others, but here are a few:

a. Unsatisfied customers

b. Internal concerns regarding, e.g., cost, quality, features, performance, delivery, packaging, etc.

c. Technological improvements

d. Demographic shifts

e. Regulatory changes

f. Serendipity/luck

g. Imagination/vision

At least several of the items on this list should make complete sense. For example, frequently, by rationally gathering, organizing, and analyzing market feedback, a company can gain critical market insights, learn where innovation is needed, and discover how best to tailor its innovations to truly satisfy the market's needs.

On occasion, innovations result from a company's pursuit of operational effectiveness, such as studying and improving its internal processes, that is, based on a *"fundamental re-thinking and radical re-design of business processes to achieve dramatic improvements in critical contemporary measures of performance"*. [18]

At other times, innovations are born somewhat spontaneously, and their innovators must search for a true market need that the innovation fulfills.

Perhaps most importantly, I have found that at least 10 to 20 valuable, protectable, and documented innovations can be generated via application of a structured 4 to 5 hour innovation session, which I describe how to implement a little later in this book (see page 63).

But regardless of how they are generated, as emerging innovations are identified, they can be tested for how effectively they function. Also, they can be analyzed for how well they can fulfill the market's actual needs, how protectable they are, and how valuable they are likely to become. Assuming an innovation meets identified criteria, including economic criteria for profitability such as risk-adjusted return on investment, strong IP protections can be sought for that innovation.

With sufficient IP protection in place or underway, your company can create and roll-out thoughtful communications that persuasively advocate an innovation's benefits to its target markets.

Leveraging the power provided by owning the rights to the IP underlying an innovation, your company can then exploit that innovation and/or its IP by any of dozens of techniques.

I will describe each of these activities of the Innovation Process in much greater detail throughout this book. But in the meanwhile, here are a few general features [19] that are common to the innovation processes of essentially all companies:

1. The Innovation Process involves combining certain crucial inputs to create novel outputs. Although they can be tangible and/or intangible, the exact nature of the inputs can vary depending on the novel outputs sought.

2. Knowledge is a crucial input to the Innovation Process.

3. Knowledge is also a vital output of the Innovation Process.

4. The Innovation Process is complex, non-linear, and risky.

5. The Innovation Process is not always predictable, yet can respond to new opportunities, insights, and serendipity.

6. Commercialization is how the Innovation Process creates economic value and the innovator obtains a return.

7. The Innovation Process often involves the following three interconnected phases:

    a. Learning and discovery;

    b. Development and implementation; and

    c. Commercialization and exploitation.

Protecting Innovations via IP

With this understanding of the Innovation Process, let's briefly consider how intellectual property fits in, recognizing that I will explore this topic much more deeply in an upcoming section of this book (see page 77).

When all goes well, the Innovation Process introduces something new, such as a new or improved product or service, that fulfills a previously unsatisfied market need. To the extent that new product or service embodies or utilizes a new intellectual asset, such as know-how, an innovation, or an artistic creation, intellectual property protection can be sought. If obtained, intellectual property protection will provide legal rights with which to exclude competitors from making, using, selling, or otherwise exploiting that new intellectual asset.

When I talk about "intellectual property" (or "IP"), I mean the property rights, defined by mechanisms such as patents, marks, and copyrights, that protect certain intellectual assets. Property rights are different from contract rights, which protect some intangible assets, such as franchises, insurance policies, securities, leases, and other agreements. In particular, the legal remedies for violating contract rights are typically limited to monetary damages alone.

The legal remedies for violating property rights, however, can include not only monetary damages, but also injunctions (court orders compelling an entity to do or stop doing something) and seizures. Sometimes, a court will issue an order requiring the violator to pay punitive damages, the attorney's fees of the IP owner, and/or other litigation-related costs. In a few situations, and unlike breaching contractual rights, violating intellectual property rights can even result in criminal penalties.

Stated differently, in general, without the corresponding legal rights provided by intellectual property, the originator of an innovative intellectual asset typically can not easily prevent competitors from exploiting that asset. So once again, *you must own the IP to own the profits*.

But while ownership is required, it is not quite enough, for ownership won't necessarily ensure that the world will beat a path to your door, gladly pay whatever price you demand, and provide you a growing pile of profits. Instead, considering the bigger picture, it becomes clear that taking a few more steps for harnessing the value and power of your company's IP can be critical to its long-term success.

Extracting Value and Power from IP

Although I address this topic in great detail under *Step 7 – Harness*, it is worthwhile to recognize now that harnessing the value and power of your company's intellectual assets and IP can take any of many forms.

For example, your company might rely on its intellectual assets and/or IP to earn enhanced profits or licensing revenues, discourage competitive activities, and/or raise the market's perception of your company's value.

Some harnessing opportunities might provide your company with market exclusivity, along with the attendant extraordinary profits and the power to obtain injunctions, exclusion orders, seizures, and monetary damages against proven infringers. Other opportunities might involve negotiating the license or sale of intellectual assets and/or IP combined with lucrative supply agreements, technical consulting, and/or know-how sharing.

Somewhat less apparent, but equally important possibilities for your company might include divesting under-utilized assets and avoiding risks, such as preventing, mitigating, and resolving disputes, lawsuits, and related liabilities.

On occasion, it can be worthwhile for a company to harness its IP power by:

    a. using IP as collateral to fund other projects;

    b. donating IP to a charitable organization; or

    c. placing IP into the public domain to prevent others from obtaining exclusive control of slight improvements or modifications to it.

Beyond measurable financial returns, the growing strength of your company's intellectual assets and IP portfolio can highlight your company's innovativeness and skills, encourage investors and early adopters, deter aggressive competitors, attract cooperative business relationships, and provide further leverage in licensing negotiations.

These are just a few cursory examples of the huge number of ways that the value and power of intellectual assets and IP can be harnessed. In fact, I describe my 70+ tactics for harnessing that value and power in *Step 7 – Harness*.

But before we investigate in greater detail how your company can exploit its intellectual assets and properties, we need to briefly cover a few other topics, including how to manage its innovation process, how to secure the resulting innovations with IP protections, and how to evaluate, tailor, and target your IP for its intended market. And to lead off that discussion, I start by considering, how your company can create and manage a high-level or strategic plan that will guide all of your company's IP-related activities.

K. C. GILLETTE.

RAZOR.

APPLICATION FILED DEC. 3, 1901.

NO MODEL.

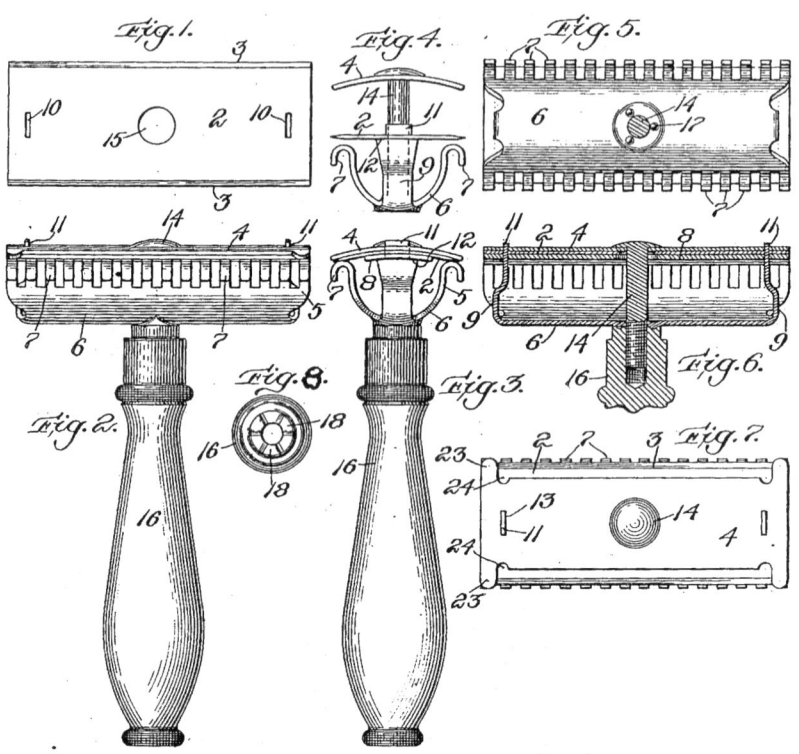

Witnesses:
Ruby M. Banfield
Margaret N. Danihew

Inventor:
King C. Gillette,
by
E. G. Chadwick,
Attorney.

STEP 2
STRATEGIZE

If you really want to learn how to **strategically manage** your company's intellectual property portfolio, so that you can empower your company to discover, grow, and fully extract its value, then this section was written for you.

What you'll learn

▸ What is strategy, and how is it determined?

▸ In what ways should your company's IP strategy be aligned with its business strategy?

▸ How can valuable innovations, know-how, and brands be converted into powerfully exploited intellectual properties that generate substantial and sustained profitability?

▸ Who should strategically manage your company's innovation process, intellectual assets, and IP?

▸ What are typical objectives for strategically managing innovations, intellectual assets, and IP?

▸ How can your company measure and nurture successful intellectual capital management?

▸ What ensures pronounced improvement of your company's innovation process, IP, and intellectual capital management?

Understanding Strategic Fundamentals

To understand strategic fundamentals, I start by answering the most fundamental relevant question: ***What is strategy?***

> *"Strategy can be defined as the determination of the long-run goals and objectives of an enterprise and the adoption of courses of action and the allocation of resources necessary for carrying out these goals."* [20]

Thus, considered most generally, strategizing involves:

1.   evaluating the current situation,

2.   defining an ideal future, and

3.   planning or mapping a possible route to that future.

As your company begins to identify its ideal future (which could be referred to as your company's ideal strategic position), your company probably should consider a few relevant thoughts of perhaps the preeminent authority on strategy and competition, Dr. Michael Porter, who remarks that beyond simply identifying a desired future and the preferred path to it:

"Strategy involves creating fit *among a company's activities. It has to do with the ways a company's activities interact and reinforce one another."* [21]

These general concepts are insightful, but what does it take to apply them in the IP context, that is, to strategically manage your company's innovation process, its intellectual assets, and its IP?

Initially, your company's top management must thoroughly understand and embrace the fact that IP is absolutely essential to the long-term well-being of your company. Thus, its innovation process and intellectual assets should be managed accordingly to ensure the company's prosperity.

That is, **your company must own the IP to own the profits**. This vital topic is covered in depth in *Step 1 – Understand.*

Once top management is firmly on-board with this fundamental concept, it is truly ready to engage in high level IP strategizing.

Taking the above-described general strategizing steps a bit deeper, it becomes clear that any effective plan for empowering your company's *strategic IP position* likely will provide significant guidance to *all* of the activities of your company's innovation process, and potentially every activity of your company. In particular, your company's *strategic IP plan* should integrate with and reinforce not only the creation, development, protection, retention, promotion, and exploitation of its valuable intellectual assets and their corresponding intellectual property rights, but potentially with all of your company's assets, along with your company's overall strategic plan.

Thus, supporting your company's strategic IP plan must be the dual management commitments that (1) each of your company's intellectual assets will further your company's overall business strategies while providing an appropriate return on investment, and (2) your company's innovation process, intellectual assets, and IP portfolio will be recognized and treated as vital profit centers.

Your company's strategic IP plan not only should fit well with your company's overall business strategies, but also should align with and reflect all of your company's directional statements, including its mission, vision, and core values. Viewed generally, these statements typically answer at least these three fundamental questions:

1. *Where does your company want to be?*

2. *How will your company get there?*

3. *How will your company measure success?*

These same basic questions apply in the IP context. For instance:

- *Does your company want to be a provider of goods and/or services, or does your company want to be a licensor of its IP, or both?*

- *Is your company willing to license its core IP to competitors, thereby earning money while raising the competitor's costs and spurring your company to continue innovating?*

- *Is your company agreeable to buying or licensing IP it needs but did not create internally?*

- *Has your company aligned sufficient backing to finance litigation if necessary to deter infringers?*

For example, if yours is what I refer to as an "operating" company that sells goods and/or services, yet also owns IP such as patents, it might be worthwhile to consider setting-up a separate IP "holding" company. That holding company would own the IP and license it to your operating company. Why shift ownership of the IP this way? If there is ever a need to pursue litigation to enforce one of the patents or marks in your IP portfolio, unlike your operating company, your IP holding company will have very few documents, witnesses, and other potential evidence that are subject to "discovery" by your litigation opponent. This discovery advantage can potentially tilt the litigation playing field profoundly in your favor, and encourage much more favorable settlement terms for you.

This example, and these challenging but important general questions hint at the vital need to understand the myriad ways that IP can be exploited to extract value and profitability. I explore my 70+ tactics for exploiting intellectual assets and properties in *Step 7 – Harness*. Go ahead and take a few minutes to review them now, as they will provide fuel for thought for the next topic, which involves exploring how your company might reach its ideal IP future.

Identifying Strategic Routes

Unquestionably, there are a vast number of routes via which a desired IP future can be achieved. But no matter what routes are selected, in general, most experts will agree that empowering IP will include at least the following broad activities:

1. recognizing your company's overall business directions, strategic position, and operational effectiveness;

2. detecting competitive, strategic, and operational opportunities and threats;

3. proposing potential shifts in factors impacting strategic position and/or operational effectiveness, particularly with respect to features, technologies, and competitors (i.e., innovating);

4. reinforcing and/or enabling your company's desired strategic position;

5. providing substantial barriers to imitating your company's strategic position and/or operations (i.e., securing its intellectual assets);

6. inducing alliances that test new positioning and operational factors, open new markets, and neutralize threats; and

7. reducing the relative power of competitive forces.

How these broad activities are actually applied can vary with the company, with its business directions, and with different types of intellectual assets.

For instance, consider know-how. Although trade secrecy can be used to protect know-how from disclosure, know-how also can be licensed to generate revenue, increase sales, and build alliances. Interestingly, oftentimes know-how is the most valuable intellectual asset in a "patent license", for the licensed know-how often can provide the highly detailed and most current knowledge of how to optimally implement and/or commercialize the patented technology. Gaining a thorough understanding of such specific knowledge can allow the licensee to much more easily reach its development, production, and/or sales goals.

Of course, patents can be used for growing your company's market share, revenues, and/or profits, excluding competitors from, e.g., making, using, and/or selling a particular innovation, and even thwarting a competitor's planned market entry, growth, and/or strategy. Patents also can be profitably licensed, leveraged to gain rights to other's innovations, or bargained in exchange for release of liability for infringing other's IP rights. Patents frequently serve to enhance the technical reputation of your company and/or its innovators, attract new investors, customers, and employees, and provide a measure of your company's value.

Another type of IP, marks, can symbolize and carry your company's reputation, image, and goodwill, serving as a reminder of all that customers value about your company, its products, and/or its services, and what differentiates your company from its competitors. Managed carefully, marks and their associated intellectual property rights can be extremely valuable, both as exclusionary tools to keep copyists and competitors alike from cashing in on your company's carefully crafted brands, as mechanisms for extending those brands to new goods and/or services, and as generators of licensing revenue from sales of goods and services even further removed from the core goods and services of your company.

And yet another form of IP, copyrights, can be used to protect your company's valuable artistic creations, from its ad copy and jingles, to its photos, blueprints, computer code, and more.

In *Step 5 – Secure,* I explore more details about the different types of IP protections, and how they can be used to secure your IP rights.

Yet it's worth repeating that with each type of IP, exploitation can rely on any of numerous tactics, including preventing competitors from operating in a protected sphere, earning licensing revenues, encouraging alliances, or raising the perception of your company's value. Less visible, but equally important IP functions can include risk avoidance, such as preventing and resolving disputes, lawsuits, and related liabilities. And these examples only barely scratch the surface. As previously mentioned, I describe my 70+ tactics for exploiting your company's IP in *Step 7 – Harness.* Sorry to be repetitive, but if you haven't already done so, skip ahead and check them out now. You'll be glad you did.

Determining Strategic Objectives

Building on this general strategic approach, more particular details of your company's strategic IP plan can be identified, explored, and documented. For example, whether referred to as objectives or goals, it can be worthwhile to arrive at more detailed strategic IP aspirations that might revolve around activities such as:

1. Periodically determining and continually monitoring your company's status regarding its:

    a. Intellectual Assets & Properties;

    b. Technologies;

    c. Products;

    d. Customers;

    e. Suppliers;

    f. Competitors; and

    g. Related Industries;

2. Nurturing and sustaining a strategically innovative environment;

3. Identifying, documenting, and assessing all of your company's know-how, innovations, brands, and works;

4. Protecting *valuable* know-how, innovations, brands, and works;

5. Identifying and weeding-out unproductive intellectual assets;

6. Implementing best practices to position valuable intellectual assets to realize their full potential; and

7. Harvesting the full value of your intellectual assets, including those protected as IP via strong property rights.

In addition to these most common activities, other activities might be great candidates for addressing via your company's strategic IP plan, such as activities related to IP risk avoidance, marketing, and/or finance.

To help round out your strategic IP plan, additional specifics, such as dates, metrics, and/or personnel, can be added to its selected activities/ objectives/goals.

But before immediately diving into such specifics on your own, note that I explore each of the above-listed activities in greater detail throughout this book. So read on!

Nurturing Strategic Implementers

Once your company has decided on some of the specifics of its strategic IP plan, it is time to identify, recruit, and empower the people that will carry the responsibility for implementing those specifics. And who are those people? Generally, top management's deep commitment to optimizing your company's intellectual assets and IP will be shared, and put into meaningful day-to-day action, by your company's *IP Team*.

When fully empowered, your company's IP Team will fulfill several vital functions, including developing, filtering, protecting, and exploiting your company's intellectual assets to achieve optimal returns on its investment in those assets, consistent with the mission, core values, and strategic directions of your company, and in full recognition of market needs, trends, and opportunities, as discovered and shaped by your innovation process.

To properly manage these vital functions, your IP Team should be staffed with, at a minimum, deeply experienced managers, innovators, and IP legal counsel. Additional backgrounds that might prove particularly helpful include high-level representatives from your finance, research, and marketing functions. But regardless of the qualifications of your IP Team, its members will be responsible for sharing and applying their complementary talents, perspectives, and wisdom to guide your company to the best possible decisions regarding its innovation process, intellectual assets, and IP.

But of course, your IP Team can't do it all. Top management must stay intimately involved and must continuously champion your company's IP strategy. By creating, promoting, and maintaining a company-wide climate that cultivates strategically-meaningful innovations and encourages the recognition, protection, and respect of intellectual property rights, top management will ensure that all levels and functions of your company provide your IP Team with a growing crop of intellectual assets to reap, and help minimize the eruption of IP-related risks, liabilities, and disputes. The desired climate can be facilitated via, for example, a multi-pronged process that includes educating, inspiring, measuring, and rewarding your company's entire workforce. Let's briefly explore that process.

To optimize its innovation process, everyone in your company needs to continually expand their understanding of IP rights, requirements, and issues. This training can be provided via any of a wide variety of formats, ranging from highly informal and impromptu chats to written materials to formal classroom-style lectures or dialogs. The key is to keep everyone's knowledge of IP ever-expanding.

This type of training can reveal opportunities that might otherwise have been missed altogether.

As an example, sometimes innovators are quick to dismiss their own concepts, making the assumption that those concepts aren't worthy of patent protection, because they don't fully understand the requirements of patentability. They think: "If I had this idea, then it must be obvious".

Yet a claimed concept is legally obvious if, and only if, at the time the concept was conceived, a person having ordinary skill in the art (the general realm of that concept) would have known of art-recognized reasons to modify or combine relevant prior art references, considered as a whole, to arrive at the entirety of that claimed concept.

Thus, although a layperson or engineer might declare that a concept seems "obvious" (typically because, after reading the claim, they can understand how the concept works or can predict that it likely will work), U.S. patent law can be rather strict about what must be proven before that concept will be deemed "obvious" from a legal perspective. So don't let your innovators dismiss their potentially valuable innovations so easily.

Coupled with educating your company's entire workforce is the need to inspire them to apply their solid IP knowledge. Simply put, management must regularly and frequently beat the drum to encourage all members of its workforce to create, disclose, protect, and respect innovations, intellectual assets, and IP.

Although I discuss each of these topics in later sections, it is worth noting that one great approach to generating innovations is via a 4 hour structured innovation session. Such innovation sessions easily can produce 10 to 20 valuable, protectable, documented innovations. I provide more information on planning and running these helpful sessions in *Step 4 – Innovate.*

Shifting gears slightly, I note that it has been said that:

> *"What gets measured gets done. What gets measured and fed back gets done well. What gets rewarded gets repeated."* [22]

That quote reminds us that measuring a process, such as your company's innovation process, can easily lead to creating, implementing, and refining valuable improvements to that process. The specific measurements chosen can vary widely, but generally should be relevant, understandable, and timely reviewed.

That quote also reminds us that to improve its innovation process, your company must reward desired behaviors. In the IP context, your company's reward system can broadly include innovation-focused contests, monetary incentives, performance evaluations, and public recognition. For example, many companies provide cash rewards to employees who submit innovation disclosures, whose innovations are reflected in filed patent applications, and/or whose innovations are protected via issued patents. Of course, reward systems can be gamed or become dysfunctional, so they need to be managed carefully to continually achieve the desired results. I'm happy to discuss how your company can customize its IP reward system to best motivate its workforce.

In summary, by nurturing your company's IP strategy, such as by building and empowering a highly-qualified IP Team, by educating your workforce on how to generate, secure, and respect IP, and by continually encouraging and motivating the desired IP-related actions, your company's top management will ensure that the foundation is solidly in place for your company to optimize its IP power.

Cultivating Strategic Implementations

Once fully empowered, your IP Team will timely recognize, investigate, and contemplate all relevant facets of your company's business, technical, and legal positions, including its strengths, weaknesses, opportunities, and threats, while determining and seeking appropriate forms of IP protection for its most promising innovations and intellectual assets, and while avoiding and correcting corresponding vulnerabilities.

Your IP Team also will periodically evaluate each of your intellectual assets, including their expected costs, revenues, timings, and risks. Based on the pertinent risk-adjusted return on investment criteria that flow from those valuations, your IP Team will thoughtfully prioritize and timely thin your company's IP portfolio, thereby channeling funds to those intellectual assets and properties showing the most promise for substantial profitability.

In addition, your IP Team will research and recommend financial tactics, such as patent assertion insurance, IP-secured credit lines, and pre-paid IP licenses, so that your company has the financial muscle to enforce its IP rights when the time comes, thereby financially positioning your most valuable intellectual assets to realize their full potential.

Finally, your IP Team will help develop persuasive communications that highlight the benefits of its securely-protected IP, targeting known market needs and players, thereby setting the stage for successful exploitation of those assets.

I have helped my clients all along the way. As one example, my powerful IP auditing tools have helped IP Teams inventory, log, and analyze all of their company's intellectual assets and properties. As another example, from an innovative concept's origin, to its protection via patent, to its emergence in the form of products/services and beyond, my unique custom databases have related and tracked innovations across their entire life cycle. In addition, my patent-pending risk analysis software has helped avoid, spot, and correct vulnerabilities in a company's patent portfolio, and exploit those of its competitors.

Harvesting Strategic Value

Beyond substantial financial returns, the growing strength of its IP portfolio can highlight your company's innovativeness, skills, and market-centric focus, attract investors and early adopters to your company and its products, deter overly-aggressive competitors, attract cooperative business relationships, and/or provide further leverage in licensing negotiations. Functioning effectively and managed well, your IP Team will vigorously pursue the most promising of those opportunities while applying resources consistent with your company's mission, core values, and strategic directions.

To optimize the return on each of your company's investments in intellectual assets and properties, your IP Team's activities will include periodically evaluating, enhancing, and implementing value extraction opportunities, such as discouraging infringers, authorizing licensees, and divesting under-utilized intellectual assets and properties. Such value extraction opportunities might provide, for example, market exclusivity, with the attendant extraordinary profits and the power to obtain, when required, injunctions, seizures, and monetary damages against proven infringers. Other opportunities can involve negotiating the license or sale of related IP and/or intellectual assets combined with lucrative supply agreements, technical consulting, and/or know-how sharing. Some IP even can be used as collateral to fund other projects.

And this list only scratches the surface! I describe my 70+ tactics for exploiting your company's intellectual assets and properties in *Step 7 – Harness*.

Enriching Strategic Resources

Not content to merely exploit your company's intellectual assets and properties, when fully empowered, your IP Team will ensure the continuous improvement of your innovation process, intellectual assets, and IP by sponsoring periodic audits of your company's intellectual portfolio, policies, and practices to identify, justify, and prioritize opportunities for improvement. These vital audits will not only enrich your IP strategy, but will also help assure that your company's IP power continues to be optimized across its entire portfolio of intellectual assets.

Considered generally, a thorough professional IP audit will systematically review how well your company has been respecting its own, and other's, IP by, for example:

1. Reviewing your company's IP-related practices, records and documents;

2. Inventorying IP controlled and/or used by your company;

3. Prioritizing your company's mission-critical IP;

4. Analyzing the scope, ownership, and vulnerabilities of that mission-critical IP;

5. Verifying that appropriate strategies, policies, and procedures are in place to optimize returns;

6. Identifying how you can mitigate liability for possible third party claims of IP infringement against your company; and

7. Recommending changes needed to optimize returns from your company's mission-critical IP.

Note that I cover auditing in greater detail in *Step 3 – Survey*. Also, I broadly explore IP risk avoidance in *Step – 6: Enhance*.

Also discussed throughout this book is one further and vital role for your IP Team. With top management's full support, your IP Team will shepherd your innovation process, encouraging your company to continuously:

1. research its desired markets;

2. innovate to satisfy unfulfilled market needs; and

3. educate the markets about how your company's strongly protected innovations valuably distinguish its goods and services from those of your competitors.

Now that we've outlined the basics of how to create and implement a typical IP strategy, let's take a closer look, starting with determining where your company currently stands.

Fig. 1.

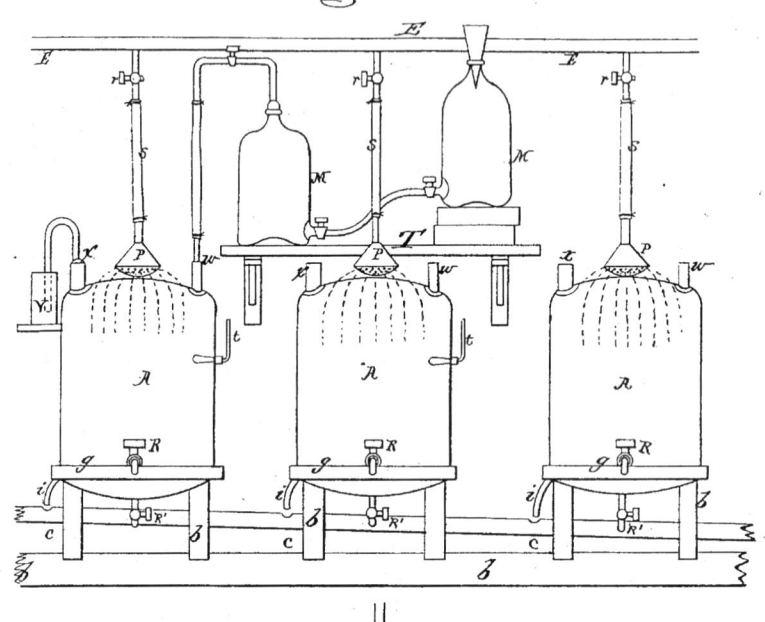

Fig. 2.

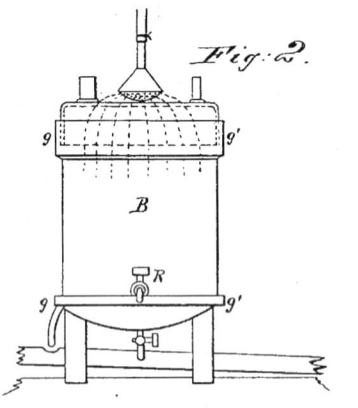

Witnesses,
E. Wolf
J. Fielbel

Inventor
Louis Pasteur
By his attorney
C. M. Keller

STEP 3

SURVEY

If you really want to know where your company stands, then *survey* its intellectual assets, customers' needs, market and technology trends, innovation opportunities, competitors' threatening activities, and potential relationships.

What you'll learn

▸ What is the best way to inventory your company's know-how and trade secrets?

▸ What 7 basic practices for performing an IP Audit can identify and help correct protections that are faulty, agreements that are flawed, and procedures that are dysfunctional?

▸ How can customer feedback lead to valuable innovations?

▸ What are the most profitable things your company can learn from analyzing the patent landscape?

▸ How can your company identify which patents, companies, and technologies are most important in a particular field?

▸ How can your company readily spot potential strategic relationships, licensees, and infringers?

▸ How can your company continuously detect competitors that are attempting to set infringement traps, legally steal its markets, or thwart its future profitability?

To truly empower your company's IP, you need to know several things, including:

- what intellectual assets and properties you have, their vulnerabilities, their value, and how to improve it;

- what your customers, prospects, and potential business partners need;

- where you stand versus your competitors;

- what trends are shaping the relevant technical, business, and legal landscapes; and

- where you have freedom to operate and where you don't.

We'll start by exploring how to learn what your company already has, how to track and manage it better, and how to continually improve it.

Knowing What You Know

The Value of Information

You undoubtedly realize that information (including knowledge and data) can be very valuable when handled correctly. Often, value can be inherent merely from aggregating otherwise discrete pieces of information. At other times, value can arise simply by virtue of certain information being kept secret from competitors while being exploited by its holder. And sometimes, the most valuable information is the knowledge of what simply doesn't work.

Thus, to facilitate understanding, I define "know-how" to include any information that provides actual or potential competitive advantage, such as, but not limited to, economic value. For example, even though its content is made available to the public, a rapidly-accessible database of current telephone numbers and addresses enables telephone companies to extract $0.50, $0.99, or more from telephone callers who dial "411".

Consequently, such a rapidly searchable aggregation of information can net tremendous revenues and profits.

Likewise , I define "trade secrets" to be know-how that has economic value, is not generally known, and is maintained via reasonable measures of security. Trade secrets derive their economic value primarily from their secrecy with respect to competitors.

Trade secrets can include many commonly encountered types of information, such as:

1. laboratory test results

2. innovative concepts

3. materials, compositions, and formulas

4. equipment specifications and drawings

5. manufacturing processes, procedures, and parameters

6. new product plans and names

7. cost and pricing data

8. contract terms

9. supplier information

10. customer lists and data

11. marketing information, plans, and methods

12. business strategies and tactics

13. financial budgets, projections, and statements

14. accounting, trading, & brokerage processes

15. computer architectures, algorithms, and code

Know-how and trade secrets also can extend to knowledge of what does not work, since avoiding the experiments needed to obtain this knowledge, and the costs associated with those experiments, can be very valuable to certain competitors.

Trade secret protection in the U.S. is governed primarily by state law. Generally, every state treats theft or unauthorized dissemination of a trade secret as an unlawful act. Theft of trade secrets also can result in criminal penalties under the federal Economic Espionage Act and/or the Computer Fraud and Abuse Act.

There is no limitation on the length of time that a trade secret can be protected. For example, the formula for Coca-Cola® allegedly has been kept secret for over 125 years!

Note that absent an enforceable contract, however, you have no right to exclude others from using "proper means" to obtain what you consider to be your trade secret (or your know-how). Proper means can include independent development, reverse engineering, obtaining from a third party who has a right to provide, or obtaining from you without breaching a contractual or other duty, such as when you have failed to exert reasonable efforts to maintain secrecy. Improper means can involve breach of contract, espionage, theft, fraud, bribery, coercion, etc.

When recognized, know-how and trade secrets are often protected by formal written agreements (e.g., Non-Disclosure Agreements, Employment Agreements, etc.), employee training, physical security, computer security, and/or other well-managed access control practices.

Nevertheless, public disclosure to even one person can destroy the secret if it then becomes more generally known. For this reason, trade secrets too frequently lose their secrecy and therefore fall into the public domain. Consequently, when feasible, many holders of valuable innovative concepts consider patent protection as a complement and/or supplement to trade secrecy.

Here's how it works. For any given innovative concept, patent protection might be sought to protect that concept. The corresponding patent application generally must enable others to implement its claimed concept. So once that patent application (or a resulting patent) is published, all hopes for trade secrecy are lost, right?

Wrong. Each U.S. patent application is required to describe the implementation details only:

- for its *claimed* concepts, rather than all valuable related concepts;

- in the best way known to the named inventors *alone*, rather than to the company as a whole;

- as known *on the effective filing date* of that patent application, rather than as learned afterwards; and

- sufficiently to enable a person having merely ordinary skill in the art to *barely* (vs. optimally) *implement* each claimed concept *without substantial experimentation.*

Furthermore, a patent application is not necessarily required to include all the valuable research data that was gathered to prove the technical and/or commercial viability of the claimed concept, or any information regarding what implementation approaches failed, did not work well, or were otherwise undesired.

So as your company learns, improves, and optimizes how to implement and commercialize the innovative concept, it can protect that know-how as trade secrets. In fact, for each of its publicized innovative concepts, your company can discover and develop tons of related and extremely valuable know-how both before and after patent protection has been timely sought. If carefully managed, your company can indefinitely maintain that know-how via trade secrecy, potentially even if patent protection is denied, or long after patent protection has expired.

These vital trade secrets can add tremendous value to your company by:

- covering more subject matter from more angles and thereby strengthening your company's abilities to exclude competitors;

- obtaining additional legal remedies for infringement; and/or

- securing backup legal rights and remedies if a primary form of intellectual property protection (e.g., patent) becomes invalid.

One way in which this extra value can be realized is when your company negotiates a license to others who seek to implement and/or commercialize the patented concepts, and who need your valuable trade secrets to facilitate that work. Simply put, patent licensees often vitally need most to all of your related know-how to successfully commercialize the patented technology. By carefully protecting that know-how, your company will be well-positioned to harness its full value.

With that brief background, you probably recognize that know-how and trade secrets are pervasive, not just in your company, but in all profit-seeking businesses. Surprisingly, just as pervasive among most companies is their lack of knowledge of the status of their know-how and trade secrets. Of course, you can't reasonably manage something until you know it exists, yet most companies have no definitive record of their know-how or trade secrets, and thus manage them rather poorly. Fortunately, the solution to this problem is simple to understand, and rather easy to implement.

Taking Stock

One of the challenges with inventorying trade secrets (and know-how) is that they often have little or no physical presence. Instead, they tend to reside in the minds of employees, hide in documents, or sometimes, are embodied in products, machines, and/or software.

Typically, trade secrets are inventoried on a departmental or functional basis. That is, each department or function of the company is responsible for listing all of its trade secrets.

But how should trade secrets be described?

One well-regarded approach to categorizing and describing trade secrets is the Subject-Format-Product (or "SFP") approach. This approach labels each trade secret according to its general subject matter, the format in which that trade secret is recorded, and the product with which it is most closely associated. The same approach works equally well for know-how.

Here are a few example SFPs that hopefully clarify the approach:

- "Trouble-shooting Flowchart for Variable Speed Drive Circuits" (where "Trouble-shooting" is the general subject matter, "Flowchart" is the format, and "Variable Speed Drive Circuits" are the product)

- "Diffusion Experiment Results for R-777 Teflon Lining"

- "Equipment Specification for Micro-housing Press"

- "Point-of-Sale Packaging Drawing for EXCEL Razor Blades"

- "Sales Projections for SURE-FIRE Rapid Injectors"

Such SFPs can provide convenient categories into which to bunch your company's know-how and trade secrets, and nearly everyone in your company will instantly recognize each SFP.

Once categorized, a given trade secret can be sequentially numbered, elaborated upon in terms of its: problem, goal, and/or objective; idea, concept, and/or solution; and specific exemplary implementations. By logging each of these details, your company will be much better positioned to track, secure, valuate, assess the patentability of, and exploit each of its trade secrets.

Assigning Value

Once categorized, know-how and trade secrets can be further characterized to better understand their potential value to your company and/or others.

For example, answers can be tallied to each of the following 7 questions:

1. To what extent is the know-how/trade secret known outside your company's business?

2. To what extent is the information known by employees of your company's business?

3. What measures have been taken to protect the secrecy of the know-how/trade secret?

4. What is the value of the information to your company?

5. How much time and cost has been spent by your company to develop the know-how/trade secret?

6. How easily can the know-how/trade secret be independently developed by others?

7. How easily can the know-how/trade secret be reversed engineered by others?

Based on the answers to these questions, your company can make decisions regarding what efforts it should make to guard the secrecy of the know-how or trade secret.

For the more cherished know-how and trade secrets, further analysis can be undertaken to try to determine their fair market value and/or useful life. Such information can provide even more guidance on how much should be expended to protect the know-how or trade secret. I typically encourage a valuation approach that relies on a risk-adjusted return on investment or a net present value of future cash flows. I describe how to implement this valuation approach in *Step 6 – Enhance*.

Know-how and trade secrets can hold a tremendous amount of value, and even can represent a majority of the value of your company's intellectual assets. But chances are that your company has other very valuable intellectual assets, some of which might be protected by intellectual property rights. And just as it can be worthwhile to inventory your know-how and trade secrets, it also can be very beneficial to tally your company's other intellectual assets, including its intellectual property. So let's briefly explore how that's done, which is via a professional IP audit.

Auditing Your IP

Upon completing a professional IP audit, your company will thoroughly learn the status of its IP (and potentially, all of its intellectual assets). In particular, a my professional IP audit will systematically review how well your company has been respecting its own, and other's, IP by:

1. Reviewing your company's IP-related practices, records and documents;

2. Inventorying IP controlled and/or used by your company;

3. Prioritizing your company's mission-critical IP;

4. Analyzing the scope, ownership, and vulnerabilities of that mission-critical IP;

5. Verifying that appropriate strategies, policies, and procedures are in place to optimize returns;

6. Identifying how you can mitigate liability for possible third party claims of IP infringement against your company; and

7. Recommending changes needed to optimize returns from your company's mission-critical IP.

Such a professional IP audit can help optimize your company's IP power by:

1. Identifying unrecognized or emergent IP;

2. Increasing the value of existing IP;

3. Reducing the costs and risks of third-party IP claims;

4. Building the value of products that reply on IP;

5. Identifying potential non-core revenue streams;

6. Inspiring additional revenue through core business licensing;

7. Increasing the value of corporate transactions;

8. Reducing costs of unused IP;

9. Suggesting tax deductions for IP donations;

10. Reducing new product development costs (product clearance);

11. Evaluating the IP of an acquisition or investment target (due diligence);

12. Assessing business direction and strength;

13. Revealing unappreciated business possibilities; and/or

14. Discovering business expansion opportunities.

It should be clear that IP audits can offer considerable value to most companies. Drilling down a level, IP audits also can benefit numerous interested parties, including:

Owners / Managers who are:

    a. Depending upon IP as a principal component of their company's value;

b. Engaging in domestic or international commerce involving IP-based products;

c. Considering an acquisition, merger, partnership, and/or joint venture with an IP-based entity;

d. Managing the IP of a subsidiary or affiliate;

e. Licensing IP from others;

f. Licensing IP to others;

g. Considering changing the tax status or accounting method for their IP;

h. Experiencing market share erosion from knockoffs or pirated copies;

i. Facing possible IP litigation;

j. Selling an IP-based manufacturing or service organization; and/or

k. Selling IP and/or IP-based assets.

Investors who are:

a. Considering funding a start-up company;

b. Financing an existing IP-based business;

c. Considering accepting a security interest in IP;

d. Entering a joint venture with an IP-based partner; and/or

e. Underwriting a public offering of an IP-based company.

Buyers who are:

a. Acquiring IP and/or IP-based assets;

b. Acquiring an IP-based manufacturing or service organization; and/or

c. Purchasing a license to make, use, and/or sell a product or process.

The scope and depth of each IP audit typically will depend on its purpose. For example, as hinted above, an audit can be limited to IP, or can encompass intellectual assets more generally, thereby including know-how, trade secrets, and agreements.

As another example, an initial audit might be limited to a few items of particular interest, or might seek to identify and evaluate all of your company's IP, policies, and practices, so that a more comprehensive list of recommendations can be determined, prioritized, and explained. Based on the groundwork already laid, follow-up audits typically will become increasingly streamlined and focused. Occasionally, non-routine audits might be triggered due to changes in technical, market, or financial opportunities or needs, business or management directions, or the legal environment. Likewise, non-routine audits might be prompted by your company's need to train staff, reduce costs, enhance profits, prepare for litigation, or perform due diligence, such as for borrowing, lending, licensing out, licensing in, fund-raising, investing, divestiture, acquisition, or merger.

As you might imagine, I have approached auditing with the same thoughtfulness and intensity that has underscored all of my work. For example, my professional IP audits have relied on my deep legal, business, and technical experience, much of has been reflected in my proprietary database of over 1500 audit checkpoints. As appropriate, I have applied the most relevant of these checkpoints to systematically review how well each audited company has been respecting its own, and other's, IP rights.

Auditing techniques can include, as appropriate:

1. Interviewing management and staff;

2. Analyzing completed questionnaires from employees who use or develop IP;

3. Inspecting your company's facilities and workplaces;

4. Reading employment contracts, non-disclosure agreements, assignments, etc.;

5. Reviewing handbooks, policy manuals, procedures, and other guidance documents;

6. Examining existing research, commercial, and legal files; and/or

7. Searching public databases including those of the United States Patent and Trademark Office (USPTO), U.S. Copyright Office, European Patent Office, etc.

With the guidance of my client's IP Team, I have typically prepared an audit plan that specifies the expected schedule, estimated budget, and needed resources for performing each audit.

How I have delivered the results of the IP audit have varied depending on the circumstances.

For example, I typically have written the audit results in a manner that could be shared throughout the company. But, when describing such findings in writing might have contributed risk, I have presented those findings verbally to top management only. I have provided very basic audit results as simple lists or tables. But due to my unique database development expertise, I have developed the ability to deliver more extensive audit results as a database having an exceptionally user-friendly design that allows for easy data entry, searching, sorting, and reporting by the IP Team and/or management.

My recommendations typically have included both general and specific remedial actions to protect and/or maintain my client's IP, increase its value, and/or avoid and/or minimize risks to that value. As warranted, I suggested and clearly explained needed and easily-implemented improvements to the company's training, policies, procedures, agreements, and/or record-keeping.

Thus, with my professional audit results in hand, my clients could thoroughly understand not only the current status of their IP (and potentially, all of their intellectual assets), but also what I recommended to substantially and cost-effectively improve that status, and thereby add significant value to their IP portfolios.

Knowing where your company's IP stands is critical. But that knowledge simply isn't enough to optimize your intellectual property power. Instead, your company will need to grow, trim, and otherwise manage its IP and intellectual assets. Of course, growing IP requires innovating. But how should your company approach that challenge?

Listening to the Market

Undoubtedly, customers will provide you with feedback, such as questions, complaints, and suggestions, regarding your products and services. You can lean heavily on that feedback to direct your future innovations.

But in some cases, relying on customer feedback, and even certain forms of market research, can turn out to be a huge mistake, leading your company to chase unprofitable goals and/or miss out on critical opportunities. But how can that be?

Henry Ford is quoted as saying that if he had asked his customers what they needed, they would have said "a faster horse". His perspective seems well-founded, particularly when considering that professional "market research" insisted that the total demand for computers would be 5 units, that copying machines would be unwanted because carbon paper would suffice, and that the Walkman would fizzle. Blatant market research failures such as these suggest a fundamental problem inherent in gathering and interpreting customer and market needs. That is, customers don't always recognize their fundamental needs or know the best ways to fulfill them, so any feedback obtained from customers must be very thoughtfully solicited, analyzed, and interpreted.

So rather than gradually collecting random feedback from your customers, over-reactively responding to whatever feedback emerges, or blindly depending on market research "experts" to tell you what to do, why not systematically and thoughtfully gather and analyze the market's real needs to identify for yourself its true innovation opportunity areas?

Although there are lots of techniques for determining market needs, here's one noteworthy approach [23] that offers the benefit of identifying what customers are actually trying to get done, rather than focusing attention solely on what they are doing currently:

1. Select a particular market and/or product;

2. Identify an exemplary customer;

3. Identify an important task the customer _wants_ to accomplish;

4. De-construct that task into a series of discrete process steps or activities;

5. Identify the metrics the customer uses to measure success in completing each of those activities;

6. Analyze the biggest challenges the customer faces in successfully completing each activity; and

7. Innovate solutions to those challenges (note that best practices for innovating are covered in detail in _Step 4 – Innovate)._

Some of these items are self-explanatory, so I won't elaborate on them. But take a closer look at item 3, which tends to set the tone for the entire process. This item encourages a pronounced focus on the customer's fundamental objective, rather than on what they are actually doing. This is a very meaningful difference from typical market research. What makes this perspective so meaningful is that it creates a climate for stepping back, thinking more abstractly, and considering alternative steps, activities, and approaches that might accomplish the same fundamental objective.

Now take a look at item 4. When de-constructing a task, it can be worthwhile to identify the specific activities (and even sub-activities) that correspond to each of the following generic activities, which tend to apply to all tasks:

    a. Defining what the task requires;

    b. Identifying and locating needed inputs;

    c. Preparing the actors, components, and task environment;

    d. Executing the task;

    e. Monitoring the task environment and the results;

    f. Maintaining, repairing, and making modifications; and

    g. Concluding the task.

To more easily de-construct a task, try starting with the execution step (d), and then identify the corresponding pre-execution and post-execution activities.

For item 7, when assessing a potential solution to the customer's challenge, try to ensure that the solution is worded in a manner that:

- identifies the most fundamental goal the customer is trying to accomplish; and

- applies to other customers performing that task.

Note that innovation opportunities can reside within any of the activities that are comprised by a given customer's task, and can target drawbacks related to efficiency, variability, and/or output quality. Also, keep in mind that throughout the task, problems can arise, requiring trouble-shooting to resolve. Innovations often can target such problems, eliminating them, recognizing them quicker, and/or solving them easier.

More generally, after identifying the specific activities that make up a customer's task, there are several approaches that can be taken for generating innovations and creating value:

- Improving the execution of an activity;

- Eliminating the need for particular inputs or outputs;

- Enabling an activity to be completed by another party, in a new location, or at a different time;

- Eliminating an activity or removing it from the responsibility of the customer;

- Addressing an overlooked activity;

- Re-sequencing the activities; or

- Easing trouble-shooting of one or more activities.

Somewhat more specifically, some common innovation themes include:

- Reducing inefficiency, delays, and/or hassles;

- Reducing hazards and/or increasing safety;

- Managing dirt, contamination, and/or scrap;

- Reducing numbers of parts;

- Reducing and/or increasing size;

- Eliminating and/or reducing spills, messes, and/or clutter;

- Eliminating and/or reducing friction, corrosion, erosion, wear, decay, and/or other sorts of entropy;

- Resisting theft, damage, and/or other diminution in value;

- Reducing costs;

- Improving quality;

- Adding features.

In summary, with this powerful market research approach, finding innovation opportunities hinges predominantly on understanding the customer's overall objective and how they will know they have succeeded.

Once you know some potentially fruitful areas for innovating, you are nearly ready to innovate. I outline a proven technique for consistently generating valuable innovations in *Step 4 – Innovate*. But before you get started with cranking out the innovations, it can be helpful to know what innovations have already been discovered and published by others, even if those innovations haven't made it to, or survived in, the marketplace. As you might expect, patent publications form the single largest and most thorough collection of innovation-describing publications. So that's where we'll turn our attention next.

Analyzing the Patent Landscape

In exchange for describing how to implement an innovative concept, a patent applicant can receive, via a granted patent, the legal rights to exclude others, for a fixed period of time, from actually implementing that concept in the country that granted that patent.

Thus, patent publications (i.e., published patent applications and granted patents) can serve at least 3 primary purposes:

1. teach how to implement new concepts;

2. warn others of the bounds of your company's innovative "turf"; and

3. guide your company in how to avoid trespassing on a competitor's protected turf.

The first of these, explaining implementation details for various concepts, can provide fertile soil for sprouting new innovations. For example, one can study patent documents in a specific field to help keep abreast of its developments, and to discover the limitations and likely problems associated with existing approaches. Via my advanced, patenting-pending, proprietary search tool, and/or using commercially-available search software, I am typically able to locate published patent documents that describe concepts of interest, or at least those patent publications that most closely describe the desired concepts

The second purpose, warning others of your property rights, can be augmented by emphasizing the "patent pending" nature of your company's concepts in all relevant communications. For example, the moment you have filed any U.S. patent application that describes your innovative concept, you are legally permitted to mark your products that embody that concept with the phrase "patent pending". Moreover, from that moment, you are legally permitted to advertise your products and/or services that implement that concept with the "patent pending" notification. Such markings and notifications not only warn competitors, but also alert suppliers, customers, and potential investors and employees of your innovations and your dedication to protecting them.

The third purpose, helping your company avoid infringing other's patents, while somewhat more challenging, is nevertheless possible via careful monitoring of the patent landscape. For example, special "watch" or monitoring services are available that report, such as on a weekly or monthly basis, all patent publications that, for example, include specific keywords, are linked to particular competitors, and/or relate to defined subject matter classifications of interest.

Spotting Trends

Although I just described 3 primary purposes for patent publications, there are several other advanced uses for patent publications. Importantly, patent publications can serve as signals of emergent technologies, companies, and competitors. Fortunately, various analytical and visualization techniques have evolved to help spot those signals relatively easily. For example, similar to that described above, monitoring services are offered that can provide your company with periodic reports of new patent publications that mention a specific keyword, are classified within an identified technical field, and/or are associated with a particular company, innovator, or earlier patent publication.

Similarly, visualizations can be provided that compare information from patent publications across different points in time, thereby allowing important changes to be identified, such as trends regarding technologies, innovators, and/or patent owners. For example, by tracking innovators associated with patent documents linked to a given patent owner over time, I can identify not only that company's most prolific innovators, but also its emerging ones. I can even determine who in that company probably knows the most about a given concept. Such insights can be invaluable when seeking to attract the "best and brightest" to join your company or when trying to assess vulnerabilities in a competitor.

As another example, by tracking the concepts described in a competitor's patent publications, I can discern that company's strategic initiatives, including those of greatest threat to your company, often long before those strategies become apparent in the marketplace. Such timely awareness can allow your company to take appropriate counter-measures, such as innovating blocking concepts and filing patent applications that "wall-off" the competitor, potentially encouraging them to abandon their threatening research and development efforts.

With that brief introduction, let's take a look at what else can be learned by studying various patent publications.

Discovering Future Relationships

Patent publications can be analyzed to help identify potential competitors, licensees, and/or infringers. For example, patent analysis software can identify parties who are very active in a given technical field, as well as those who are recent entrants, those who have fallen behind (and might need your help to get back in the game), and those who have pursued patents on concepts that are potentially complementary to yours. As hinted previously, analyzing patent documents can highlight prolific innovators, including those who have been willing to change employers in the past, thereby suggesting potential future hires. A careful analysis of patent publications also can suggest potential suppliers, customers, and/or acquisition targets.

For example, tracking recent entrants to a field of particular interest to your company, can help you spot innovative start-ups and small competitors that might make good acquisition or investment targets. Partnering with and/or purchasing such businesses, or licensing their innovations, can help you rapidly improve your product and/or service offerings, with much lower risks of R&D failures. Similarly, investing in such firms can provide you with opportunities to guide nascent technologies while earning above-market returns.

As another example, analyzing the patent publications of potential suppliers can help your company learn of potential solutions to long-standing market needs long before those suppliers are ready to offer completed solutions to the marketplace, including your competitors. Thus, by joining forces with such suppliers while they are still honing their innovations for the marketplace, you can guide the supplier to providing an optimized solution for your needs and those of your customers. Moreover, by gaining advanced notice of your supplier's innovations, you potentially can secure an exclusive licensing arrangement with that supplier, possibly locking-out your competitors from accessing that supplier's most important innovations or from competing directly against your solutions that implement those innovations.

There is clearly a tremendous amount of potentially valuable information that can be learned from analyzing patents. Yet we still haven't covered perhaps the most valuable thing that a careful study of patent publications can teach – how to stay out of serious legal trouble.

Avoiding Infringement Traps

A careful and periodic review of the relevant patent landscape can help your company continuously identify those patents that your current and/or potential products and/or services might infringe. With such patents identified, further analysis, such as via my powerful, patent-pending, document analysis tool, can identify whether any patents of concern have sufficient vulnerabilities to allow you to proceed with much reduced infringement liability risk, or whether cost-effective design-arounds, or possibly taking a license, might be the more prudent approach. It's also possible to research the litigation history of a given patent owner, to learn whether they are likely to ignore, negotiate with, or attack perceived infringers, thus informing your tactics for dealing with them.

For example, via my innovative software, I have developed the ability to analyze any of over 100 metrics, including numerous risks and benefits springing from the specifics of how a patent application was written and/or prosecuted (negotiated to issuance) in the USPTO. Simply stated, these metrics can have a huge impact on the value of the resulting patent. But this isn't just my opinion. To factually evidence their impact, I have linked these metrics to some of the many court cases that criticize the corresponding risky drafting and prosecution practices and punish the patents that demonstrate those risks. My ground-breaking tool includes a powerful search engine that can analyze nearly any English-language patent document, such as a draft, as-filed, and/or published patent application, or even an issued patent, for evidence of these metrics, and then grade that document accordingly, thereby providing a meaningful quantitative measure of just how severely the value of the corresponding patent had been compromised by risky drafting and/or prosecution choices.

Such information can prove invaluable for assessing your ultimate risk of being held liable for infringing that patent, and can greatly help with bracketing the potential damages if liability is found. Moreover, my innovative analytical results can help define the full range of design-around possibilities, helping you identify which are technically feasible and most economical, so that you can identify appropriate ways to compete without substantial risk of infringement liability.

Sometimes (although rarely), my analysis has indicated that a given patent has been written and prosecuted rather well, such that, assuming the scope and validity of its claims are not at issue, the risks of ignoring or designing-around it were unpalatable. In those cases, the vulnerability feedback provided by my innovative patent-pending software has helped me negotiate much better licensing terms that if those vulnerabilities had not be systematically determined, documented, and explained.

Hopefully, you now know the importance of surveying your company's IP power, as well as that of others, and you have a greater appreciation for the some of the many valuable uses for that information. With that background understanding, you are ready to learn some best practices for innovating.

O. & W. WRIGHT.
FLYING MACHINE.
APPLICATION FILED MAR. 23, 1903.

3 SHEETS—SHEET 1.

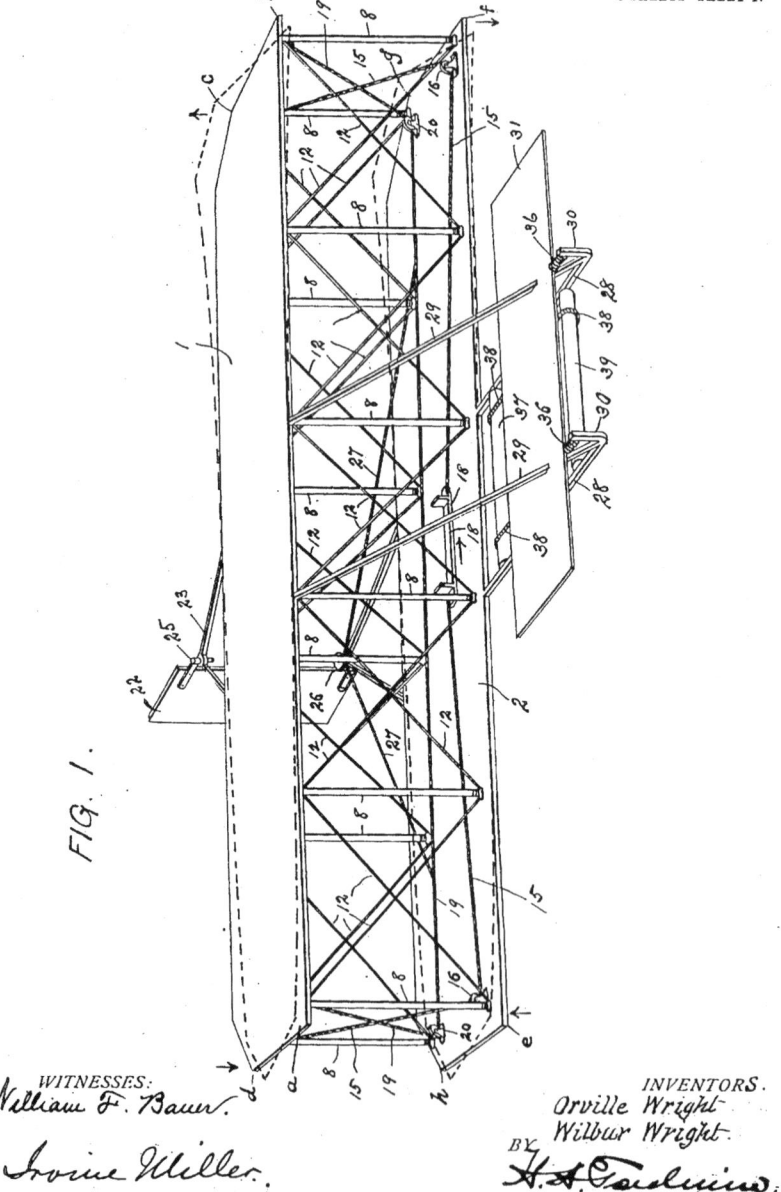

FIG. 1.

STEP 4
INNOVATE

If you really want to discover how your company can easily *innovate* many valuable solutions that meaningfully differentiate your company from its competitors and lead to sustained profitability, then you will definitely want to look over this section.

What you'll learn

▶ How can a 4 hour structured innovation session produce 10 to 20 valuable, protectable, documented innovations?

▶ What are the keys to preparing for innovating?

▶ How should your company structure an innovation session?

▶ In what ways should innovations be captured?

▶ How should innovations be filtered?

▶ By what criteria should innovations be prioritized?

▶ How should innovations be documented and protected?

Appreciating the Challenges

In *Step 1 – Understand*, you learned why sustained profitability hinges on not only innovating, but obtaining property rights in the fruits of your innovation process. In many cases, those property rights will be defined by patents.

Ideally, your company's patent portfolio seamlessly covers its entire business spectrum, leaving no gaps unprotected, and thereby prevents your competitors from gaining even a toehold via which to pilfer your hard-earned market share, revenues, and profits. More realistically, many gaps will exist or emerge, and the need to extend the edges of your portfolio will endure.

Of course, not every gap needs to be filled. But leaving opportunities to competitors might give them just what they need to gain critical leverage over your company, perhaps forcing you into taking a license to their innovative concepts that you wish you had created, giving them a license to your crown jewels to avoid IP warfare, or retreating from an otherwise cherished market.

Also, not every gap need be filled by your own innovations, but instead sometimes can be addressed by acquiring or taking a license to other's patent rights where expedient and/or prudent. Just the same, you will want to at least explore most of the gaps in your portfolio, and consider whether and how you can fill them easily.

While exploring those gaps, you will likely encounter a number of potential drivers of innovative concepts, including:

1. Solving known problems;

2. Applying technology trends to a particular field;

3. Creating breakthrough and/or disruptive technologies;

4. Developing new revenue streams;

5. Building strategic patent portfolios;

6. Designing around an existing patent; and/or

7. Anticipating, or participating in, creating an industry standard.

But no matter what drives your company to innovate, successfully filling the gaps in your company's patent portfolio will be hugely dependent on the specific approach it takes to innovating. That is, simply collecting your most talented folks and asking them to "brainstorm" innovative solutions will unlikely lead to anything more than frustration and a waste of time, due to competition, criticism, and lack of follow-through.

Yet by following some simple guidelines and best practices, you can quickly learn to hold pleasant 4-5 hour structured innovation sessions that can consistently yield upwards of 10 to 20 valuable, protectable, and documented innovative concepts that can help you efficiently fill the gaps in your patent portfolio in relatively short order.

Preparing to Innovate

Before planning your first structured innovation session, complete the following 7 relatively simple preparation tasks:

1. Designate an innovation leader;

2. Pick some problems/opportunity areas;

3. Select the innovation team;

4. Choose a few innovation starters;

5. Sample the relevant prior art;

6. Learn a few patent concepts; and

7. Arrange the session logistics.

Let's briefly explore each of these tasks.

1. *Designate an innovation leader*

Like nearly everything else in business, for systematic innovation to proceed, it needs to have a leader who takes responsibility for the process, has the clout to marshal resources to pursue that process, and intimately knows the business, both internally and externally.

2. *Pick some opportunity areas*

The directions in which your innovation process can flow are nearly infinite, but relatively few innovative solutions have a high potential to result in sustained competitive advantage and profitability for your company. So it can be very worthwhile for the innovation leader to focus the innovation process on innovative concepts that will solve a few (and perhaps only one) thoughtfully chosen real-world problems and address your company's strategic business objectives. I explain a process for selecting such real-world opportunity areas under the heading *"Listening to the Market"* in *Step 3 – Survey.*

3. *Select the innovation team*

A comfortably-sized innovation team will preferably number 4 (or possibly 5) people. If you involve more participants than that, the logistics will begin to become cumbersome, social aversions likely will shut-down several participants, and valuable concepts (i.e., ideas, solutions, innovations, etc.) will be stifled or lost.

One of the team members can serve as the session Facilitator, and the same person (or perhaps another) will serve as the Record-keeper. The chosen Facilitator should be thoroughly experienced in participating in such sessions, well-trained in facilitating them, and reasonably knowledgeable about the opportunity area. To avoid stifling their input, the Facilitator should not be the supervisor of any of the team members.

The participants/team members should be chosen based on the selected opportunity areas. For any given innovation session, appropriate attendees will likely include technical experts and business experts associated with the opportunity area, and possibly one from outside the opportunity area, or even outside your company (e.g., academicians, consultants, customers/suppliers, etc., working under an appropriate agreement) to help inspire some out-of-the-box thinking. Often, a savvy marketing person can inspire well-chosen technical folks to propose excellent insights and solutions to real-world challenges and opportunities.

Innovation team members should be picked based predominantly on the fit between their skills and the identified opportunity area, so try to minimize the number of participants chosen for purely political reasons. Also, team members should be selected in recognition of not only their skill sets, but also their personalities, which should be manageable by their team's Facilitator.

Perhaps your innovation disclosure program already rewards innovators for submitted disclosures, filled patent applications, and/or issued patents. If not, now might be the time to address that opportunity/ deficiency for incenting the desired behaviors.

Alternatively, consider what might be needed to seriously motivate every attendee to fully participate in the innovation session. Should you award gift certificates to those team members who submit the most concepts? Permit innovation teams from different sessions to compete for prizes? Allow the conceiver of any innovation that gets implemented to choose the product's or service's name or aesthetic features, such as shape, color, or non-functional packaging attributes? All of the above?

In any event, when you invite the participants, at the very minimum, let them know of the importance of the innovation session, that each invitee has been selected based on their highly regarded skills, and that receiving thoughtful contributions from each and every one of them is vital to the success of your company.

4.   *Choose innovation starters*

Within each selected opportunity area, choose a few relevant innovation starters well before the innovation session gets underway. These starters can be questions that better define the opportunity (i.e., problem) and/ or limit the corresponding concepts (i.e., ideas, insights, innovations, solutions, etc.). That is, the chosen innovation starters should help define the outer boundaries of the desired concepts, keep participants on track, and encourage concepts that refine, expand, and/or improve on other proposed concepts. But depending on where those boundaries are drawn, innovations starters can lead to mediocre insights, provoke a flood of outrageous and disjointed ideas, or stimulate precisely the desired level of creativity while preventing the session from devolving into a whimsical competition to generate concepts of increasing outlandishness and decreasing relevance to one another or the chosen opportunity area.

Innovation starters that generate big, radical, high-risk concepts tend to differ considerably from those that produce incremental, ordinary, low-risk ones. Thus, the key to choosing innovation starters that will lead to the desired concepts is to recognize that, by systematically and thoughtfully constraining the scope of their innovation discussion, the participants will be much more likely to fully explore the defined opportunity, which will produce a lot of reasonable and related concepts, and sometimes a few outstanding ones. Over-constrain the topic, and only boring, low value concepts are likely to emerge. Under-constrain the opportunity area, and the participants likely will have too many options to consider, throw out a few disjointed ideas, become frustrated, and then shut-down due to the uncertainty of not knowing which of those ideas to pursue.

Consequently, the most productive innovation starters tend to blend creativity with discipline, by focusing the participants on just the options that differ dramatically from those explored before, leading the participants to valuable unconsidered needles in the haystack of possible concepts.

A critical prerequisite for choosing effective innovation starters is determining whether your company is seeking merely to patent its innovative concepts, or whether it also plans to implement each innovative concept and bring that implementation to market. Because patents can have a life of up to 20 years (and possibly a bit longer) from their filing date, even if the innovative concepts they claim might not be market-ready for many years to come, owning the legal rights to exclude competitors from eventually marketing such innovations can nevertheless be very valuable. On the other hand, if your company is leaning strongly toward pursuing only those innovative concepts it can bring to market soon, then the budget, resources, and timing of those needs will and should constrain the chosen innovation starters.

Regarding the logistics of concept generation, keep in mind that the very best ideas tend to emerge from a combination of individual and group processes. Thus, consider distributing the chosen innovation starters to the innovation team members well before the innovation session, so that they can come prepared with at least a few well-considered responsive concepts.

Consider starting off the innovation session with 1 or 2 really simple innovation starters to get the team's creative juices flowing, help the participants become accustomed to the process, and teach the "rules" for participating in an innovation session.

As an example of a simple innovation starter, consider asking *"What do Rollerblades, Ben & Jerry's ice cream, and Spider-Man movies have in common?"* After a brief pause, provide the answer: *"they are all based on reproducing something children love in a more expensive form for adults"*. Explain that the same general business concept has led to lots of new product categories, including gourmet candies, fantasy sports, iPad games, etc. Now ask your participants, *"what else can you think of that was emotionally powerful to you as a child, and that can be reproduced in an expensive form for adults?"*. This brief exercise should help get the process rolling.

Here's another exemplary introductory starter that is simple, but perhaps a bit more relevant to your company: *"What would be a great service anniversary gift, costing under $500, for an employee who has been with the company for 5 years?"*.

For more help with selecting innovation starters, read over the process outlined for selecting opportunity areas under the heading *"Listening to the Market"* in *Step 3 – Survey*.

5.　*Sample the relevant prior art*

By establishing the boundaries of each opportunity area, a brief prior art search potentially can be performed before the innovation session. Presenting a reasonable sampling of the resulting prior art can inform the innovation session participants of known solutions to that opportunity/ problem, thereby allowing them to suggest concepts that are likely to be different from those known solutions.

6.　*Learn a few patenting requirements*

At the beginning of an innovation session, it can be very helpful to briefly explain to the participants the basic requirements of patenting, and particularly the requirements of novelty and enablement.

In a nutshell, to be patentable, an innovative concept must be novel, that is, must have some difference from what has come before, either in its structure or in how it is used.

Also, the concept must be described in the patent application in a way that enables a person having merely ordinary skill in that realm to implement it, at least crudely, without the need to engage in experimentation. There is no need to actually build that implementation; simply describing in writing how to implement it will suffice for patenting.

70

7. *Arrange the session logistics*

Heeding the following logistical considerations can help ensure successful innovation sessions:

a. Each innovation session should take place in a room that is relatively spacious, secure, and free from outside distractions (e.g., phone calls, text messages, smartphone games, etc.);

b. Participants should be comfortably seated around one or more round or elliptical tables having an interesting focal point so that participants can avoid eye contact with other participants when desired;

c. A good audio recorder should be utilized to help capture and/or clarify concepts that slip by the Record-keeper;

d. At least one easel, multiple pads of flip chart paper, and a half-dozen or more colored marking pens should be made available to the Facilitator and/or Record-keeper. Also, a mechanism (e.g., masking tape, tacky strips, etc.) should be provided for hanging each completed flip chart page on the walls of the room for everyone to easily see (i.e., so the concepts on that page can inspire additional concepts). Computers and/or overhead projectors are not currently recommended, as they typically do not allow participants to easily and independently see or modify concepts on earlier "slides", charts, or pages;

e. Each participant should be issued a highly visible name tag bearing their initials, so that the Facilitator and/or Record-keeper can easily identify each concept by its creator's initials, thereby making attributing inventorship that much easier;

f. Each participant also should be issued a few colored marker pens and a pack or two of 3" x 3" (or larger) sticky note paper, so that they can quietly and easily elaborate or improve upon any concept previously listed on a flip chart page without disturbing the current flow of the session (remembering to include their initials on each completed sticky note); and

g. A clock should be easily visible to all participants so that they can help the Facilitator keep the session on schedule.

Here are a few additional best practices for scheduling an optimal innovation session:

a. Verify that top management has communicated its strong support for the session to all supervisors before requesting that their employees serve as participants;

b. Plan for a 4-5 hour innovation session;

c. Consider eating out together or catering a meal to allow the participants a chance to socialize with one another, preferably before the session gets underway;

d. Defer the session until all selected participants can be available for the entire 4-5 hour session;

e. While the innovation session should not be spread across multiple meetings, as too much continuity and value will be lost, follow-up meetings are encouraged if needed to advance a great concept;

f. Provide appropriately spaced breaks for snacks, restrooms, checking and returning urgent calls, etc.; and

g. Because the participants will be mentally spent after a round of serious concept generation immediately followed by another round of concept evaluation, don't try to "enhance" the session by extending the idea-generating phase or the overall session time. Instead, schedule additional complete innovation sessions, each having its own selected problem/opportunity areas, participants, and innovation starters.

Holding the First Session

The most successful innovation sessions tend to follow a proven process, implement a well-considered structure, and follow thoughtful rules. Such best practices guide how, within such innovation sessions, the innovations are nurtured, captured, filtered, prioritized, documented, and initially protected. Although I have laid the groundwork for teaching these best practices, they really need to be seen in action to be learned well and truly appreciated.

By carefully implementing my best practices, you can reasonably expect that your company's 4-5 hour structured innovation sessions will consistently produce upwards of 10 to 20 valuable, protectable, and documented innovative concepts.

Crowd-source Opportunities

Along with holding innovation sessions, your company can tap the insights of strangers to identify problems your company might be able to innovatively solve. Whether your company has identified challenges in need of solutions and/or solutions in need of applications, a number of organizations utilizing crowd-sourcing have sprouted up that could help your company transform creativity into true innovation.

Both the X Prize Foundation (www.xprize.org) and InnoCentive (www.innocentive.com) work to match up challenges (ranging from simple idea gathering to tackling huge global issues) with crowd-sourced solutions, that is, solutions proposed by nearly anyone, especially via the web. Using contests that award cash prizes, commercial, government, and non-profit organizations can essentially increase R&D capacity without all of the associated risks and costs. Taking the opposite approach, the folks at Marblar (www.marblar.com) work with universities and corporations to identify dormant IP, then present that IP to its members, seeking crowd-sourced potential new uses and/or commercialization strategies, and even spawning start-ups. The site was also designed to make the process playful and fun. Members (or "marblars") can earn points ("marbles") for identifying new applications for inventions and sometimes even cash prizes for their efforts.

These and other crowd-sourcing mechanisms can be valuable tools to help bridge the gap between idea and innovation.

Now that you a familiar with some of the basics of generating valuable innovative solutions to true market opportunities, we next turn to how to best secure and protect your company's valuable innovations and other types of intellectual assets.

(12) **United States Design Patent**
Akana et al.

(10) **Patent No.:** **US D636,392 S**
(45) **Date of Patent:** ** **Apr. 19, 2011**

(54) **ELECTRONIC DEVICE WITH GRAPHICAL USER INTERFACE**

(75) Inventors: **Jody Akana**, San Francisco, CA (US); **Bartley K. Andre**, Menlo Park, CA (US); **Freddy Anzures**, San Francisco, CA (US); **Jeremy Bataillou**, San Francisco, CA (US); **Imran Chaudhri**, San Francisco, CA (US); **Daniel J. Coster**, San Francisco, CA (US); **Daniele De Iuliis**, San Francisco, CA (US); **Evans Hankey**, San Francisco, CA (US); **Richard P. Howarth**, San Francisco, CA (US); **Jonathan P. Ive**, San Francisco, CA (US); **Steve Jobs**, Palo Alto, CA (US); **Duncan Robert Kerr**, San Francisco, CA (US); **Shin Nishibori**, Portola Valley, CA (US); **Matthew Dean Rohrbach**, San Francisco, CA (US); **Peter Russell-Clarke**, San Francisco, CA (US); **Christopher J. Stringer**, Woodside, CA (US); **Eugene Antony Whang**, San Francisco, CA (US); **Rico Zörkendörfer**, San Francisco, CA (US)

(73) Assignee: **Apple Inc.**, Cupertino, CA (US)

(**) Term: **14 Years**

(21) Appl. No.: **29/376,051**

(22) Filed: **Sep. 30, 2010**

Related U.S. Application Data

(63) Continuation of application No. 29/360,036, filed on Apr. 19, 2010, now Pat. No. Des. 627,778, which is a continuation of application No. 29/359,260, filed on Apr. 7, 2010.

(51) **LOC (9) Cl.** **14-02**
(52) **U.S. Cl.** **D14/341**; D14/485
(58) **Field of Classification Search** .... D14/341–347, D14/137, 138, 138.1, 138 AA, 138 R, 138 AB, D14/138 G, 138 A, 496, 426, 429, 129, 130, D14/420, 439 441, 448, 125, 147, 156, 218, D14/250, 336, 203.1, 203.3, 203.4, 203.7, D14/315, 388 390; D21/324, 329, 330; D10/65, 104; D18/6–7; 345/169, 901, 905, 345/156, 157, 168, 173; 361/680, 686, 679.27, 361/679.3; 379/433.04, 433.07, 433.11, 379/916, 433.01, 433.06
See application file for complete search history.

(56) **References Cited**

U.S. PATENT DOCUMENTS

D297,518 S   9/1988 Yuen

(Continued)

FOREIGN PATENT DOCUMENTS

EM   000569157-0005   9/2006

OTHER PUBLICATIONS

"LG KE850 Prada," http://www.gsmarena.com/lg_ke850_prada-1828.php. Downloaded Feb. 20, 2007. 4 pages.

(Continued)

Primary Examiner — Cathron C Brooks
Assistant Examiner — Barbara Fox
(74) *Attorney, Agent, or Firm* — Sterne, Kessler, Goldstein & Fox PLLC

(57) **CLAIM**
The ornamental design for an electronic device with graphical user interface, as shown and described.

DESCRIPTION

FIG. **1** is a bottom front perspective view of an electronic device with graphical user interface thereof showing our new design;
FIG. **2** is top front perspective view thereof;
FIG. **3** is a top rear perspective view thereof;
FIG. **4** is a bottom rear perspective view thereof;
FIG. **5** is a front view thereof;
FIG. **6** is a rear view thereof;
FIG. **7** is a top view thereof;
FIG. **8** is a bottom view thereof;
FIG. **9** is a left side view thereof; and,
FIG. **10** is a right side view thereof.
The shade lines in the Figures show transparency and not surface ornamentation.
The broken lines in the Figures show portions of the electronic device and portions of the graphical user interface which form no part of the claimed design.

1 Claim, 8 Drawing Sheets

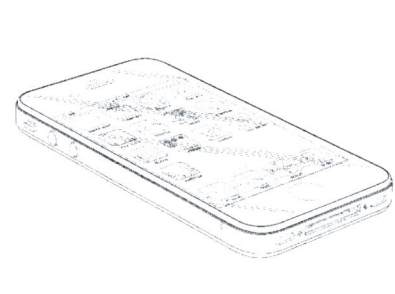
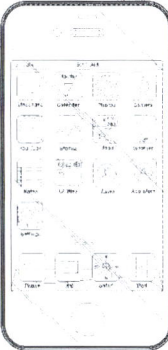

(12) **United States Design Patent**

Clark et al.

(10) Patent No.: **US D572,144 S**

(45) **Date of Patent:** ** **Jul. 1, 2008**

(54) **CONTAINER**

(75) Inventors: **Andrew James Clark**, Morristown, NJ (US); **Deborah A. Lyzenga**, Long Valley, NJ (US)

(73) Assignee: **Kraft Foods Holdings, Inc.**, Northfield, IL (US)

(**) Term: **14 Years**

(21) Appl. No.: **29/283,452**

(22) Filed: **Aug. 15, 2007**

(51) **LOC (8) Cl.** **09-01**

(52) **U.S. Cl.** **D9/623**; D9/643

(58) **Field of Classification Search** D9/600, D9/614, 616, 619–620, 623, 628, 643–644, D9/500–50; 206/457, 822; 215/400; 220/890; D3/270, 271.1, 271.9; D7/514–515, 619.2, D7/628; D21/623; D11/160

See application file for complete search history.

(56) **References Cited**

U.S. PATENT DOCUMENTS

D99,333	S	*	4/1936	Rowse D9/623
D143,576	S	*	1/1946	Claypool D9/623
D250,758	S	*	1/1979	Braddock D11/160
D254,717	S		4/1980	Mascia et al.
D254,718	S		4/1980	Mascia et al.
D254,719	S		4/1980	Mascia et al.
D254,777	S		4/1980	Mascia et al.
D265,022	S	*	6/1982	Parker D21/623
5,056,674	A		10/1991	Swartley
5,067,622	A		11/1991	Garver et al.
5,407,086	A		4/1995	Ota et al.
5,598,941	A		2/1997	Semersky et al.
5,758,790	A		6/1998	Ewing, Jr.
6,554,146	B1		4/2003	DeGroff et al.
6,585,125	B1		7/2003	Peek
D479,396	S		9/2003	Altemus
7,051,890	B2		5/2006	Onoda et al.
7,073,675	B2		7/2006	Trude
D531,903	S	*	11/2006	Haubein D9/500
D532,311	S	*	11/2006	Yourist D9/538
7,228,981	B2		6/2007	Chisholm
2005/0211661	A1		9/2005	Galownia et al.
2005/0252881	A1		11/2005	Zhang et al.
2006/0289379	A1		12/2006	Ozawa et al.
2007/0039917	A1		2/2007	Yourist

FOREIGN PATENT DOCUMENTS

JP	2000-231352	8/2000

OTHER PUBLICATIONS

GoAntiques.com Mr. Peanut Limited Edition decanter Jar, made 1991. www.goantiques.com/detail,peanut-limited-edition,1577149.html.*

ebay.com Mr. Peanut Cookie Cracker Jar with Lid Glass, made 1990. http://cgi.ebay.com/mr-peanut-cookie-cracker-jar-with-lid-glass-1990_WOQQitemZ200214261695QQihZ010QQcategoryZ38 94QQssPageNameZWDVWQQrdZVViewItem.*

* cited by examiner

Primary Examiner — Sandra Morris

(74) *Attorney, Agent, or Firm* — Stites & Harbison PLLC; Marvin Petry

(57) **CLAIM**

The ornamental design for a container, as shown and described.

DESCRIPTION

FIG. **1** is a front elevational view of a container according to our new design.

FIG. **2** is a right side elevational view thereof.

FIG. **3** is a left side elevational view thereof.

FIG. **4** is a rear elevational view thereof; and,

FIG. **5** is a top plan view thereof.

The bottom view forms no part of the present design.

1 Claim, 4 Drawing Sheets

STEP 5

SECURE

If you really want to **secure** your company's distinctive market position, such as by capturing and strongly protecting its intellectual assets, acquiring valuable intellectual properties, and avoiding costly infringements, this section was written for you.

What you'll learn

▸ Which IP protections can be obtained instantly and inexpensively?

▸ When are trade secrets a better bet than patents?

▸ What are the benefits, costs, and risks of seeking a patent?

▸ What are the 7 steps to obtaining a valuable patent?

▸ In what foreign countries does patenting make the most sense?

▸ How can infringement liability be avoided, reduced, and resolved?

▸ What are the benefits, costs, and risks of registering trademarks and copyrights?

Intellectual Assets

What are intellectual assets?

As explained in *Step 1 – Understand*, I define *intellectual assets* to be valuable, recorded, intangible assets. And I define *intangible assets* as non-monetary things of potential value that typically are thought of as not requiring physical storage space, such as a company's knowledge, skills, data, software, organizational structure, employee motivation and flexibility, R&D, legal and marketing activities, brands, reputation, goodwill, agreements, and relationships, etc. With that background, let's now take a closer look at intellectual assets and how and when to protect them as *intellectual property*.

What are the major types of intellectual assets?

1. Know-how

2. Trade Secrets

3. Patents

4. Marks

5. Domain Names

6. Copyrights

7. Agreements

Below, I explain in detail the nature of each of these types of intellectual assets, when to pursue them, and how to protect them. Note that although I describe them separately, many types of intellectual assets can complement and supplement each other, bolstering the protection and value that would be provided by employing only a single type of intellectual asset.

Know-how and Trade Secrets

Know-how can include any information (including data and knowledge) that provides competitive advantage. Of any given company's intellectual assets, its know-how typically accounts for the vast majority of those assets, yet often goes unrecognized, unappreciated, and rather poorly protected.

Although not necessarily secret or unknown to others, know-how can be quite valuable. Here's an example I presented earlier (see page 40). Even though its content is made available to the public, a rapidly-accessible database of current telephone numbers and addresses can enable telephone companies to extract $0.50, $0.99, or more from callers to "Information" or "411". As another example, in many patent licensing deals, it is the know-how, the detailed nuts-and-bolts knowledge of how to implement the patented subject matter, often in an optimized way, that can be the most valuable part of the deal.

Trade secrets, which are a particular form of know-how and the oldest form of intellectual property protection, are defined as information that is not generally known, provides economic value to its owner, and is kept secret via reasonable measures of security. Trade secrets can include, for example:

1. innovative concepts, whether patentable or not

2. formulas and manufacturing processes

3. material and equipment suppliers

4. cost and pricing data

5. customer lists and data

6. marketing information, plans, and methods

7. business strategies and tactics

8. financial statements and projections

9. accounting, trading, & brokerage processes

10. computer software code

Of particular interest to trade secret owners is not only positive know-how (how to accomplish something), but also negative know-how (what not to do and/or why not to do it), as such negative know-how can reflect the tremendous resources expended and/or the valuable knowledge gained through unsuccessful experiments and/or implementations.

Notably, trade secrets aren't protected by government registration or certification. They are protected by being kept secret.

For any given trade secret, which secrecy measures are considered reasonable often depends on the context, such as industry practices, the value of the secret, and the costs to secure it. Generally, however, the following measures are commonly implemented to protect trade secrets:

- explaining the company's trade secret policies in writing to all relevant audiences (e.g., employees, contractors, partners, etc.);

- including a confidentiality obligation in all relevant agreements;

- avoiding improper exposure to the trade secrets of competitors;

- memorializing trade secrets in writings marked as "proprietary and confidential";

- limiting and tracking access by employees, contractors, and partners to the company's trade secrets;

- screening potential disclosures, such as via plant tours, speeches, publications, and electronic device and network vulnerabilities;

- preventing public access (both physically and electronically) to the company's trade secrets; and

- conducting exit interviews with departing employees.

Trade secret misappropriation quite often arises within companies and their close associations. Today's mobile workforce, computer technology, and the increased use of contractors, consultants, and outsourcing have all significantly increased the risks of misappropriation.

Not all misappropriations are intentional. Often, employees may simply not view the information they work with everyday as being the highly-valued trade secret material it is. Sometimes this is due to management's lack of educating employees about the confidential nature of their work. Not surprisingly, continuous and consistent education regarding trade secret protection tends to have more staying power than a message delivered once at hiring. Proper training and accountability are key, and also happen to be incredibly cost-effective.

Of course, deliberate theft also occurs. A 2007 survey [24] revealed that a primary threat to proprietary information is the deliberate action of current and former employees.

That same survey indicated that all types of business transactions and trade secrets stored in all kinds of formats are targeted. Beyond the financial harm and competitive advantage lost, a company's reputation also can be on the line when trade secrecy is misappropriated.

Not only that, but the U.S. economy and national security also can be threatened by the loss of trade secrecy. While difficult to measure the full extent of the problem, a 2011 study [25] by the National Intellectual Property Rights Coordination Center noted that trade secret theft encompasses both private and national economic and technological losses and may threaten national security - particularly when civilian trade secrets are applied to defensive uses. To be sure, theft of U.S. trade secrets happens most often from within in the U.S. by U.S. actors, but among international offenders, China tops the list and is a growing priority for the U.S. Trade Representative. [26]

Unfortunately, all too many companies wait until the unthinkable happens to begin taking measures to continuously identify, valuate, and better protect their trade secrets.

Trade secret protection in the U.S. is governed primarily by state law. Generally, every state makes theft or unauthorized dissemination of a trade secret an unlawful act. Most states have adopted some form of the Uniform Trade Secret Act (UTSA), which allows for the recovery of both the plaintiff's actual losses and the amount the defendant has benefited as a result of the misappropriation.

Theft of trade secrets also can result in criminal penalties under the federal Economic Espionage Act and/or the Computer Fraud and Abuse Act. A case is said to be a matter of economic espionage when a foreign government, instrumentality, or agent directs or benefits from the trade secret theft.

There is no limitation on the length of time that a trade secret can be protected (e.g., the formula for Coca-Cola® allegedly has been kept secret for over 125 years). Trade secrets don't expire and they can be licensed indefinitely. Note however that, absent an enforceable contract, you have no right to exclude others from using "proper means" to obtain what you consider to be your know-how or trade secret. Proper means can include independent development, reverse engineering, obtaining from a third party who has a right to provide, or obtaining from you without breaching a contractual or other duty, such as when you have failed to exert reasonable efforts to maintain secrecy. In contrast, improper means can involve breach of contract, espionage, theft, wiretapping, fraud, bribery, coercion, etc.

As mentioned above, know-how and trade secrets are often protected by formal written agreements (e.g., Non-Disclosure Agreements, Employment Agreements, etc.), employee training, physical security, computer security, and/or other well-managed access control practices.

Regardless of the precautions taken, public disclosure to even one person can destroy its secrecy if the information then becomes more generally known. For this reason, trade secrets too frequently lose their secrecy and therefore fall into the public domain. Trade secrets can be fragile. Consequently, many holders of such information often consider patent protection when feasible.

When they do, patenting is sometimes chosen instead of trade secrecy. At other times, both forms of protection are used, because patent protection can both supplement and complement trade secret protection. For example, once a patent application is filed, there is no obligation or ability to update it as implementations of the innovation are optimized. Therefore, such optimization details can be maintained as trade secrets. As another example, while developing and/or optimizing an innovation, considerable information about what approaches don't work can be gathered and maintained via trade secrecy.

Below are a few basic factors that can be considered when weighing trade secrecy and patenting.

Factors suggesting trade secrecy vs. patenting	
Trade secrecy	**Patenting**
Used only internally	Feature of commercial product
Short commercial life	Long commercial life
Leakage easy to prevent	Leakage difficult to prevent
Easily designed around	Not easily designed around
Not easily reverse engineered	Easily reverse engineered
Independent development unlikely	Independent development likely
Seems unpatentable	Appears to be patentable
Infringement difficult to detect	Infringement easy to detect
Limited value to competitors	Large value to competitors

Sometimes information that is extremely valuable to a company just simply isn't patentable. Yet it's that information and knowledge that is vitally needed for the business to run and/or distinguish itself from its competitors. Some argue that the creation of trade secret information is the primary business activity of most companies in today's economy, making trade secrecy a very high priority among intellectual property strategies.

Finally, because of the risk of being on the *wrong end* of an allegation of trade secret misappropriation, I recommend that companies have policies in place that address how information is obtained, who owns it, and whether any duties or obligations attach. Understanding confidentiality and/or non-compete obligations of new employees, maintaining good documentation of the company's own know-how and independent development, and keeping confidentiality agreements with other parties to a minimum are all good ways of reducing the risks of misappropriating the trade secrets of others.

Patents

What is a patent?

Generally, a patent is written document that;

- is granted by a government;

- describes, to a person having ordinary skill in the corresponding field of endeavor ("the art"), in an enabling manner and without requiring substantial experimentation, how to make and/or use one or more "inventions"; and

- legally defines each "invention" via a "claim".

Most governments grant patents to encourage detailed and empowering written descriptions of innovations to the public, thereby continually increasing the public's knowledge base. Thus, the description section of most patents typically includes both text and drawings, and sometimes tables, equations, and/or charts. Videos are not permitted, photos are rarely permitted, and generally, the entire contents of the patent must be clearly reproducible on paper, such as via a copying machine or printer.

Once granted, a patent generally provides its owner with the right to exclude others from making, using, or selling anything that falls within the scope of any valid unexpired claim of that patent. Claims can endure for up to a specified period of time, which is typically 20 years from the filing date of the initial application that led to that patent. In the United States, a patent also provides its owner with the right to exclude others from offering for sale or importing the claimed subject matter.

Generally, except as noted, my communications focus on U.S. patents.

What are the classes and types of patents?

In the U.S., there are three basic classes of patent applications:

1. Utility: for functional innovations;

2. Design: for aesthetic (ornamental) innovations; and

3. Plant: for asexually reproduced plant variety innovations.

Because the Utility class is by far the largest (roughly 96% of all U.S. patent applications), except where noted, it is the primary focus of my communications. I will address utility patents first, and then briefly discuss design patents and plant patents.

The Utility class includes two types of applications:

- the provisional (a.k.a. "informal") patent application; and

- the non-provisional (a.k.a. "regular" or "formal") patent application.

I discuss both provisionals and non-provisionals below.

Utility Patents

What do utility patents protect?

The range of patentable subject matter is very wide. For United States utility patents, patentable subject matter can include nearly anything that involves or results from a human-caused transformation and that is reasonably categorized within any of these 4 broad classes:

1. "Process"

- that is, a novel method of transforming nearly anything

- the method can involve manufacturing, engineering, physics, chemistry, biology, business, information, or software

- examples include: an innovative method for transforming iron oxide into pigments, or a new procedure for transforming raw accounting data into a required value on a tax return

2. "Article of Manufacture"

   • that is, a new good or product resulting from a transformation

   • examples include: an innovative device, such as a light bulb, mouse trap, or modem

3. "Composition of Matter"

   • that is, a novel material resulting from a transformation

   • examples include: a innovative chemical compound, drug, or gene sequence

4. "Machine"

   • that is, a new system or combination of devices for causing a transformation

   • examples include: an innovative assembly for making a new or old flashlight, biodiesel fuel, or nano-particle

What is required for an innovation to be patentable?

Within these 4 classes, the USPTO is required to grant/issue Utility Patents on non-provisional patent applications that adequately describe how to implement the useful, novel, non-obvious subject matter ("concepts") that they properly claim.

A claimed concept is not considered sufficiently useful if it is a law of nature, a physical phenomenon, or too abstract (has no described implementations). Also, the patent application must identify a beneficial use for the claimed concept (other than acting as, for example, a boat anchor, paperweight, or research curiosity).

A patent application's claimed concept is not novel (new) if it was:

- known or used by others in the U.S., or patented or described in a printed publication anywhere in the world, before its conception date by the inventors named in that patent application;

- patented or described in a printed publication anywhere in the world, or in public use or on sale in the U.S., more than one year before the filing date of that patent application;

- invented by someone other than the named inventors.

Generally, the novelty of a claimed concept is determined based on a comparison to what is "taught" (described and enabled) by the prior art, which is basically everything that was known (effectively, everything published) before the origination of the concept.

A claimed concept is considered legally obvious if, at the time it was conceived, a person having ordinary skill in the art (the general realm of that concept) would have known of art-recognized reasons to modify or combine relevant prior art references, considered as a whole, to arrive at the entirety of that claimed concept. Thus, although a layperson or engineer might exclaim that a claimed concept seems "obvious" (typically because, after reading the claim, they can understand how the concept works or can predict that it likely will work), U.S. patent law can be rather strict about what must be proven before that concept will be deemed "obvious" from a legal perspective.

A Patentability Search often can help reveal whether a concept is novel (and sometimes whether it is non-obvious).

A patent application's description of a claimed concept is considered adequate if, as of the application's effective filing date, that description reasonably empowers a person having merely ordinary skill in the art to successfully (even if non-optimally or crudely) implement that concept without requiring substantial experimentation to do so, and in the best manner known to the innovators, and reasonably demonstrates that the innovators actually had that concept in mind.

What are the benefits of owning a patent?

Although in *Step 7 – Harness*, you will learn 70+ tactics for harnessing the power of intellectual assets, including patents, I will highlight a few of the most patent-relevant tactics here.

Some of the most common tactics to exploit a patent include:

Distinguishing its innovators and owners, such as by:

- Publishing and promoting their technical prowess, innovativeness, productivity and skill;

- Creating an aura of innovativeness, intelligence, and skill;

- Attracting investors, customers, licensees, and business alliances;

Creating and enhancing revenue, such as by:

- Requiring competitors to pay licensing fees and royalties for the right to use or sell the patented innovation;

- Landing related deals;

- Carving out exclusivity in the marketplace;

- Enabling enhanced downstream pricing & terms (sole seller); and/or

- Empowering enhanced upstream pricing & terms (sole buyer).

Discouraging competitors from entering or staying in a market, such as via:

- Injunctions

  – e.g., shutting down competitor's research, production, distribution, marketing, website, etc.

  – e.g., seizing and destroying imported knock-offs

- Damages

  – at least a reasonable royalty

  – possibly the patent owner's lost profits

  – possibly up to triple damages for willful infringement

- Costs & attorneys fees (in exceptional cases)

If desired, a patent sometimes can be legally enforced against potential and/or actual competitors to prevent the making, using, offering for sale, and/or selling in, and/or importing into, the country in which the patent is in force, anything that falls within the scope of one or more valid unexpired claims of that patent.

Such enforcement often can be achieved outside the judicial system, such as via a simple "Patent Pending" notice on the patent owner's goods. At other times, enforcement can require the threat and/or filing of a lawsuit alleging infringement of the patent. If the parties are unable to settle the dispute early in the suit, the litigation costs can become very expensive and time-consuming for both parties. Thus, the vast majority of patent infringement suits settle relatively quickly.

For those who do not have the financial means for enforcement, patent assertion insurance sometimes can be purchased that will provide the financial muscle to litigate all the way to an enforceable judgment, even after being upheld on appeal, if necessary.

Patent rights only arise upon issuance of a patent. That is, only the claims of an issued patent can be legally enforced against perceived infringers. I would be happy to discuss how I can assist with preparing for enforcing, and actually enforcing, your company's patent rights.

Often, a patent's owner is willing to allow competitors to make, use, and/or sell implementations of a patented concept, provided that the competitors pay the patent owner for the right to do so. A document that provides for the grant of such rights and the associated payments is called a "Licensing Agreement".

Sometimes, a patent publication can serve as an advertisement of the technical capabilities of the innovators and/or the patent owner. The audience for that message can be potential investors, customers, employees, competitors, and/or suppliers, etc.

How long does it take to obtain a patent?

The amount of time that elapses from the time a non-provisional patent application is filed, until that application issues as a utility patent, can vary considerably from one application to another. Factors that can effect this patent "pendency" include:

- the technology area of the claimed subject matter;

- the USPTO's backlog and staffing in that technology area;

- the quality of the patentability search;

- the breadth of the claimed subject matter;

- how close the prior art is to the claimed subject matter; and/or

- the tenacity of the applicant to fight for all subject matter to which they are legally entitled versus capitulating to the examiner and potentially seeking broader claims via a follow-up application.

Although it has very wide variability, and although there are several ways to greatly accelerate examination (see 153), average pendency in the USPTO is now roughly 4 years. Of this average, approximately 2 to 3 years is spent waiting for examination. Actual substantive examination, with its volleying of Office Actions and responses seeking consensus on the scope and language of the claims, tends to require roughly 1 to 2 years on average. But again, there is wide variability associated with each of these averages, so check with me before assuming a pendency for any particular patent application.

What are the costs of seeking a patent?

From the perspective of most individuals, (utility) patents are relatively expensive to obtain.

For example, by the time the USPTO actually issues a U.S. patent, a typical patent applicant will have spent a total of at least $15,000 (and possibly considerably more) on government fees and the costs of preparing, filing, and, although somewhat deferred, prosecuting (negotiating with the USPTO to convince them to issue a patent) the underlying U.S. non-provisional patent application.

In particular, my charges (attorney fees) to prepare a non-provisional patent application for filing typically fall in the range of $5,000 to $9,000. For good reasons, the cost sometimes can edge higher, particularly if, for example:

- the disclosure is excessively lengthy, confusing, or complex;

- the disclosure includes numerous drawings;

- multiple innovations are disclosed;

- the known prior art is particularly "close" to the innovation;

- an inordinate amount of re-work is required;

- communications are particularly challenging; or

- detailed explanations of many attorney decisions are requested.

It should be apparent that most of the above-listed cost-increasing factors can be controlled by the client. In any event, once prepared, the costs to file a non-provisional patent application can vary depending on, for example, the jurisdictions in which that application is filed (e.g., U.S. only, PCT, foreign, etc.), its page count and/or claim count, and/or the number of people employed by the applicant, etc. Expect the filing fees for a U.S. non-provisional to be at least roughly $500, and sometimes considerably more.

Although most prosecution costs do not begin to be incurred until roughly 1 to 3 years after a non-provisional patent application is filed, prosecuting a U.S. version of that application will typically cost from $1,000 to $6,000, and potentially much more if, for example, the scope of protection sought is relatively broad, the claimed subject matter is particularly valuable and/or complex, and/or the cited prior art is quite close to the desired subject matter, etc.

The filing and prosecution costs in countries foreign to the U.S. can be lower, but in several cases can be greater than those in the U.S., due to, for example, translation costs, annuities, and/or foreign counsel fees, etc.

Fortunately, a significant chunk of the prosecution costs can be deferred until long after the patent application is prepared and filed.

What are the risks in seeking a patent?

No matter how much money any company spends, or what degree of professional assistance it obtains, the potential risks associated with the patenting process are substantial and should be carefully considered before and while pursuing that process.

Although most of these risks can be managed, it can be very difficult to predict with any reasonable accuracy, for example, how the USPTO will respond to a given patent application, how much time or effort will be needed to convince the USPTO to issue a patent, or what the scope of the claims of the issued patent will be.

And even if a patent examiner asserts an illegal or factually-unsupported position, there is no valid general guarantee that efforts to overcome that position will be successful, or that the desired patent will result.

Similarly, although most of these risks can be well-managed, there are no certainties as to, for example, how the market will react to an innovation, whether a company will be able to successfully license or enforce its patent, and/or whether the company will obtain a reasonable return on its investment in the patenting process.

These and other potential risks associated with the innovation and patenting processes are significant and should be taken into account before and while pursuing those processes.

Utilizing the services of a competent patent attorney often can help lessen some of these risks, but not all of these risks can be eliminated entirely.

Thus, it is important that your company recognizes, weighs, and maintains realistic expectations of the potential costs, potential benefits, and potential risks, throughout the innovation and patenting processes, and beyond.

What are the alternatives to seeking a patent?

Although other forms of protection should always be at least briefly considered to supplement patent protection, patenting is not the best approach in certain situations. For example, sometimes it is more advantageous to:

- maintain an innovation as a trade secret than to seek a patent to protect that innovation (this can sometimes be safer in industries with just a few competitors keeping close watch on each other);

- seek protection of only a product's aesthetic aspects via a design patent;

- exploit superior supply chain management to exclude competitors from key resources;

- use branding to associate a product or service with a desirable lifestyle or traits; and/or

- rely on rapid market entry, "first mover" status, and/or superior marketing communications to establish market leadership.

For example, relying on trade secrecy can be the best approach when:

- your company's innovation lends itself to secrecy because it is very difficult for competitors to arrive at the innovation, such as via independent discovery or reverse engineering based on one's marketed products and/or services, and

- your company is willing to take appropriate and substantial measures to maintain the innovation's secrecy, recognizing that the average trade secret loses its secrecy, and thus its trade secret status, within relatively few years.

If speedy protection is needed, particularly from copy-cat pirates, then initially obtaining design patent protection of a product's ornamental features might make more sense than waiting years for a utility patent to issue that protects the product's functional features. And keep in mind that, compared to utility patents, enforcing design patents can be much quicker and cheaper too. On the flip side, design patents can be much easier for a competitor to successfully "design around", so typically, they are most useful only against rather blatant knock-offs.

On occasion, a company can land a valuable supplier agreement that, for example, locks-out competitors from access to a critical component or service, provides very favorable long-term pricing, and/or secures other highly beneficial terms (involving, e.g., features, financing, inventory management, delivery, co-marketing, service, warranty, indemnity, etc.). The possibilities here are nearly endless, and once in a while, can provide even stronger leverage than patenting.

Branding and/or marketing techniques sometimes can be more effective than patenting, particularly where tremendously strong goodwill is generated and can be maintained for a brand. Generating such strong goodwill usually requires a substantial and sustained investment. Maintaining that goodwill often mandates careful and highly responsive brand management, for events can rapidly arise that tarnish a brand, thereby quickly eroding the goodwill and corresponding investment in that damaged brand.

When considering these alternatives to utility patents, keep in mind the guidance and caveats raised in *Step 1 – Understand*. In particular, if you remember nothing else, remember my bottom line advice: ***you must own the IP to own the profits***.

Should a patent be sought?

The decision to seek a patent should be thoroughly and carefully considered. The patenting process can be expensive, lengthy, risky, and frustrating. Yet, the rewards can be substantial.

Generally, one should seek a patent if the expected risk-adjusted return justifies the investment in the patent. For some, merely having their name on a patent, or a patent number on their product, is incredibly valuable, particularly when marketing their capabilities to potential employees, investors, customers, etc.

For others, the opportunity to obtain royalties or other forms of licensing revenue from those who wish to manufacture, sell, and/or distribute the patented product or service is an ample justification to pursue patenting.

For still others, the right to exclude competitors from making, using, importing, or selling the patented innovation can provide a sufficient reward for their investment in obtaining the patent.

Despite the beckoning of these potential benefits, I urge you to recognize that the patent process is moderately risky. For example, not all patent applications result in issued patents. Although the percentage varies from year-to-year, roughly 65-70% of original patent applications are eventually granted, while the remaining patent applications are abandoned, with their subject matter potentially dedicated to the public domain. Keep in mind that this percentage includes all original patent applications, including:

- applications for which no patentability search was performed, and thus fail to describe or claim a truly patentable innovation;

- applications filed by innovators who represent themselves before the USPTO, without the assistance of a competent patent attorney, and who eventually become frustrated with the patenting process and quit;

- applications directed toward subject matter that, while patentable, is no longer in sync with the company's chosen business directions; and

- applications filed by those who ultimately lack sufficient financial resources to prosecute the application to issuance.

Thus, when sufficient resources are properly applied, the likelihood of success with the patenting process can be greatly improved with respect to this 65-70% metric. Generally, the better the patentability search, the better the preparation of the patent application, and the better the prosecution of that application, the greater the odds are that the application will be issued, assuming the applicant remains committed to obtaining that patent. Similarly, the better the business plan, and the better the implementation of that plan, the greater the likelihood that a substantial return will be earned on the issued patent.

Applying appropriate patent valuation techniques, such as those described in detail in *Step 6 – Enhance*, potential returns, investments, and risks, along with the likely timings of each of those financial events can be determined. Then, an appropriate business plan can be developed for obtaining the optimal return on your patent investment.

What are the time limits for seeking a patent?

To protect rights in a valuable innovative concept, it is often worthwhile to file some form of patent application as soon as possible. Doing so will provide a filing date that defines what "prior art" can be used against the claims of any non-provisional patent application filed (now or later). Because one never knows when uncomfortably close prior art might emerge, time might be of the essence.

Those patent applications for which each claim has an effective filing date of 15 March 2013 or earlier are subject to the "first-to-invent" ("FTI") rules. Under those FTI rules, the U.S. allows a one-year grace period from the date of an offer for sale, commercialization, or non-confidential disclosure of a concept until a U.S. utility patent application describing that concept must be filed if a U.S. utility patent is desired that is permitted to claim that concept.

Those patent applications for which any claim has an effective filing date of 16 March 2013 or later are subject to the "first-to-file" ("FTF") rules. Under those FTF rules (which have yet to be clarified by the courts), many grace periods have been eliminated.

The table below lists the available U.S. grace periods under the FTI rules and under the FTF rules. Note that once the grace period expires on a given concept, no valid initial patent application can be filed seeking to protect that concept.

Activity	FTI	FTF
Discuss Concept (verbally)		
Confidentially	Unlimited	Unlimited
Non-Confidentially	1 year	None
Present Concept (visually)		
Confidentially	Unlimited	Unlimited
Non-Confidentially	1 year	None
Describe Concept (in writing)		
Confidentially	Unlimited	Unlimited
Non-Confidentially		
Not published	1 year	Unlimited
Published (accessible to public)		
Within U.S.	1 year	None
Outside U.S.	1 year	None
Use Concept		
By inventors		
Experimentally		
Confidentially	Unlimited	Unlimited
Non-Confidentially	1 year	None
Commercially		
Confidentially	Unlimited	Unlimited
Non-Confidentially	1 year*	None
By un-connected others		
Confidentially	Unlimited	None or Unlimited***
Non-Confidentially	1 year	None
Offer Concept for sale		
By inventors		
Within U.S.		
Confidentially	1 year**	None or Unlimited***
Non-Confidentially	1 year**	1 year

Activity	FTI	FTF
Outside U.S.		
Confidentially	Unlimited	None or Unlimited***
Non-Confidentially	Unlimited	1 year
By un-connected others		
Within U.S.		
Confidentially	1 year	None or Unlimited***
Non-Confidentially	1 year	None
Outside U.S.		
Confidentially	Unlimited	None or Unlimited***
Non-Confidentially	Unlimited	None
File patent application describing Concept		
Within U.S.		
By un-connected others	up to 1 year	None
By inventors	N/A	N/A
Outside U.S.	1 year	1 year
Obtain patent describing Concept		
Within U.S.	1 year	None
Outside U.S.	1 year	None

Includes when confidential process produces a product that is non-confidentially used or sold

*** Must be a commercial offer & ready for patenting*

**** Currently disputed*

Moreover, many countries bar patenting of a concept if there is any public disclosure (and sometimes any attempt at commercialization) of that concept before the filing of a patent application. So generally, the patenting process encourages a "race to the patent office" to protect innovative concepts.

Thus, if there is a desire to preserve the right to file a patent application outside the U.S. (and potentially within the U.S.), I recommend that you file at least a well-written provisional (and preferably a non-provisional) patent application before **any** non-confidential disclosure, offer for sale, or commercialization of the innovation occurs.

A U.S. non-provisional seeking to benefit from the submission of a U.S. provisional patent application must be filed within 12 months of the filing date of that provisional.

Once an initial non-provisional patent application is filed in most countries (including the U.S.), any desired foreign or international patent applications must be filed typically within no more than 1 year.

In summary, many companies prefer to file a provisional U.S. patent application as soon as possible after an innovation is identified, thereby obtaining a relatively early date for defining prior art and lowering the likelihood of violating a patent filing time limit. They then follow-up as soon as possible (and within 12 months) by filing a non-provisional patent application in each desired country/jurisdiction.

What are the 7 steps to obtaining a valuable patent?

With documentation of your innovation in hand, the general process for obtaining a valuable patent on that innovation is:

1. describe your innovation, including an identification of a problem that seems to be uniquely solved by your innovation;

2. with your description in hand, self-perform a brief innovation search, which will "knock out" your innovation from further consideration if it appears to be publicly known already;

3. draft a thorough description of how to implement your innovation;

4. professionally investigate your described innovation for acceptable:

   □ *patentability;*

   □ *risks; and*

   □ *value;*

5. draft a strong patent application that properly describes and claims your desired innovations, and, within the required time limits, prepare and submit a proper U.S. patent application, PCT patent application, and/or foreign patent application(s);

6. prosecute each patent application through examination to allowance and grant; and

7. receive, maintain, and exploit the granted patent.

I routinely help my clients with each of these steps of the patenting process, which is explained in detail in several sections below.

I also remind them that, because I am authorized to practice law only in the United States, my general communications, such as this one, tend to focus on securing U.S. intellectual assets, such as via U.S. patents. Nevertheless, I am nearly always happy to discuss how I have aided in obtaining strong patents (and other intellectual assets) in typically-sought foreign countries via my vast network of foreign patent professionals.

How should an innovation be documented initially?

Before deciding whether a given innovative concept justifies patenting, that innovation must be properly described in writing. When describing and documenting an innovation, keep in mind that to better protect the innovation, facts pertaining to it should be provable.

The best kind of evidence of such facts is evidence that removes any question of after-the-fact modification.

Here are some helpful tips for documenting innovations:

- If working on paper, use ink rather than pencil.

- Avoid erasing. Instead, strike-through any needed deletions, being sure to add the date and a note about the revision.

- Don't leave big areas of blank space in your working documents - cross them out, removing the possibility of later modifications.

- Use audit logs, time stamps, and modified dates for electronic records.

- All original drawings, notebooks, data, samples, records, etc., no matter how simple, should be dated, signed by the innovator(s), properly witnessed, and carefully preserved.

- Preferred witnesses are those who are not co-creators or co-inventors, yet are qualified to understand the content of the innovation documentation, and are likely to be available to testify in the event of a dispute.

Note that these tips are equally applicable to know-how, including trade secrets. By properly documenting and storing a record of your know-how, you obtain well-secured written evidence of when, where, why, and how that know-how was created and and who within your company created it. Such evidence can help your company thwart anyone who obtains that know-how via improper means from asserting that they already knew it before they improperly obtained it from your company.

What is a problem/solution statement?

Properly drafted, a problem/solution statement succinctly describes a concept that uniquely solves a given problem, and thereby can serve as an outstanding starting point for patentability searches, claim drafting, and valuation.

Here is a whimsical problem/solution statement to help better illustrate their nature:

> *The problem of male pattern baldness-induced hair loss is uniquely solved by gently applying at least 1 fluid ounce of organic apple blossom honey to the scalp for approximately 10 minutes each day.*

Here is a more serious exemplary problem/solution statement that provides additional context for its problem, and should describe a rather familiar concept:

The problem of transporting a person, across land, a net horizontal distance of several miles and a net vertical (uphill) distance of several hundred feet, without the use of human, animal, or wind power, is uniquely solved by mounting an engine to a platform having wheels and applying energy generated by the engine to rotate the wheels.

Rarely is a problem/solution statement drafted perfectly on the first attempt. Instead, problem/solution statements are typically revised repeatedly and as needed to optimally define their concept.

When drafted too generally, a problem/solution statement describes a problem that is solved by the prior art, and thus the stated concept is not new, not unique, and not inventive, and thus not patentable. Also, a problem/solution statement is too generally drafted if a person having ordinary skill in the art, faced with the same problem, would have a good reason to combine the teachings of the relevant prior art to arrive at the described solution.

When drafted too narrowly, a problem/solution statement includes implementation details that are unnecessary to distinguish the innovative concept from the prior art, and thereby unnecessarily restricts the scope and value of that concept.

When drafted optimally, a problem/solution statement can add tremendous value to the patenting process, by serving as the basis for a number of important tasks, including: innovation analysis, patentability searches, claim drafting, valuation analyses, marketing communications, and/or IP exploitation. With regard to a patent application alone, a well-written problem-solution statement can very helpfully inform both innovators and patent attorney regarding what to search, what to claim, and what to describe.

What is an innovation search?

It often can be helpful for an innovator to self-perform a very brief and basic search to see if their innovation is already known to the public. This step can help avoid wasting time preparing a detailed description of an innovation that is not patentable.

Yet before embarking on an innovation search, it often can be helpful for the innovator to prepare a rough problem/solution statement to guide that search. As explained just above, properly drafted, a problem/solution statement succinctly describes an innovative concept that (hopefully) uniquely solves a given problem.

Here is an example of a problem/solution statement:

> *For many of those who suffer from arthritis that substantially inhibits their use of both of their hands, the problem of adequately gripping a can opener is uniquely solved by sizing each handle of the can opener to have a minimum cross-sectional dimension of between roughly 1.0 and 1.5 inches.*

Most innovators find that with a well-written problem/solution statement in hand, a strong innovation search can be performed much more easily. Many innovation searches rely on searchable databases of published United States Patent Applications and granted United States Patents, which are available from:

- The USPTO at patft.uspto.gov

- FreePatentsOnline at www.freepatentsonline.com

Both of these search engines allow you to enter relevant keywords (such as those used in the problem/solution statement), and find patent publications that utilize those keywords.

FreePatentsOnline also allows you to specify proximity searches, such as when one keyword must appear within a specified number of words of another. Check out its syntax instructions here: www.freepatentsonline. com/help/topic/Syntax-Examples.html

If preferred, a competent patent professional can perform an innovation search, or a more extensive patentability search.

How should an innovation be described for patenting?

I refer to an innovator's detailed written description of their innovation as an "innovation disclosure".

A well-written innovation disclosure can form a solid foundation for analyzing patentability, risks, and value, and help build a high-quality patent application.

It can be tempting for innovators to provide their patent attorney with a laundry list of trumpeted and fluffed-up attributes of their innovations and call it an innovation disclosure.

Unfortunately, such platitudes, while fine for sales and marketing efforts, usually don't provide a patent attorney with the relevant information required to build a high-quality patent application.

Instead, at a minimum, a reasonable innovation disclosure typically should provide a:

1. list, ranked by innovator-perceived value, of the concepts the innovator(s) believes are innovative;

2. simple explanation of the background and nature of the problem each listed concept is believed to uniquely solve, possibly drafted as a "problem/solution" statement;

3. brief identification, for each listed concept, of its unique str features, unique functions, and unique results, and how they help solve the problem;

4. sketches, if particularly helpful, to illustrate those unique aspects;

5. summary of the most significant difference(s) between each listed concept and any particular innovator-known previous solutions to the problem and/or closely related problems;

6. description that:

    • explains how to make and use the full scope of each listed concept in the best way any of the innovator(s) currently know; and

    • is sufficiently detailed to empower one of ordinary skill in the field to successfully make and use the full scope of each listed concept without experimentation to obtain the unique results;

7. for each listed concept, all currently available evidence, if any, of:

    • recognition of a problem not recognized by others (e.g., competitors);

    • long-felt but unmet need in the market for a solution to the problem;

    • failed attempts by others to solve the problem;

    • skepticism of experts that this concept solves the problem;

    • discouragement or teaching away from this concept by others;

    • praise by competitors or others for this concept; and/or

    • any unpredictable results/benefits achieved by this concept.

In the Appendix, you will find my Innovation Disclosure Form, which can be a helpful tool for communicating information regarding an innovation, particularly from an innovator to a patent attorney. Although this form is very detailed, think of it as a guide indicating what information often proves helpful to the patent attorney rather than mandating what information must be provided.

While preparing a description of the innovation, whether freestyle or using my Innovation Disclosure Form, consider these additional writing suggestions:

1.   *Identify the problem and its solution*

All true innovations solve some problem. Those that are patentable solve that problem uniquely. So describe the problem(s) solved by your innovation, and explain how it uniquely does so.

2.   *Describe embodiments*

Clearly explain how to make and use your innovation. If your innovation is an object, such as a device, machine, and/or composition, specify the details of how to make it, identifying any preferred suppliers/brands/models/types of components, as well as potential alternatives. Factually describe how those components relate to one another structurally, spatially, functionally, temporally, etc.

If your innovation is a process, such as a method, procedure, and/or any combination of activities, detail what objects are acted upon, by whom, under what circumstances, in what order, and why. Include alternative activities and approaches and indicate any aspects that tend to be repeated within the process.

Regardless of the type of innovation, tell how to implement it in the best way you currently know how, as well as any reasonable alternatives that come to mind. In doing so, *describe only facts and avoid opinions.*

3.   *Explain functions*

While explaining how to make and use your embodiments, try to explain the function of *every* component and/or activity involved.   Doing so should help you visualize more alternatives, and will provide me with the grist I need to more broadly claim your innovation, thereby expanding its potential value.

4.   *Provide experimental data*

Although not necessarily required for patenting, if you have it, provide any data evidencing that your solution at least crudely works as intended. Likewise, if you have any evidence showing how well your innovation works, by all means include it with your disclosure. Although not needed when a person having ordinary skill in the art would find the performance of the innovation to be predictable (often the case with mechanical, eletrical, and software innovations), such experimental and/or performance testing data can be extremely helpful for unpredictable innovations (particularly those involving chemistry and life sciences).

5.   *Consider the audience*

Assuming your company elects to pursue your innovation via a patent application, keep in mind that patent applications, and any resulting patents, will be evaluated from the perspective of a person having merely ordinary skill in the art (that is, the realm of the claimed subject matter). So when writing-up a description of your innovation, don't assume that person has a high degree of familiarity or competence with your innovation's concepts, jargon, or other particulars. Dumb it down a bit.

6.   *Ignore other's formats, sections, and styles*

You are *describing* your innovation, not drafting a patent application, which is the job of your patent attorney. Thus, any formats, sections, or styles shown in other's patent applications or patents are irrelevant to the task at hand. Moreover, most such documents were written in the mind-set of a long-extinct legal era, and from today's perspective, contain numerous unnecessary legal risks. Likewise, the USPTO offers several risk-filled drafting guidelines that you really should completely ignore. Instead, stick to my suggestions to substantially lower your risks.

7.   *Avoid phrases like "prior art", "known", and "traditional"*

Try to bypass phrases such as "prior art", or what is "known", "traditional", "conventional", etc. Such phrases can invite undesired and/or damaging comparisons between what your (eventual) patent claims and the infringing product or service. Instead, limit any comparisons of your innovation to particular products, services, or publications.

Once you file a U.S. non-provisional patent application, there is a duty to disclose all the material prior art of which you are aware to the USPTO. But I will remind you at the right time, request that information from you, and prepare and submit it to the USPTO in the special way they require.

8.   *Don't use "invention"*

From a patent law perspective, the word "invention" is confused, confusing, and highly loaded with legal risk. Don't use it. Ever. Please.

9.   *Replace closed verbs with open*

Most innovators are technically trained and/or experienced. That background has taught them to write in clear, active tense, using precise verbs. Yet from a patent law perspective, doing so can add unnecessary legal risk. So although in other contexts it might be preferable to write "***Connect*** the widget to the gadget" or "The widget ***is*** connected to the gadget", the more expansive, vague, and less risky approach is to state that "The widget ***can*** be connected to the gadget". Although your 10th grade English teacher would probably strenuously object, this is the one place where vague, passive, imprecise verbs are your friend, as they support broader, more valuable claims in any patent that eventually emerges from your innovation disclosure.

10. Avoid restrictive adjectives

This theme of expansiveness also should be reflected in your choice of adjectives. Do not use restrictive language such as "required", "necessary", "key", "must", etc., as doing so invites infringers to argue that your otherwise broad patent claims are limited by how you initially described your innovation, thereby potentially spoiling the value of your patent. When you feel compelled to use restrictive adjectives, consider softening their edges a bit by preceding them with phrases such as "usually", "typically", "often", "sometimes", etc.

11. Broaden numerical values

With our goal of expansiveness, it should be clear that although it is good to quantify measurable aspects of your innovation, presenting those quantities as relatively broad approximate ranges of numerical values is even better. For example, compare *"heat the solution to 212 degrees F"* with *"heat the solution to approximately 195 degrees F to approximately 220 degrees F"*. Which is more likely to be easier for a competitor to design around, i.e., literally avoid while still implementing its essence?

12. Explain terms of art

If your disclosure relies on any special terms that have particular meanings, define or otherwise explain those meanings as clearly as possible. Include those explanations or definitions in your patent application, as they can help expand and/or contract the scope of your claims to avoid invalidating prior art and/or capture infringing implementations.

Finally, keep in mind that when describing a new innovation, to preserve your rights in that innovation, facts pertaining to its conception must be reasonably provable. The best kind of evidence is that which removes any significant question of after-the-fact modification. So if working on paper, use ink rather than pencil. Avoid erasing. Instead, strike-through any needed deletions, being sure to add the date and a note about the revision. Don't leave big areas of blank space in your working documents

- cross them out, removing the possibility of later modifications. Use audit logs, time stamps, and modified dates for electronic records. All original drawings, notebooks, data, samples, records, etc., no matter how simple, should be dated, signed by the Innovator(s), properly witnessed, and carefully preserved. Preferred witnesses are those who are not co-inventors, are qualified to understand the content of the innovation disclosure, and are likely to be available to testify in the event of a dispute.

What is a professional patentability search?

Before making a substantial investment in a patent application, it often can be helpful and very cost effective to obtain a professional patentability search. These searches attempt to identify prior publications that describe most or all of the major features of the concept of interest, thereby showing that the concept is not new or inventive. The timely recognition of such relevant "prior art" can lead to a reasoned professional determination of unpatentability, thereby helping to avoid wasting money trying to patent what might be an unpatentable concept.

A basic version of a professional patentability search typically can be completed within 3 to 10 days, and usually costs between $800 and $1200.

Yet there are very good reasons to spend considerably more on an initial professional patentability search. Here's why:

- Although it can run considerably higher, the cost to prepare and file a typical U.S. non-provisional patent application is typically at least $6,000 to $9,000 (including government fees).

- The cost to prosecute a typical U.S. non-provisional patent application to the point where the USPTO's best available prior art has been revealed, and the applicant decides to abandon the application, is typically at least $3,000 to $5,000.

- Thus, the cost to prepare, file, and prosecute a typical U.S. non-provisional patent application to the point where the applicant chooses to abandon the application is typically at least $9,000 to $14,000, and sometimes more.

- Roughly 30-35% of all original U.S. non-provisional patent applications are abandoned during prosecution and therefore do not issue as patents.

- Consequently, one could reasonably justify spending $2,700 (30% x 9,000) to $4,900 (35% x $14,000) to determine up front that any given innovation is unpatentable or not worth patenting, thereby avoiding the costs of preparing, filing, and prosecuting its corresponding U.S. non-provisional patent application.

Regardless of the budget that has been determined for a professional patentability search, before I start on the search itself, I prefer to reach consensus with the innovator on a problem/solution statement that reasonably describes how their concept differs from the prior art already known to the innovator.

As discussed above, a typical problem/solution statements reads:

"The problem of ____ is uniquely solved by ____."

For example, with reference to the safety seals on half-gallon and gallon-sized plastic milk jugs, a reasonable problem/solution statement might read:

"the problem of a consumer purchasing a jug of milk in a plastic container and later finding that the primary safety seal for the container's cap has been prematurely yet inadvertently compromised is uniquely solved by including a secondary safety seal that completely covers the opening of the container and is completely covered by the container's cap."

Well-written problem/solution statements serve to clarify the problem that the innovator has addressed, specify the structures and/or activities that uniquely solve the problem, and limit the scope of the search, thereby constraining costs.

What is a provisional patent application?

Provisional (sometimes referred to as "informal") U.S. patent applications expire 12 months after they are filed, typically contain no Innovator's Declaration, formal drawings, or claims, and thus are not examined by a government patent examiner. Consequently, provisionals do not mature into patents. Instead, their basic purpose is to act as a time stamp for the subject matter they properly describe. Also, preparing and filing a provisional can defer some of the costs associated with preparing and filing a non-provisional ("formal") U.S. patent application.

Taking the provisional application approach will create a 12 month window during which your company can:

1. explore the patentability of its described innovation;

2. improve upon that innovation;

3. mark "Patent Pending" on any product embodying the innovation;

4. determine the value of the innovation; and/or

5. raise or budget funds to cover the cost of preparing and filing any desired non-provisional applications that rely on the description and filing date of the provisional.

Before the expiration of that 12 month window, your company hopefully will be in a good position to decide whether to prepare and file at least one non-provisional patent application that:

1. was filed within 12 months of the filing of the provisional;

2. properly references the provisional;

3. describes how to at least crudely make and use the same innovation that was described in the provisional;

4. describes how to make and use that innovation in the best way any of the innovators know;

5. will be treated as having been filed on the date of the provisional for evaluating whether the innovation was novel as of that date;

6. claims the described innovation; and

7. will receive an examination of those claims and possibly their description.

Interestingly, a 2012 study revealed that while the number of provisional applications filed with the USPTO continues to rise each year, the number of abandoned provisionals (i.e., those not relied upon for a priority claim) also grows each year. The study estimates that for 2011, about 48% of provisional filed were abandoned. From personal experience, I know that some of those provisionals were re-filed.

Keep in mind that a provisional secures a filing date only for the innovation that it describes sufficiently to empower ("enable") one of ordinary skill in the field of endeavor (the "art") to at least minimally successfully implement ("practice") the full scope of that innovation without substantial experimentation and in the best manner known at that time to any of the innovator(s). Thus, the description must empower an average, unimaginative, and non-expert practitioner in the art to at least crudely implement the innovation for which patent "protection" will be sought or "claimed". Note that any claimed innovation in a non-provisional that was not sufficiently described in an earlier-filed related provisional is not entitled to the filing date of that provisional, and to be claimed, must be described in the non-provisional in the best manner then known to any of the innovators. Thus, when there is any doubt about the quality of the description in the provisional, the description should be enhanced prior to filing the provisional, or in one or more promptly-filed follow-up provisionals.

This correctly suggests that there can be a serious benefit in not waiting until an innovation is optimized before filing a provisional, particularly if any aspect of that optimization can be protected as a trade secret. That is, assume a barely operable implementation of an innovation is described in a provisional patent application that is filed today. Then, over the next month lots of valuable know-how is developed to optimize that implementation. Importantly, there is no requirement to include any of those valuable optimization details in any non-provisional that claims the benefit of the provisional. Instead, your company can keep that valuable know-how secret, thereby substantially enhancing the value of any license offered to the combination of the non-provisional patent application or any patents that result from it, and the know-how that can allow the licensee to optimally implement the your patented innovation.

The cost and time required to prepare a proper U.S. provisional patent application varies widely, depending primarily on the quality of the description provided by the innovator. Sometimes, only about 0.5 to 2 days of elapsed time and $1000-$3000 worth of my legal services are needed for me to review the written description, make needed adjustments to minimize legal risks, prepare the filing paperwork, and file the provisional application. In other situations, the time required (and cost) can be substantially greater, particularly if considerable effort must be expended to extract a sufficient description from the innovator. Fortunately, the client is generally in control of the availability of the innovator and the quality of the description, and thus the provisional's timing and preparation cost.

The government's filing fee for a U.S. provisional patent application is typically in the neighborhood of $100 for a Small Entity, and about $200 for a Large Entity (I explain Small Entity status beginning at page 193).

What is a non-provisional patent application?

Contrast provisionals with non-provisional (sometimes referred to as "formal" or "regular") U.S. patent applications, which must include one or more "claims" that each legally define an "invention", typically have their claims examined by an "examiner" from the USPTO, and often result in the issuance of a patent by the USPTO. As with provisionals, non-provisionals also create the right to mark "Patent Pending" on anything that embodies any innovation that has been enablingly described in the application. If a provisional was filed, and a non-provisional is desired that claims subject matter that was properly described in that provisional, the non-provisional must be filed within 12 months of the filing date of the provisional.

Prepared properly, non-provisional patent applications require the dedication of a substantial amount of time for very careful claim drafting, thoughtful defining of phrases that appear in the claims, and skilled avoidance/reduction of legal risks. In addition, numerous additional preparation formalities must be addressed, including properly preparing drawings, fulfilling rigid document formatting requirements, and correctly referencing any priority documents.

As mentioned above, my charges (attorney fees) to prepare a non-provisional patent application for filing typically falls in the range of $5,000 to $9,000. For good reasons, the cost sometimes can edge higher, particularly if, for example:

- the disclosure is excessively lengthy, confusing, or complex;

- the disclosure includes numerous drawings;

- multiple innovations are disclosed;

- the known prior art is particularly "close" to the identified innovation;

- an inordinate amount of re-work is required;

- communications are particularly challenging; or

- detailed explanations of numerous attorney decisions are requested.

This preparation cost is essentially the same regardless of where a non-provisional patent application is filed (e.g., only in the U.S., as an international (PCT) application, and/or in various foreign patent offices, etc.). That is, once prepared, an application can be filed in any number of jurisdictions, and the cost for doing so is only the incremental filing cost associated with each jurisdiction (plus the costs of translations, if needed).

Just as with a provisional, the client can manage this preparation cost downward by providing a good quality textual description, a few drawings that are adequate to illustrate the concept, and an innovator who is reasonably available, understandable, and cooperative. Moreover, much of my work to prepare and file a provisional can be applied toward preparing the non-provisional, thereby lowering my charges for the non-provisional. The details of each specific situation will determine the extent of the cost reduction.

If a non-provisional is filed only in the U.S., the government's filing fee will be at least $500 for a Small Entity (and $1000 for a Large Entity - explained below), and more if a large number of claims or pages are included. If the application is filed as an international (or PCT) application, the government's filing fee will probably range from about $3500 to about $5000, depending primarily on the number of pages of the application. Thus, total preparation and filing costs for an application filed only as a PCT application can range from roughly $8500 to $14,000 or more, inclusive of the government's fees.

The amount of time I need to prepare non-provisional patent applications varies widely. Occasionally, I can prepare non-provisional patent application in less than 1 week, if the quality of the provided materials is exceptionally high, the innovator is readably available, and other pending matters can be delayed. More typically, I begin preparing each non-provisional application several months before its due date, thereby hopefully allowing adequate time for thorough consideration of the application's claims and descriptive material, recognizing the typically busy schedules of all involved.

What is a PCT patent application?

There are roughly 196 countries in the world. Currently, 146 of them, which includes nearly every major industrialized country (except Taiwan and several that are relatively unindustrialized and/or have relatively small economies, such as many Latin American, Middle Eastern, and African countries), are signatories to the Patent Cooperation Treaty ("PCT"). That UN-sponsored treaty defines a process for filing, searching, and examining an "international" (or PCT) patent application.

A PCT application does not directly result in a patent. Instead, filing a PCT application typically causes a government-employed patent examiner to search for relevant prior art to the subject matter of the claims and to issue a written opinion of the perceived patentability of those claims.

The examiner's written search report and opinion typically are provided roughly 19 months from the "priority date" (a.k.a., "effective filing date", which is the earlier of the actual filing date of the PCT or the actual filing date of the earliest filed application from which the PCT application properly seeks to benefit, such as a provisional U.S. application filed no more than 12 months before the PCT's actual filing date).

The PCT application also is published at roughly 19 months from its priority date. If examination is requested, the examiner prepares an examination report, which sometimes is more detailed than the written opinion. Examination reports are usually received between 19 and 28 months from the priority date.

At one time, filing a document called a "Demand" was required, but it is now effectively optional. Filing a Demand will buy another Patentability Report and the opportunity to file certain amendments prior to the examiner drafting the Examination Report (which typically mirrors the latest Patentability Report).

If it is filed, a Demand must be filed before 19 months have elapsed from the effective filing date of the International application.

Whether a Demand is filed or not, the International Stage of the PCT process will end 30 (and sometimes 31) months from the effective filing date, at which point National Stage applications must be filed in the desired jurisdictions.

If a Demand is filed, the International Stage of the PCT process will proceed in the same manner, at the same pace, and with the same deadlines as if no Demand were filed, except that before the 30 month date, we should receive a second Patentability Report. Sometimes, however, such second Patentability Reports or the Examination Report arrive long after the 30 month date, making those reports rather useless to us.

In any event, if a second Patentability Report or Examination Report is positive (finds the claimed subject matter to have utility, novelty, and inventive step (non-obviousness), some of the National Stage examiners might feel more confident in granting a patent in their respective jurisdiction, but others might still prefer to perform their own independent search and examination.

If requested by the client, by 30 (or sometimes 31) months from the priority date, for each client-selected country, I arrange for a localized "National Stage" patent application that corresponds to the PCT application to be submitted by foreign counsel to the national patent office of that country.

The PCT search results, written opinion, and examiner's report (if any) can assist each corresponding national patent examiner with determining if a patent should and will be issued for their country. When particularly positive, those PCT documents sometimes can inspire a national patent examiner to not perform an additional search or a rigorous additional examination of the claims.

Thus, potential benefits of the PCT process include:

- deferring the decision (and the associated costs) to file a patent application in a PCT signatory country for up to 18 additional months from the PCT's priority date;

- obtaining a relatively quick search report and patentability opinion for the claims; and

- obtaining an examination report that sometimes will strongly influence at least some of the national patent examiners;

- while costing only a relatively modest government fee (considering the potential expenses associated with early filing in a number of foreign patent offices).

The costs of filing "national" patent applications varies considerably from country to country, and is impacted substantially by whether a certified translation of the priority or PCT application is required by a given country (in other words, whether the English language patent application must be professionally translated into that country's official language).

In some situations, if no delay and less than 4 or 5 countries are desired, it can be advantageous (from a cost perspective, but perhaps not from other perspectives) to file directly in those countries and skip the PCT process. This issue should be resolved as early as possible so that cost estimates can be timely obtained.

In what foreign countries does patenting make the most sense?

Frequently, companies believe they must seek and maintain patent protection throughout the industrialized world. Yet given that there are roughly 196 countries in the world, doing so can be very expensive, ultimately costing hundreds of thousands of dollars. As a result of those phenomenal costs and the corresponding diminishing returns associated with many of those countries, taking the "patent everywhere" approach can actually undermine the return on the resulting family of patents.

Fortunately, sales of patent-protected implementations in large markets can often generate sufficient profits to, where legally allowed, subsidize competition-discouraging pricing of those implementations in many smaller, unpatented markets. So prior to deciding where to patent, your company should carefully analyze the geographical distribution of the expected global market for implementations of an innovation, and seek to estimate demand, pricing, and profitability in *each* country of interest.

Various ranked lists of countries, which are freely available on-line, can assist with these estimates. Here are a few potentially helpful ranked lists of countries:

- *Population*

    - en.wikipedia.org—List_of_countries_by_population

- *Gross domestic product (GDP)*

    - en.wikipedia.org—List_of_countries_by_GDP_(PPP)

- *Average wages*

    - en.wikipedia.org—List_of_countries_by_average_wages

- *Household income*

- – en.wikipedia.org—List_of_countries_by_household_ income

- **GDP by sector**

  - – en.wikipedia.org—List_of_countries_by_GDP_sector_ composition

- **Future GDP per capita (PPP)**

  - – en.wikipedia.org—List_of_countries_by_future_GDP_per_ capita_estimates_(PPP)

- **Various lists of countries by per capita values**

  - – en.wikipedia.org—Category:Lists_of_countries_by_per_ capita_values

In addition, the CIA's World Factbook, available from www.cia.gov— rankorderguide.html, provides dozens of ranked lists of countries, by topics such as: GDP growth rate, investment, inflation rate, industrial production growth rate, exports, imports, population growth rate, birth rate, life expectancy, education expenditures, internet users, military expenditures, etc.

Based on those estimates, determine the risk-adjusted return on investment ("RARE") value associated with obtaining patent protection in that country, using the techniques described in *Step 6 – Enhance*. Per the principles guiding those techniques, patent applications should be filed in only those countries having associated RARE values that exceed a reasonably-chosen threshold.

For my clients, once the desired countries were determined, through my carefully managed network of skilled foreign patent professionals, I have ensured that appropriate patent applications were correctly filed, prosecuted to issuance while mitigating prosecution-related risks, and properly maintained in each of those countries. I also have helped my clients with licensing or otherwise exploiting their foreign patent rights, such as by using some of the tactics outlined in *Step 7 – Harness.*

Likewise, when the time came to enforce or litigate those foreign patents, based on my substantial experience with foreign patent litigation, I have helped my clients identify, weigh, and select the best foreign counsel, strategies, and tactics for their particular needs. So just as with their U.S. patents and other IP rights, they have relied on my expertise, techniques, and contacts to help them optimize their IP power around the globe.

What are the U.S., PCT, and foreign filing options?

There are lots of options for filing patent applications in both the U.S. and foreign countries. For a U.S. resident, those options include:

A.   Filing a U.S. application and the desired foreign applications simultaneously;

B.   Filing a U.S. application and then later (within 1 year) file the desired foreign applications;

C.   Filing a foreign application and then later (within 1 year) file an international (PCT) or U.S. application;

D.   Filing a U.S. and then later file a PCT, claiming priority to the U.S.;

E.   Filing a U.S. and PCT simultaneously;

F.   Filing a PCT and then later file in the U.S. as a National Stage of the PCT; and

G.   Filing a PCT and then later file in the U.S. as a Continuation of the PCT.

Walking down through these options, options A and B typically work best when only a few (typically less than 3 or 4) foreign countries are desired and funding is readily available. Options A, B, and C also can be beneficial for obtaining prompt examination from those countries (e.g.,

UK, Australia) where it typically is available. Option C can make sense when none of the inventors is a U.S. resident. Finally, options B and C can be a good route if funds are initially scarce.

Unless steps are taken to expedite U.S. prosecution, it typically takes 2 years or more until a U.S. application is examined. So if option D or E is taken, by the time the PCT Search Report is received, there typically is still time to amend the U.S. claims before examination, thus potentially speeding-up the U.S. examination process.

On the other hand, if funds are initially scarce, but protection is desired in several (typically 4 or more) foreign countries, options F and G can be favored, since most of the costs (i.e., National Stage filings and any accompanying translations) are deferred for at least 18 months, and potentially up to 31 months.

The 2012 World Intellectual Property Indicators report published by the World Intellectual Property Organization (WIPO) revealed that in 2011, China's patent office, for the first time, received more patent applications than any other in the world. Topping the list of countries with the most in-force patents in 2011 were U.S., Japan, China, Korea, and Germany.

What are export controls?

Since we're talking about foreign patenting, this is a great opportunity to briefly discuss export controls, which surprisingly have important ramifications for IP.

If your company exports, it is responsible for determining whether those exports require a license from either the U.S. Department of Commerce's Bureau of Industry and Security (BIS) or the U.S. Department of State. Determining whether you need an export license depends on the export's technical characteristics, its use and end-user, and the destination (i.e., whether it appears on any of the variety of lists of sanctioned countries and parties).

Note that exports include any transfer of technology, equipment, information, software, or services, including transfer to foreign nationals within the U.S. (referred to as a "deemed export").

The BIS implements and enforces the Export Administration Regulations (EAR) that control the export and re-export of most commercial items, and in particular "dual use" items (i.e., those with a predominantly commercial use, but with potential uses in military, intelligence, and/or law enforcement).

The Department of Commerce has categorized and coded types of exports (assigning each export type an Export Control Classification Number or "ECCN") and compiled a list of their licensing requirements, known as the Commerce Control List ("CCL"). Determining whether your export has an assigned ECCN is a good place to start when researching BIS license requirements. However, the export's use, end-user, and destination must still be taken into consideration.

A good introduction to export controls can be found at the BIS's website:

http://www.bis.doc.gov/licensing/exportingbasics.htm.

Further information about ECCNs and the CCL is available at export.gov, the International Trade Administration's website, and particularly on this page:

http://export.gov/logistics/eg_main_018803.asp.

The Commerce Control List is available online here:

http://www.bis.doc.gov/policiesandregulations/ear/ccl_index.pdf.

The U.S. State Department regulates the export of items that have a predominantly military application, by administering the "International Traffic in Arms Regulations" (ITAR). ITAR's export control list is known as the "Munitions List" and can be obtained from:

http://www.pmddtc.state.gov/regulations_laws/
documents/consolidated_itar/ITAR_Part121.pdf.

Finally, to view a training presentation providing a reasonably good general explanation of export controls, visit:

*http://www.wpi.edu/Images/CMS/ORA/WPI_Export_*
Control_Slides-web_training.pdf.

Note that somewhat different rules apply to "exporting" the information found in a patent application by filing that application in a foreign country. In this situation, the USPTO will grant a foreign filing license once it has had an opportunity to review the application's and ensure that it doesn't contain overly sensitive military/defense-related content. One good way to obtain such a foreign filing license is to prepare and file a U.S. provisional patent application that describes the most sensitive concepts as least as well as they will be described in the foreign-filed application.

Perhaps the most important thing to know about exporting from the U.S. is that non-compliance with its export control laws can mean heavy fines, temporary or permanent loss of exporting privileges and/or licenses, and even criminal sanctions. Because of the many complex factors involved and the risk of serious consequences, it is of utmost importance to rely on legal counsel with solid expertise in this field (fortunately, when needed, I have been able to refer my clients to a colleague having outstanding skills in this area). Counsel having such export control expertise may also be able to advise regarding tax incentive programs for exporters that can, among other things, potentially reduce the federal tax rate applicable to export income by almost 50% and/or indefinitely defer taxes payable on up to $10 million in annual export sales.

Likewise, experienced export control counsel can advise regarding:

- Foreign laws that override express contract provisions;

- Foreign laws that declare important and common U.S. contractual provisions to be "unfair trade practices", unlawful restraints on competition, etc.;

- Loss of trademark and other IP rights due to:

  - Failure to take steps required (e.g., register trademark in U.S. exporter's name);

  - Forign laws that allow squatting; and/or

  - Deficient or flawed foreign laws and/or systems.

How is a patent application typically prepared?

Working closely with the innovator(s), I often can relatively rapidly prepare and file a patent application that not only will meet with eventual approval by the relevant patent office, but also will result in an issued patent that is easily recognized as being highly likely to survive the rigors of litigation, and thus will be respected by competitors without the need to litigate.

To prepare such a strong non-provisional patent application, these are the general steps that I typically follow (usually with a well-written innovation disclosure and a solid patentability search report in hand and with appropriate innovator assistance and feedback):

1. clearly describe the problem apparently uniquely solved by each desired concept;

2. strategically draft claims to the desired concepts (the claims define the legal rights that can be enforced via the resulting patent);

3.   thoughtfully generate definitions for each phrase used in the claims (which I've been able to do for my clients via my innovative, proprietary, and patent-pending claim definition software);

1.   carefully prepare drawings and a textual description (the "specification") that are adequate to enable a person having ordinary skill in the field of endeavor (the "art") of the claimed subject matter to at least minimally successfully make and use the full scope of the claimed concepts without substantial experimentation and in the best manner currently known to any of the innovators;

5.   properly present the claims, definitions, drawings, and textual description in a draft patent application that meets the legal requirements of the desired patent offices;

6.   skillfully integrate all relevant innovator feedback regarding that application; and

7.   correctly file the resulting patent application and required paperwork in the desired patent office(s).

With some of the most commonly-asked questions regarding non-provisional patent applications in mind, here are a few tips:

- A utility patent application can be filed in the U.S. without ever building a working prototype of the innovation.

- Generally, it is advantageous, although not necessarily required (yet), to file a patent application before disclosing the innovation non-confidentially or attempting to commercialize the innovation (including confidentially offering it for sale).

- Sometimes in the rush to file a patent application, innovators overlook that perhaps the biggest key to filing a powerful patent application, whether provisional or non-provisional, is to fully meet the legal requirements for describing their innovative concept.

• In particular, at a minimum, every U.S. patent application must describe to a person having ordinary skill in the art how to at least crudely make and use the full scope of the innovation without significant experimentation, and in the best manner known to any of the innovator(s) at the time of the application's filing. Because failing to completely fulfill this requirement seems to be at the root of many patent-related disappointments, and is under the nearly total control of the innovators/client, I really can't emphasize this point enough.

How are patent claims typically drafted?

Because the claims of each non-provisional patent application define its subject matter, are searched and examined before a patent can issue, and ultimately give rise to the specific legal rights held by the owner of the patent, the claims are a critical component of each patent application.

Assuming that the results of the professional patentability search were hopeful, then given adequate time and an appropriate budget, a highly skilled patent attorney can typically draft numerous claims that have a reasonable likelihood of eventually receiving a favorable reaction from the relevant patent office, and shortly thereafter will be issued in a patent.

If special care is taken in the searching and drafting stages, at least some of these issued claims can have a good chance of being upheld if challenged via litigation. Because poorly-drafted claims can be refused by the examiner as unpatentable, or can result in issued claims that are held not infringed or even invalid, claim drafting should be left to a highly skilled patent attorney.

Such a highly skilled patent attorney will typically draft numerous claims of several different types, and of varying scope. Typically, the professional will draft claims for devices, systems, compositions, and/or methods. In certain technology areas ("arts"), additional claim types are sometimes presented. For example, in the software realm, claims have been drafted for unique data structures, user interfaces, and waveforms. For biotechnology-related innovations, claims for vaccines, assays, and diagnostic kits are common.

Claims are classified as independent or dependent. An independent claim refers to no other claim. A dependent claim refers to another claim and further limits the subject matter of that other claim. Non-provisional patent applications must contain at least one independent claim, and typically include many dependent claims.

Most jurisdictions charge additional fees when more than a specified number of claims are filed. In the U.S., the basic filing fee permits a patent application to present up to 3 independent claims and 20 claims in total before an extra claims fee is assessed.

After leading off with a "preamble" that indicates its type and whether it is independent or dependent, a typical claim will usually present a "transition" term, followed by a "body". In most cases, the transition term is "comprising", which has been legally defined to mean "including, but not limited to". On rare occasion, a claim will transition via "consisting of", which legally means "including only".

Often, the body of a claim will contain what appears to be a description of the innovation in rather arcane language and using a run-on structure, both of which are traditional, required, and/or expected by examiners.

If a good quality patentability search has been performed, and with a healthy dose of good luck, the broadest claims presented in a patent application will include at least one feature that adequately distinguishes their claimed subject matter from the prior art. Yet because it is essentially impossible to predict whether a given patentability search has found all the relevant prior art, additional measures can be taken to increase the odds of patentability. For example, additional distinguishing features can be added to the broadest claims, with the understanding that doing so also shrinks the scope of those claims, and potentially their value. Before I discuss some other approaches, let's take a short step back.

Why include dependent claims in a patent application?

In an ideal world, there is no need at all for dependent claims. That is, ideally, I file one independent claim of each appropriate type (device, method, composition, etc.), which is allowed without rejection or amendment, and is enforceable and valid throughout the life of the patent.

But realistically, we rarely know with absolute certainty that a just-filed independent claim is patentable (i.e., novel and non-obvious). That's because, regardless of the quality of any patentability search performed prior to filing, there remains a significant possibility that prior art will emerge that can be used to defeat the patentability of the claim, but simply could not have been found during the patentability search.

Here's why. Under current U.S. law, a patent application can function as prior art as of its effective filing date. Yet, that patent application typically will not be published until *at least* 18 months after that effective filing date, meaning that it is kept in confidence throughout those 18 months, and possibly much longer.

So consider this hypothetical scenario. Assume that a patent application owned by a competitor was filed 7 months ago, and exactly describes your company's brand new innovation. Assume the competitor has carefully maintained the secrecy of their patent application, so that no matter what resources you expend searching for prior art to your new innovation, you simply will not discover the competitor's patent application. Yet after you file your patent application, and once the competitor's patent application has been published by the USPTO, it very likely will be cited by the USPTO to defeat the patentability of your claims. As frustrating as it is for patent applicants, this sort of thing happens with substantial frequency. And even if the USPTO fails to cite it to reject your claims, the competitor's published patent document nevertheless will exist as invalidating prior art for the claims of any patent the USPTO eventually grants to you.

So just in case one or more of your independent claims aren't patentable, as either determined during prosecution, or much later, during enforcement, Always include some dependent claims in each non-provisional patent application I file. That way, if the corresponding independent claim turns out to be not patentable, perhaps the added limitation(s) of one or more of the dependent claims will be patentable, and infringed, thereby preserving the value of some of your investment in the patenting process.

From that perspective, the most valuable dependent claims are those that would not likely be obvious or taught by a prior art reference that defeats the corresponding independent claim. That is, the best dependent claims define truly novel, non-obvious, and valuable features, assuming that the subject matter of their independent claim is not novel and non-obvious.

On the other hand, generally less valuable are those dependent claims that, assuming their independent claim was found to be unpatentable, only cover features that would be considered well-known, trivial, or non-valuable.

How is a patent specification typically drafted?

Each patent application must include a "specification" that, in addition to including the claims, must "teach" a person having ordinary skill in the art how to as least crudely implement the claimed subject matter without undue experimentation, in the best manner known to any of the inventor(s).

The specification typically includes a textual Description portion, and frequently several drawing figures, that together should communicate how to make and how to use the claimed subject matter. This communication should be directed at someone who understands the basic concepts and jargon of the technology, but who is not necessarily an innovator or creative thinker.

Although most patent applications are drafted by patent attorneys, highly experienced patent attorneys typically will rely on the innovator's input, assistance, and/or verification to assure that each concept and phrase that appears in the claims is:

- thoughtfully defined or explained;

- described thoroughly, both structurally and functionally;

- elaborated upon via helpful examples; and

- expanded by thoroughly describing known alternatives.

Claims to subject matter in what are considered to be unpredictable technology areas, such as chemistry, biology, and some cutting-edge areas of physics, typically are supported by experimental data that appears in the Description portion and that evidences at least limited operability of the claimed subject matter. Also, typically provided is an explanation of the practical utility of such subject matter.

Claims to subject matter in what are considered to be predictable technology areas, do not require experimental data to evidence the operability of that subject matter. Nevertheless, at least a brief mention of the practical utility of that subject matter should be included in the specification.

According to U.S. law, the specification must also include a Title, a Brief Description of the Figures, and an Abstract of the Disclosure.

Contrary to the "traditional" approach slavishly followed by many patent attorneys and agents, U.S. law does not require a "Field of the Invention", "Background", or "Summary" section, any mention of an "invention", or comparisons of the claimed subject matter to the "prior art", such as discussions of any perceived "advantages" of the claimed subject matter. Moreover, on many occasions, opposing litigators have used such thoughtless writings and/or other poorly-considered written statements submitted during prosecution to destroy the resulting patent (i.e., convince a court to issue a judgment that the claims are not infringed and/or are invalid (or worse)).

What are the requirements for patent drawings?

For certain innovative concepts, clients can substantially reduce the cost to prepare a patent by providing good quality drawings showing the features I request. Generally, patent drawings should meet the following criteria for submission in a patent application:

- sized to fit 8.5 inch x 11 inch paper with 1" margins all around;
- presented as black ink on a white background (preferably laser printed or suitable for laser printing);
- highly legible;
- no more detailed than necessary to describe claimed innovation;
- lettering at least 1/8" in height (typically 12 point and above);
- no hidden lines, shading (hatching is OK), or extraneous marks;
- no dimensions required;
- not required to be to scale; and
- if provided electronically, in PDF, JPG, bit map, Word, or PowerPoint file format.

The style of the drawing can vary depending on its subject matter:

- if a method, a simplified block flowchart containing connected boxes describing primary activities of the claimed method;
- if a mechanical structure, preferably perspective views, but can include front, top, side, full cross-sectional, assembly, etc. views, showing the claimed structure;

- if an electrical or communications network, a simplified block diagram; and

- if a chemical structure, a chemical structure drawing (e.g., ChemDraw or the like).

What's required to file a U.S. patent application?

We file all U.S and PCT patent applications electronically via the USPTO's Electronic Filing System.

For U.S. provisional patent applications, the filing requirements include submitting a copy of the patent application in PDF format and a cover sheet, along with instructions regarding payment of the filing fee.

For U.S. non-provisional patent applications, the filing requirements include submitting a copy of the properly-written and properly-formatted patent application in PDF format and an Application Data Sheet, along with instructions regarding payment of the filing fee. The Application Data Sheet identifies:

a. the inventors;

b. the address to which the USPTO should send correspondence regarding the application;

c. some information specific to the application (e.g., title, page count, attorney reference, number of drawing sheets, etc.);

d. whether the application should be published (see below);

e. what attorney is representing the applicant(s);

f. any applications to which the current application claims priority; and

g. the applicant;

If not filed with the application, relatively soon after filing the USPTO will require submission of an Inventor's Declaration (described below) for each inventor. Although optional, many applicants seek to have the inventors sign an Assignment document, and then seek recordation of that Assignment in the USPTO. I describe Assignments below.

The filing of PCT applications is considerably more complicated, so I won't go into its details here.

When should a patent application be published?

Generally, all U.S. non-provisional patent applications are published at roughly 18 months after their effective filing date. Beginning on the publication date, a copy of a published application can be obtained at www.uspto.gov/patft/ or www.freepatentsonline.com by entering the publication number.

The primary alleged advantage of publication is that, if the claims that issue are substantially identical to those published, and if a competitor practices the claimed subject matter after publication and before issuance, the patent owner can earn in damages a reasonable royalty from the publication date to the issue date. Another feature, which might be viewed as an advantage or a disadvantage, depending on the situation, is that the subject matter of the application can be discovered by potential competitors, investors, etc., and thus loses its confidentiality.

For those who prefer to keep the subject matter of their company's patent application confidential for as long as possible, there fortunately is a way to do so. When that patent application is filed, the applicant has the option to request that it not be published. This option is available if the applicant swears that no corresponding foreign or international application has been filed or is expected to be filed. If non-publication has been requested and a corresponding foreign or international application directed to the claimed or described subject matter is filed, the applicant must notify the USPTO within 45 days of that filing and allow the U.S. application to publish, otherwise the U.S. application will be regarded as abandoned and the claims of any patent that happens to issue from that application will be treated as invalid.

Generally, to be safe, I request non-publication of non-provisional patent applications I file, unless you notify me otherwise or I already know of corresponding one or more PCT or foreign-filed applications. Note that a non-publication request can be retracted at any time, thereby causing the application to be published per the timing explained above.

What is an Inventor's Declaration?

A U.S. non-provisional patent application receives a filing date upon its receipt by the USPTO. But for the USPTO to consider that application ready for examination, the USPTO also must receive a signed Inventor's Declaration for each inventor, that is, for each person who contributed to the conception of the subject matter of at least one claim presented in the patent application.

Via an Inventor's Declaration, an inventor essentially states each of the following, under penalty of perjury:

- their name, residence, mailing address, and citizenship;

- they believe they are an original and first inventor of the claimed subject matter;

- they have reviewed and understand the content of the patent application; and

- they have a duty to disclose material non-cumulative information to the USPTO (see "What is the duty of disclosure?", below).

Also, via an Inventor's Declaration, an inventor optionally can assert the benefit of one or more identified, prior filed:

- foreign patent applications (if any);

- U.S. provisional patent applications (if any); and/or

- U.S. non-provisional patent applications (if any).

Usually included in each Inventor's Declaration is a grant of limited Power of Attorney, which enables the named patent attorney(s) to represent the inventor before the USPTO for the purposes of prosecuting the identified patent application.

Typically, I prepare the Inventor's Declarations and send them electronically to my contact, who distributes them to the identified inventors. The signed Inventor's Declarations are then returned to me electronically, via fax, or in hard copy form. To motivate its inventors, some companies withhold patent incentive payments until all necessary paperwork, such as Inventor's Declarations, have been signed and provided to me.

Although Inventor's Declarations can be submitted at the same time that a non-provisional patent application is filed with the USPTO, I have found that the better practice usually is to submit them afterwards. That way, the Declaration contains the application number (ensuring that it won't be lost by the USPTO), and the inventors are more likely to have had sufficient time to actually review and understand the content of the application (as the Declaration states), without the pressure of a filing deadline hanging over their heads.

Once I receive signed copies of all the Inventor's Declarations, I file them in the USPTO, typically in response to a Notice of Missing Parts that was sent by the USPTO and that explains that submission of the Inventor's Declarations is required. Note that the Inventor's Declarations must be filed within 2 months of the mailing date of the Notice to File Missing Parts. This due date can be extended for up to 4 additional months via payment of an Extension Fee with the filing, that Extension Fee effectively doubling for each month of extension required.

Acceptance of the submitted Inventor's Declarations will result in the USPTO issuing an updated Official Filing Receipt, which verifies the filing date of the application, indicates that it is ready for examination, and assures that each inventor's name will appear on any published patent application and any resulting patent.

What is a patent assignment?

Each U.S. patent application is filed in the name of its identified inventors, and those inventors own that patent application unless and until they transfer ("assign") their ownership rights.

A well-drafted Employment Agreement will assign all intellectual assets developed using company resources or within the company's field(s) of endeavor to the company.

Similar to how a clerk's office in a county court records real estate transfers, the USPTO can record Assignments and other conveyances of U.S. patent applications and patents, thereby providing a public record of those conveyances. Such a public record can prevent the situation where an inventor or other "assignor" assigns their rights to both a first "assignee" and a second assignee, the second assignee being unaware of the first assignee's rights. In that case, if the first assignee did not timely record their assignment, the second assignee is awarded the rights, otherwise the first assignee wins. In either case, one of the assignees will be left with no patent rights, and only a claim for monetary damages to pursue against the assignor. In summary, checking and recording Assignments can be crucial to avoid being swindled!

Although U.S. patents often list an "assignee" on their first page, this information is often unreliable, since published U.S. patents are not updated to reflect changes in their assignment status. Instead, to better understand the ownership status of a given patent, the USPTO's current assignment records should be searched.

Only the recorded owner of a patent, or its exclusive licensee, can enforce a patent. Thus, when either of those parties needs to quickly obtain an injunction to halt an infringer, any delays while waiting to record an assignment can prove very costly.

Delays in obtaining and/or recording Assignments also can be very frustrating for your company. Such frustrations can become apparent when an inventor leaves your company on unfriendly terms, divorces, dies, or becomes incarcerated, incapacitated, or otherwise unwilling, unavailable, or unable to sign the Assignment.

I have prepared and recorded literally hundreds of Assignments. But rather than merely copying Assignment language that has been handed down through the generations, I created the language for my Assignments by starting with that used by several Fortune 50 companies, and then blending and improving from there. So although there's possibly some room for improvement, I believe my Assignments do a relatively superb job compared to most.

Typically, I have prepared Assignments and sent them electronically to the inventors. Although not required, I generally have encouraged that Assignments be signed in the presence of a notary, because doing so reduces the risk that the assignor's signature will be challenged later.

Note that the original of a signed Assignment for a U.S. patent application should not be sent to me, but instead should be treated like the title to a house or car, and stored in a secure location, such as a safe deposit box. In contrast, sometimes foreign patent offices require that I provide them with an original signed Assignment for the corresponding foreign patent application, and I will alert you if this is the case.

A copy of each signed Assignment can be returned to me electronically, via fax, or in hard copy form. To motivate its inventors, some companies withhold patent incentive payments until all necessary paperwork, such as Assignments, have been signed (and notarized if desired) and provided to me.

Upon receipt, I electronically submit a copy of the signed Assignment along with a Recordation Request, to the USPTO. Typically, within a few days, the USPTO will record that Assignment and send a Notice of Recordation, which I promptly will report to you.

What is the process for obtaining a patent?

When our best practices are followed, most U.S. patent applications we prepare and prosecute tend to advance according to the general process laid out here and depicted in the flowchart on page 152. Note that the flowchart numbers track the step numbers presented below.

1. Conceive concept.

The process starts with the creation of a concept. That moment in time, which is called "conception", exists when written evidence is available showing that an idea of a specific, complete, and operative implementation of the innovative subject matter was known first to the alleged inventor. Although innovating isn't always easy, by following some simple guidelines and best practices, you can quickly learn to hold pleasant 4-5 hour structured innovation sessions that can consistently yield upwards of 10 to 20 valuable, protectable, and evidenced innovative concepts. Please see *Step 4 - Innovate* for details.

2. Describe concept.

Next, succinctly describe a problem that seems to be uniquely solved by your innovation. I refer to this description as a "problem-solution statement", and describe it in detail on page 103. Augment your problem-solution statement with a thorough description of how to implement your innovation.

3. Evaluate patentability.

Then, with your description in hand, self-perform a brief innovation search, which will "knock out" your innovation from further consideration if it appears to be publicly known already. If you're unable to knock it out, commission a professional investigation of your innovation for acceptable: patentability, risks, and value.

Assuming it's warranted, the next step is to draft a strong patent application that properly describes and claims your desired innovations, and, within the required time limits, prepare and submit a proper U.S. patent application, PCT patent application, and/or foreign patent application(s).

4.   *Decide whether to file a U.S. provisional patent application.*

Provisional (sometimes referred to as "informal") U.S. patent applications expire 12 months after they are filed, typically contain no Innovator's Declaration, formal drawings, or claims, and thus are not examined by a government patent examiner. Consequently, provisionals do not mature into patents. Instead, their basic purpose is to act as a time stamp for the subject matter they properly describe. Provisionals do create the right to mark "Patent Pending" on anything that embodies any innovation that has been enablingly described in the application.

Contrast provisionals with non-provisional (sometimes referred to as "formal" or "regular") U.S. patent applications, which must include one or more "claims" that each legally define an "invention", typically have their claims examined by an "examiner", and often result in the issuance of a patent. As with provisionals, non-provisionals also create the right to mark "Patent Pending" on anything that embodies any innovation that has been enablingly described in the application.

If a provisional is filed, and a non-provisional is desired that claims subject matter that was properly described in that provisional, the non-provisional must be filed within 12 months of the filing date of the provisional.

5.   *Prepare and file provisional application.*

Preparing and filing a provisional can defer some of the costs associated with preparing and filing a non-provisional patent application. Taking the provisional application approach will create a 12 month window during which your company can:

1. explore the patentability of its described innovation;

2. improve upon that innovation;

3. mark "Patent Pending" on any product embodying the innovation;

4. determine the value of the innovation; and/or

5. raise funds to cover the cost of preparing and filing any desired non-provisional applications that rely on the description and filing date of the provisional.

6. *Decide whether to file a foreign patent application.*

Frequently, companies believe they must seek and maintain patent protection throughout the industrialized world. Yet doing so can be very expensive, ultimately costing hundreds of thousands of dollars. As a result of those phenomenal costs and the corresponding diminishing returns associated with many of those countries, taking the "patent everywhere" approach can actually undermine the return on the investment in the resulting family of patents.

Fortunately, sales of patent-protected implementations in large markets often can generate sufficient profits to, where legally allowed, subsidize competition-discouraging pricing of those implementations in many smaller, unpatented markets. So prior to deciding where to patent, your company should carefully analyze the geographical distribution of the expected global market for implementations of an innovation, and seek to estimate demand, pricing, and profitability in each country of interest.

7. *Prepare and file foreign application.*

Once the desired countries are determined, through the patent professional's carefully managed network of skilled foreign patent professionals and with the client's input, appropriate patent applications are correctly filed, prosecuted to issuance while mitigating prosecution-related risks, and properly maintained in each of those countries.

8. *Decide whether to file PCT application.*

Nearly every major industrialized country is a signatory to the Patent Cooperation Treaty ("PCT"). The few non-members of that UN-sponsored treaty include Taiwan and a number of countries that are relatively unindustrialized and/or have relatively small economies, such as many Latin American, Middle Eastern, and African countries. So for most companies, with the possible exception of Taiwan, the non-member countries of the PCT are irrelevant from a patenting perspective.

In short, the PCT defines a process for filing, searching, and examining an "international" (or "PCT") patent application. Yet a PCT application does not directly result in a patent. Instead, filing a PCT application typically causes a government-employed patent examiner to search for relevant prior art to the subject matter of the claims and to issue a written opinion of the patentability of those claims.

If desired, by 30 (or sometimes 31) months from the priority date, for each country selected, a localized "National Stage" patent application that corresponds to the PCT application can be submitted to the national patent office of that country by competent foreign counsel.

The PCT search results, written opinion, and examiner's report (if any) can assist each corresponding national patent examiner with determining if a patent should and will be issued for their country. When particularly positive, those PCT documents sometimes can inspire a national patent examiner to not perform an additional search or a rigorous additional examination of the claims.

9. Prepare and file PCT application.

Preparing and filing a PCT application can potentially provide the following benefits:

- deferring the decision/requirement to file a patent application in a PCT signatory country for up to 18 additional months from the PCT's priority date;

- obtaining a relatively quick search report and patentability opinion for the claims; and

- obtaining an examination report that sometimes will strongly influence at least some of the national patent examiners;

- while costing only a relatively modest government fee (considering the potential fees for early filing in a number of foreign patent offices).

10. Prepare and file U.S. Non-Provisional Patent Application or U.S. National Stage Non-Provisional Patent Application based on a PCT application.

Prepared properly, a non-provisional patent application requires the dedication of a substantial amount of time for very careful claim drafting, thoughtful defining of phrases that appear in the claims, and skilled avoidance/reduction of legal risks. Somewhat similar to provisionals, a non-provisional must describe the desired subject matter, and particularly the claimed subject matter, in a manner that enables a person having ordinary skill in the relevant art to implement (make and use) that claimed subject matter. In addition, numerous additional preparation formalities must be addressed, including properly preparing drawings, fulfilling rigid document formatting requirements, and correctly referencing any priority documents. Fortunately, once a non-provisional has been prepared, it can be filed as a U.S., PCT, and/or foreign patent application, often with relatively few or even no changes (except for the possible need to translate it to a different language).

Working closely with the innovator(s), I often can relatively rapidly prepare and file a patent application that not only will meet with eventual approval by the relevant patent office, but also will result in an issued patent that is easily recognized as being highly likely to survive the rigors of litigation, and thus will be respected by competitors without the need to litigate.

Once a non-provisional patent application is filed with the United States Patent and Trademark Office (USPTO), it enters the "prosecution" stage, during which it is examined (usually after considerable delay) by an "examiner", who often challenges the originally-filed claims using various "rejections", some of which can be based on alleged prior art references.

During prosecution, the application might be amended and/or re-filed (yet keep the benefit of its original filing date). When appropriate, a final decision of the examiner might be appealed. For a minority of applications, the applicant might decide to abandon further prosecution. There are numerous other contingencies possible, thereby making a detailed explanation of the prosecution stage rather long and tedious. However, I provide a very general description of patent prosecution next.

Early on, the USPTO first checks the filed application for compliance with numerous formalities, such as the submission of all Inventor's Declarations and compliant drawings. Once all formalities are met, the USPTO sends the application to an "Art Unit", which assigns the application to one of its many examiners.

11. Restriction Requirement.

Sometimes, even before the claims of a U.S. non-provisional patent application have been examined for patentability, the assigned examiner issues what is referred to as a "Restriction Requirement". This document mandates that the applicant elect certain claims to prosecute, and others to either "withdraw" from examination for the time being or cancel from the application. As allowance of the remaining claims becomes imminent, the examiner sometimes can be convinced to re-consider and also allow the withdrawn claims. Cancelled claims can be pursued via a follow-up "Divisional" application that contains the same descriptive content as the non-provisional application, and receives the benefit of its effective filing date.

12. Prepare and file response to Restriction Requirement.

It is possible to fight a restriction requirement, but the USPTO's rules can make it somewhat difficult and expensive to do so. Consequently, most applicants capitulate and go with the flow.

13. Non-Final Office Action.

After a substantial delay (typically 9 to 30 months while the examiner addresses a mountain of earlier-filed applications, and currently averaging roughly 20 months across all art units), the assigned examiner performs a search for prior art publications (typically published patents and patent applications) that reasonably relate to the subject matter claimed (and elected if a Restriction Requirement was issued) in the filed application.

Based on that prior art search, the examiner prepares and sends a first substantive communication, commonly called an "Office Action". In that first Office Action, the examiner explains his or her initial viewpoint on the patentability of the claims, which unfortunately is typically negative, poorly explained, and weakly supported in fact and law.

14. File Response: Amendments and/or Arguments.

Regardless of the quality of an examiner's justifications for "rejecting" the claims, with input from the inventors (if necessary), I usually can overcome those rejections via negotiations with the examiner. Via those negotiations, which nearly always include multiple written "Responses" (or "Replies"), I attempt to persuade the examiner to reconsider his/her evidence and/or reasoning or I amend the claims to avoid prior art that is just too close to the claimed concepts. In any given Response, I might amend the specification, drawings, and/or claims, and/or present legal and/or technical arguments challenging the examiner's position.

15. Final Office Action.

As suggested above, multiple volleys of Office Actions and Responses can be required to obtain "allowance" of the claims of the patent application. Often, after filing a Response to a first Office Action, the examiner will issue a "Final Office Action" that again rejects the claims. Note however, that "Final" is a misnomer, meaning only that the applicant must pay an additional fee to continue prosecuting the application, or must appeal the examiner's claim rejections.

16. File Response: RCE with Amendments and/or Arguments.

If you are inclined to modify the claims in the hopes of appeasing the examiner, or are willing to submit an expert's declaration that explains why the examiner's assertions are factually incorrect, then along with filing a "Request for Continued Examination" ("RCE"), I can file a Response containing those claim amendments, presenting the expert declaration, and/or providing accompanying arguments.

17. File Appeal.

If you really want a patent to issue that includes claims having precisely the same language as that of some (at least twice) rejected claims, the next step is to appeal the examiner's rejections of those claims to the Patent Trial and Appeal Board. Note that appeals can be somewhat pricey, and currently are taking 2 years or longer for the Board to decide.

18. Appeal Decided.

If the Board's Decision overturns all the examiner's rejections, the examiner often will allow the claims without further resistance. If any of the examiner's claim rejections are upheld, I can re-open prosecution, amend the corresponding claims to overcome those rejections, and continue trying to convince the examiner to allow all of the claims.

Alternatively, I can ask the Board to reconsider its position, and can even appeal the Board's decision if my client feels particularly strongly that the Board erred. In either case, if the USPTO realizes it has made a mistake, it will then relent, otherwise the appeal will move forward.

No matter how it turns out, unless the application is abandoned, at some point, the patent application should be allowed.

19. Allowance.

Typically, within about 33 months [27] of the filing date, and after several rounds of Office Actions and Responses (i.e., within about 12-24 months from the mailing of the first of those Office Actions), the examiner becomes comfortable with the claims and sends a "Notice of Allowance and Issue Fee(s) Due".

A recent study indicates that original non-provisional applications have about an 89% chance of eventually being allowed to issue as a patent. [28] Of those, some are eventually re-filed as Continuation applications (see step 21 below) before allowance is obtained.

20. Pay Issue Fee.

Assuming that the allowed claims, reasons for allowance, and fulfillment of other requirements are acceptable, with my client's authorization, I pay the required Issue Fee.

21. Decide whether to file Continuation.

Quite frequently, a follow-up "Continuation" patent application is filed that claims an innovation described in a previously-filed ("parent") application, but that was not defined by the claims of that parent application. For instance, Continuation applications often claim one or more described concepts more broadly than their parent application, and in some cases, more precisely, particularly when "aiming" their claims at a known infringer. In any event, every Continuation application must be filed before its parent application issues, and preferably no later than the date the Issue Fee is paid on that parent application.

About 65-70% of Continuation applications eventually issue. Around 30% of them issue in less than 2 years and about half issue in under 5 years. [29]

22. Patent Issues.

Anywhere from 3 to 12 (or more) weeks after I pay the Issue Fee, the USPTO issues, publishes, and mails the corresponding United States Patent, complete with gold seal, red ribbon, and signature of the USPTO's Director.

Note that all patent offices charge some form of fee or tax for keeping in force a patent application or resulting patent. In most countries, this fee is referred to as an annuity (because it must be paid each year). In the U.S., this fee is referred to as a maintenance fee, and must be paid at roughly 4, 8, and 12 years after the patent is issued to keep the patent in force. Generally, if a required annuity and/or maintenance fee is not timely paid, the patent application or patent will be deemed abandoned, and only sometimes can be revived if prompt action is taken.

Finally, recall that provisional patent applications themselves are not prosecuted and thus, do not directly result in issued patents (or require you to pay issue fees or maintenance fees), and instead expire automatically 1 year after they are filed.

23. Exploit Patent.

To highlight some of the ways I can help you harness, extract, and exploit the value and power of your company's intellectual properties, including its patents, I have compiled over 70 tactics in *Step 7 – Harness*.

PROSECUTING A U.S. UTILITY PATENT APPLICATION

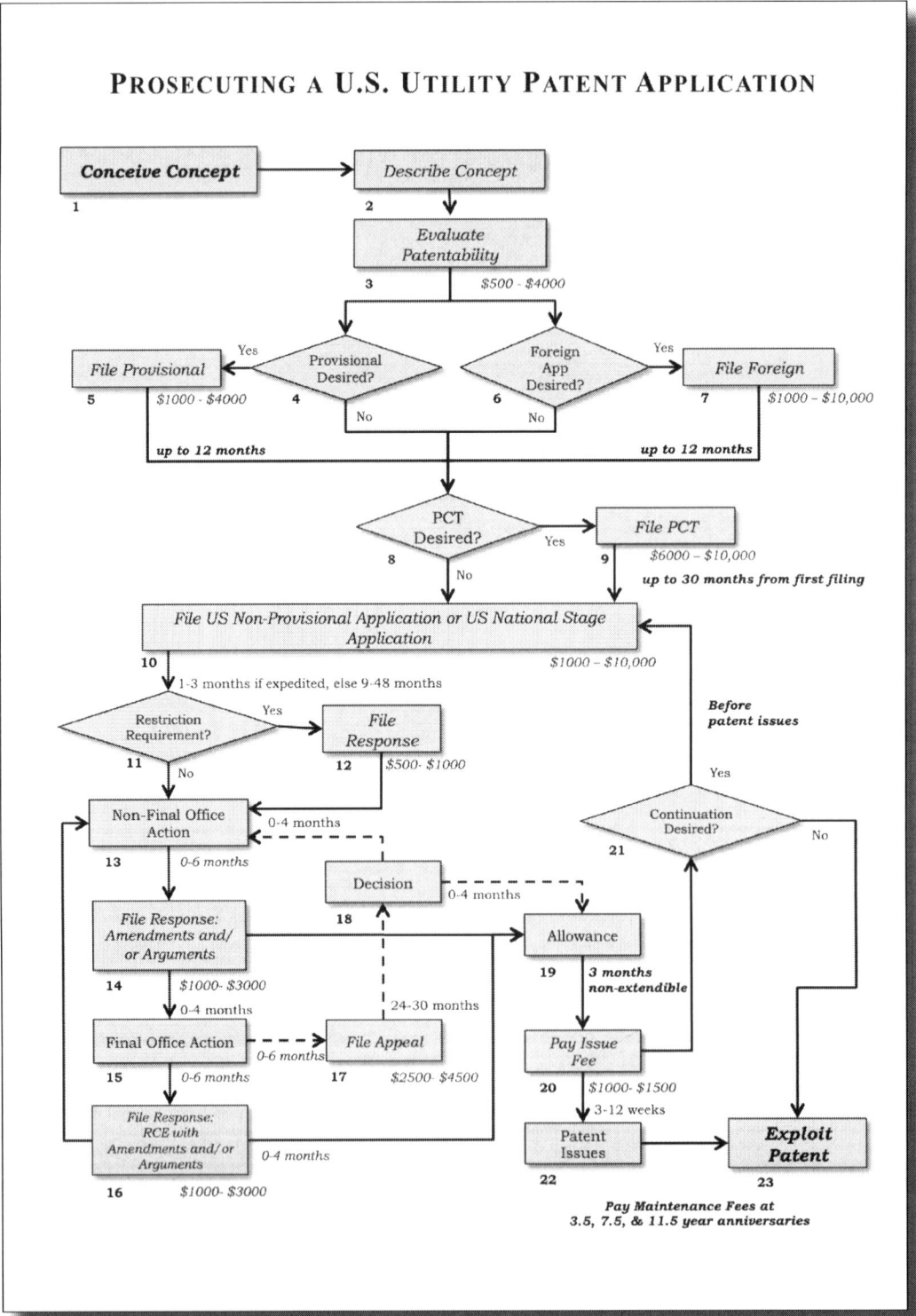

To what extent can a patent application be revised?

Once a patent application is filed, only very limited aspects of its content can be changed. In particular, its claims can be revised or "amended", but only to the extent that the remainder of the application describes the particular amended subject matter, and how to implement it. Also, formal drawings can be substituted for the original drawings. Sometimes, amendments can be made to the text of the application, but typically only to correct obvious typographical errors, or to describe in writing precisely what is shown in the drawings. The general rule of thumb is that no new subject matter can be added to a filed U.S. patent application. Thus, when new subject matter arises that "deserves" to appear in a patent application, a new patent application must be filed describing and/or claiming that new subject matter.

Is there any way to accelerate examination?

Although there are situations where delay is valuable, sometimes a U.S. patent applicant is not content to wait roughly 3–4 years (the current average) for the USPTO to complete examination of an application and issue the patent. To counter some of that delay, there are currently 4 primary ways to request the USPTO to expedite the examination of your patent application.

The quickest examination approach is called "Track One", which sometimes is referred to as "prioritized examination". Once a request for Track One examination has been filed, the USPTO will decide whether to grant that request within an average of about 2 months. Once the USPTO grants a request for Track One examination, it must either allow or finally reject all of the claims of that application within the following 12 months. The USPTO will grant only 10,000 Track One requests per fiscal year. Currently, the USPTO is allowing or finally rejecting all of the claims of the typical Track One application within about 6 months. So on average, in under 8 months, the corresponding patent has been granted, or the

Track One application's claims have been finally rejected, a decision that can be appealed and potentially reversed.

Yet Track One isn't for everyone, especially considering the relatively large additional fee (currently $4000 for large entities, $2000 for small entities, and $1000 for micro entities) and the following additional requirements:

1. The number of claims in the filed application is limited to 4 independent and 30 total;

2. All required inventor declarations must be filed with the application; and

3. The Track One request must be filed at the time the application is filed.

Also, the application will lose its prioritized status if any of the following occur:

A. The number of claims expands beyond 4 independent claims or 30 total claims;

B. The applicant files a request for extension of time;

C. The applicant files a request for continued examination (RCE);

D. The applicant files a notice of appeal;

E. The applicant files a request for suspension of action;

F. The USPTO mails a notice of allowance;

G. The USPTO mails a final office action; or

H. The applicant abandons the application.

Nevertheless, in some situations, Track One might be very appropriate (e.g., pending licensing and/or potential infringement litigation). This approach not only speeds up examination, but compared to regular examination, also can result in a lower overall out-of-pocket cost for getting the patent application through examination to issuance. Note that to best exploit Track One, the applicant should have first performed a strong patentability search and written the claims to easily avoid any found prior art. Otherwise, the USPTO might finally reject the claims, which potentially can be overcome via appeal and/or continued prosecution via an RCE, but will lead to a loss of Track One status.

The next quickest technique is called the "Patent Prosecution Highway" (PPH) and is nearly always the least expensive approach. This tactic relies on the prior search or examination results for a corresponding patent application (foreign or PCT), those results generated by a PPH participating patent office (either a foreign patent office or the USPTO acting as the search or examination authority for a PCT application).

The PPH requirements are relatively straightforward. Consider two patent applications, "application A" and a corresponding "application B"). Generally, for application B to enter the PPH:

1. Application A was filed initially in a participating patent office;

2. Application A received an indication that at least one of its claims is patentable;

3. Application B was filed after application A was filed;

4. Application B is substantially identical to application A;

5. Application B's claims are substantially identical to application A's; and

6. Application B has not yet been examined.

There is no additional USPTO fee for requesting PPH examination, and examination results are typically received 2-3 months from the grant of the request.

In general, the PPH approach can work really well when a company is willing to first file the same application in a relatively quick-to-examine foreign patent office, such as those of the UK and Australia (and sometimes a PCT application, as explained below). Currently, the USPTO has pilot PPH programs with over 20 foreign IP Offices. Note that in some situations, allowance in the U.S. may likewise help accelerate examination of corresponding foreign applications.

Just as with Track One applications, to best exploit the PPH, the applicant should have first performed a strong patentability search and written the claims to easily avoid any found prior art. Otherwise, the initial patent office might not promptly indicate the patentability of one or more of the claims, leading to a delay or inability to enter the PPH.

As hinted above, the USPTO also has expanded the PPH program to allow applicants to leverage a favorable PCT Written Opinion or International Preliminary Report on Patentability issued by a participating International Authority to accelerate examination in a corresponding U.S. application. Given that PCT applications typically receive search results relatively quickly (by 19 months from their priority date, which is often about 7 months after they are filed), this can be a very effective way to accelerate examination in the U.S. (and may also be a great way to accelerate examination in other PCT-PPH-participating jurisdictions).

It's important to realize that receiving special status as a PPH application may help accelerate the examination process, but it does not change the U.S. standards for patentability. In other words, the USPTO isn't going to give your application a "free pass" to allowance simply for driving on the Patent Prosecution Highway. Interestingly though, allowance rates for PPH applications have tended to be considerably higher the allowance rate for non-PPH applications.

Turning away from the PPH, a bit slower is a technique that is misnamed "Accelerated Examination" (AE). The USPTO petition fee for requesting

AE is currently $130. However, the applicant must conduct its own search and supply the USPTO with not only search results, but a "support document" that summarizes and characterizes those results. This approach can be more expensive than regular examination, and due to the support document requirement, can introduce several serious legal risks that are typically very unacceptable from my perspective.

Finally, the least effective approach for expediting examination is to file what is called a "petition to make special". There is no USPTO fee for the applicant to file such a petition if it asserts any of the following as its reason for granting the petition:

1. one of the inventors is over the age of 65 or is ill to the point where they may not be available to assist in the prosecution of the patent;

2. that the invention will materially:

   a. Enhance the quality of the environment;

   b. Contribute to the development or conservation of energy resources; or

   c. Contribute to countering terrorism.

A petition to make special also can be filed, along with a relatively modest USPTO fee (currently $130), if the petition asserts any of the following reasons for granting the petition:

1. the patent will enable manufacture of the invention;

2. the patent is being infringed (although asserting this reason can carry additional legal risks);

3. the patent relates to any of superconductivity, recombinant DNA, cancer, HIV/AIDS, and terrorism; and

4. the patent relates to biotechnology that is a major asset of a "small entity" (typically a company with less than 500

employees), the development of that biotechnology dependent on expedited examination of the patent application.

Note that any application can be made "special" if the head of a government agency requests it. Also note that even when petitions to make special are granted, although examination of the corresponding application might begin within as little as 6 months, it still takes an average of over 2 years to reach allowance, requiring nearly as many volleys with the examiner to convince the examiner to grant the patent as is required for a regular application. So on average, petitions to make special tend to work best for technologies that tend to experience long delays before and during examination, such as those related to computer software and business methods, yet where the applicant can not afford the USPTO's Track One fee.

In summary, when available, the PPH is the clear winner. When PPH is not available, if there is a strong reason for expediting examination, most clients will obtain the greatest return on investment by seeking Track One examination. And although I've not yet heard a good reason to follow the Accelerated Examination path, in a few situations a Petition to Make Special still makes sense.

What is the duty of disclosure?

Under U.S. law, everyone (inventors, attorney, patent agent, etc.) associated with the filing and prosecution of a U.S. non-provisional patent application has a duty of disclosure to the USPTO. Although a relatively recent court case (*Therasense, Inc. v. Becton, Dickinson & Co.*) has modified that duty in some contexts, the duty remains very relevant to patent applicants, at least under current USPTO rules.

More specifically, according to the US patent rules (37 C.F.R. 1.56 in particular), your company's legal requirement is to submit to the USPTO any information of which it is aware that is material to patentability.

Information is considered material to patentability when:

1. It is not cumulative to information already of record or being made of record in the application, and

2. It establishes, by itself or in combination with other information, a *prima facie* case of unpatentability of a claim; or

3. It refutes, or is inconsistent with, a position the applicant takes in:

    (i) opposing an argument of unpatentability relied on by the Office, or

    (ii) asserting an argument of patentability.

I realize this legal-speak, so I'll try to translate it to everyday English.

Generally, everyone to whom the duty applies must submit any documented information (e.g., a publication (such as a article, book, patent, web page, brochure, etc.), photograph, etc.) of which they are aware if a U.S. patent examiner reasonably can use that documented information (we'll call it a "reference") to reject a claim of the application and if that reference is not simply repetitive of a reference already submitted or a reference already cited by the examiner of the application.

So there is no need to submit any reference that is only repetitive of what's in the other references previously cited, submitted, or planned to be submitted. There is a need to submit any reference that is not repetitive and reasonably can be used to reject a claim.

When can a reference be used to reject a claim?

1. If it provides, to a person having ordinary skill in the field, an enabling description of how to implement the entire subject matter of any claim of the application; or

2. If it, when properly modified or combined with another reference, provides, to one of ordinary skill in the field, an enabling description of how to implement the entire subject matter of any claim.

The first criteria is a simplified explanation of a *prima facie* case of unpatentability due to anticipation. The second is a simplified explanation of a *prima facie* case of unpatentability due to obviousness.

Although obviousness has never been particularly easy to understand, recent Supreme Court decisions, and USPTO interpretations of those decisions, have nevertheless managed to muddy the unclear waters even further. Although the following explanation of how to establish obviousness has potentially been loosened, it remains somewhat helpful:

> "To establish a prima facie *case of obviousness, three basic criteria must be met. First, there must be some suggestion or motivation, either in the references themselves or in the knowledge generally available to one of ordinary skill in the art, to modify the reference or to combine reference teachings. Second, there must be a reasonable expectation of success. Finally, the prior art reference (or references when combined) must teach [explicitly or inherently]... all the claim limitations. The teaching... to make the claimed combination and the reasonable expectation of success must both be found in the prior art, and not based on applicant's disclosure."* In re Vaeck, 947 F.2d 488 (Fed. Cir. 1991).

Trying to apply the above explanation typically leads one to conclude that it is far easier to just submit every known reference that seems reasonably close to the claimed (and perhaps even the described) subject matter.

Although a very recent court case has modified the law in this area, the consequences of failing to fulfill the duty of disclosure can be very severe. For example, if it is proven that anyone failed to fulfill their duty of disclosure, not only can the patent arising out of an application be invalidated, but so can every other patent that is related to that application.

From solely this legal perspective, one might conclude that researchers/innovators might be better served by resisting the temptation toward providing overly-inclusive bibliographies in any papers or disclosures describing their innovations.

Why are claims restricted?

Sometimes, before the claims of a U.S. non-provisional patent application even have been examined for patentability, the assigned examiner issues what is referred to as a "Restriction Requirement". This document mandates that the applicant elect certain claims to prosecute, and others to either "withdraw" from examination for the time being or cancel from the application.

On their face, the USPTO's ostensible goals for restricting patent claims seem reasonable enough, namely:

1. to avoid overwhelming the examiner with multiple "inventions" (which might prevent quality examination since the examiner is being paid to examine only a single "invention");

2. to avoid issuing one patent for multiple "inventions" (which might deprive the USPTO of needed fees (filing, prosecution, issue, maintenance, etc.) to cover the costs of examining the multiple "inventions"); and

3. to avoid issuing multiple patents for a single "invention" (which might create a situation where some of those patents are owned by different owners, and thus an alleged infringer might be liable to multiple parties for a single act of infringement).

Yet respect for these goals is currently undermined by the USPTO intentionally distorting and misinterpreting the laws authorizing restriction, falsely asserting more "inventions" than are claimed, and providing little to no means for easily challenging these illegal antics.

In particular, although U.S. patent laws authorize the USPTO to restrict claims, to do so properly the examiner must show that each alleged invention (a given group of one or more claims of the application) is both "independent *and* distinct" from each other alleged invention. Yet as demonstrated in nearly every case, the USPTO's examiners have been trained and encouraged to ignore this requirement, and instead restrict merely on the basis that the alleged inventions are "distinct". As you might imagine, it is downright simple for an examiner to show that two or more alleged inventions are distinct from each other, and thus the examiner always "wins" this lop-sided charade. Consequently, applicants far too often are initially forced to divide their claims into multiple groups, and elect to pursue only one of those groups in the filed application.

It is possible to fight a restriction requirement, but the USPTO's rules can make it somewhat difficult and expensive to do so. Consequently, most applicants capitulate.

Fortunately, this isn't the end of the road. First, the applicant can pursue each of the unelected groups of claims in additional applications, which are referred to as "divisional" applications. Each divisional application is identical to the original application, except that it presents only a unique one of the groups of unelected claims. If the applicant desires to pursue an unelected claim group via a divisional, that application must be filed while the original application, a "continuation" of it, or another divisional of it are still pending in the USPTO. Of course, by forcing the applicant to file a divisional to pursue a group of claims, the USPTO assures itself of additional filing fees, and potentially additional prosecution, issue, and maintenance fees.

Also, fortunately, there is no need to file a divisional application for a claim group if, during the prosecution of the original application, the examiner can be convinced that any allowed claim is "generic" to the claims of an unelected group. So often, applicants defer filing a divisional application until shortly before the original application issues, just in case I can convince the examiner to "re-join" some or all of the unelected groups of claims.

Why are claims rejected?

Once the patent examiner examines the claims of an application for patentability, he/she reports her opinion of that patentability via a document commonly referred to as an "Office Action".

Traditionally (about 95+ percent of the time), the first Office Action includes a rejection of all the claims, sometimes for good reasons, but typically for not-so-good reasons. In most of those cases, by doing so, the examiner is essentially inviting the applicant to explain how the claimed subject matter differs from what is described (not necessarily claimed) in the cited "prior art" references.

From the "mailing" date of an Office Action, the applicant typically has 3 months within which to file a "Response" or "Reply" that presents evidence and/or arguments debunking the faulty reasoning of the Office Action, and/or presents amendments to the claims or other portions of the application that actually need to be adjusted to fulfill the patentability requirements or that the applicant wants to revise for other reasons. That due date can be extended in 1 month intervals, for up to a total of 3 months, by the payment of a corresponding "extension fee" with the filing of that "late" Reply. Note that each additional month that the Reply is delayed results in approximately a doubling of the extension fee.

Often, after filing a Reply to a first Office Action, the examiner will issue a "Final Office Action" that again rejects the claims. Note however, that "Final" is a misnomer, meaning only that the applicant must pay an additional fee to continue prosecuting the application, or must appeal the examiner's claim rejections.

According to a recent study [30], U.S. patent examiners may be motivated by the USPTO's examiner incentive system to either over-willingly allow claims or to over-willingly reject claims, regardless of the objective patentability of those claims.

That incentive system awards an examiner a "count" (performance credit) not only for each new application they examine, but also for each application they finally reject, and for each application they allow to issue as a patent. Examiners also earn a count for any application that is abandoned. The greater the examiner's counts, the greater his or her "production" bonus (pay).

When an RCE is filed, the examiner earns another count for examining that application, even though the examiner typically doesn't have to spend nearly as much effort as they would searching and examining a new application.

Thus, contrary to the legal requirement for the USPTO to issue patents, an examiner can early plenty of counts (and the corresponding pay), avoid negative management attention, and unnecessarily delay allowance of an application. As shown in the study, some examiners seem to take precisely that approach, forcing the applicant to file several RCEs before allowing the patent to issue. Yet other examiners take the opposite approach, only forcing the applicant to file an RCE when truly needed to arrive at claims that indeed seem patentable.

Assuming the study's findings to be true (which my experience strongly validates), it might be worthwhile to approach U.S. patenting with an expectation that a significant proportion of examiners will delay allowance simply out of self-interest.

But let's assume for a moment that an examiner's motivation for rejecting claims is appropriate. In basic terms, what are the legal reasons that claims might be rejected? I will answer that question shortly, but before I explain the most common types of claim rejections, I first will provide some brief background information.

The U.S. patent system is empowered by the U.S. Constitution, Article 1, Section 8, which states that:

"Congress shall have the power to... promote the progress of science and the useful arts by securing for limited times to authors and inventors the exclusive right to their respective writings and discoveries...."

To implement this power, Congress long ago decided that the U.S. patent system would be examination-based, and established a Patent Office to perform those examinations in accordance with various laws, regulations, and rules.

Currently, unless withdrawn beforehand, each filed U.S. non-provisional patent application will be examined by the USPTO to verify that it complies with the legal requirements for a U.S. patent. Those legal requirements are defined in the U.S. patent statute (Title 35 of the United States Code and in Title 37 of the Code of Federal Regulations), as interpreted by the U.S. federal court system, and revolve around several core notions.

First, to be entitled to a patent, your patent application must properly "claim" an "invention". An "invention" is a useful, new, and non-obvious concept. A "claim" is a textual definition of a concept. A granted claim defines the scope of your concept and establishes limits on your legal right to exclude others from implementing that concept. Note that each claim must define a different concept from each other claim, even if that difference is only slight.

Second, to earn a patent, your patent application must properly "teach" (adequately explain) how to implement each of your claimed concepts. This is the basic exchange that is contemplated by the Constitution for our patent system. Very generally, you teach society how to implement each of your claimed concepts ("promote the progress"), and in exchange, receive the right to exclude society from doing so for a limited period of time.

This exchange of information for a patent is premised on the beliefs that it will:

- allow you to earn an attractive return on your research and development investment in your concepts;

- inspire more R&D investments (by you and/or others); and

- bring even more concepts to market (again, "promote the progress").

These two notions, properly defining a concept, and properly teaching how to implement it, serve as the basis for the 7 primary reasons that examiners allege for rejecting a claim of a U.S. non-provisional patent application. I will briefly explain those 7 reasons, and how I typically overcome each of them.

1. *Statutory Subject Matter*

A patent claim must be directed toward one of the 4 broad types of subject matter identified in the patent statute (Section 101 of Title 35 of the United States Code).

In particular, although it might not use these particular words in the claim, each claim must be directed at a "manufacture", "machine", "composition of matter", or "process".

The first of these, "manufacture", covers any claim directed toward a "device", "apparatus", or a particularly named "thing" that reasonably falls within the scope of these words. By far the bulk of the statutory subject matter rejections regarding "manufacture" claims involve claims that are directed toward computer software that is stored on a machine-readable medium, such as a hard drive, optical disk (CD, DVD), flash drive, etc. I can usually easily overcome such a rejection either via brief discussion with the examiner and/or a minor amendment to the claim language.

The next of these, "machine", covers any claim directed to a combination of "devices", such as an "assembly", "system", or the like. I rarely see statutory subject matter rejections regarding such claims, and as with "manufacture" claims, these rejections are usually easy to resolve.

Even more rarely seen are statutory subject matter rejections regarding "composition of matter" claims, which are directed toward "substances", "mixtures", "solutions", "materials", "gene sequences", "molecules", and so forth. These rejections only tend to arise when the examiner interprets the claimed subject matter as a product of natural, rather than human-caused, transformation.

Until recently, the most frequently seen statutory subject matter rejections targeted "process" claims, which are often presented as "methods", "procedures", "activities", etc. More specifically, such rejections typically targeted "process" claims that were directed toward mathematics, "business methods" and/or software. But in response to a June 2010 Supreme Court decision, the USPTO has dramatically reduced such rejections, and I typically can handle any remaining ones rather easily. Generally, the key here is to only claim concepts for which operable implementations are described, thereby avoiding allegations that the claimed subject matter is too "abstract".

In summary, well-written patent applications rarely encounter statutory subject matter rejections that are truly serious, because I can easily settle nearly all that arise in the patent applicant's favor.

2. *Utility*

A patent claim must be directed to subject matter that has "utility" (according to Section 101 of the patent statute). This means, that the application must describe an implementation of the claimed concept that is practical, beneficial, and operable.

The first utility category is "practical" or "specific" utility. Rejections involving this requirement typically arise for chemical compositions for which no use has yet been described (other than possibly serving as a "research subject", "intermediate", or "ballast", none of which count as a "practical" utility). To avoid such rejections, the application should describe a particular meaningful purpose for the claimed subject matter. If such a purpose has not yet been determined, the filing of the application should be deferred and the compositions kept secret in the meanwhile.

All that is required to fulfill the "beneficial" aspect is that the claimed subject matter be capable of providing some meaningful benefit to society. It's hard to write a patent application and not describe a beneficial aspect of the claimed subject matter. Thus, I've not yet encountered a rejection asserting that a claim wasn't directed to something "beneficial".

The USPTO is presented with quite a few claims to perpetual motion machines, cold fusion, and other incredible concepts that appear to violate fundamental laws of nature, so the USPTO needs the ability to weed out the nonsense. They do so via the "operable" standard of the utility requirement, which allows them to reject claims that credibly can not be implemented in any manner that will work. Nevertheless, claimed subject matter is presumed to be operable, and the USPTO has the burden to prove otherwise. Therefore, these sort of utility rejections are rare. And the few times I have seen one, the subject matter that was intended to be claimed was indeed operable, so only a slight tweak of the claim language was needed to more clearly or logically claim the concept that was intended.

Operability-type utility rejections are more common for certain "arts" than others. For the "predictable" arts, such as mechanical, electrical, and software-oriented technologies, utility rejections are truly rare, since most patent attorneys won't involve themselves with innovations that are clearly inoperative. For the "unpredictable" arts, however, such as chemical, biological, and certain very cutting edge technologies, utility rejections are more common, if simply because the examiner believes that whether the claimed concept will work for its intended purpose (i.e., is operable) is generally unpredictable.

I typically can avoid such operability-type utility rejections for unpredictable technologies by providing data showing that the claimed concept indeed works, i.e., is at least barely operable. On some occasions, and although a somewhat risky approach, rather than being included with the application, such data can be generated and submitted after the utility rejection is received.

To summarize, in my experience, utility rejections are rather rare, and can be avoided by following best practices for disclosing innovations and drafting patent applications.

3. Indefiniteness

To fulfill section 112 of the patent statute, a patent claim must be "definite", meaning that the scope of subject matter it covers must be clearly understandable by a person having ordinary skill in the "art" (the well-recognized and broader realm that includes that subject matter).

In my experience, the vast majority of "indefiniteness" rejections stem from the examiner not reading the application, or not having sufficient technical literacy or competence to understand what has been read.

In other words, the nature and bounds of the claimed subject matter usually are clearly understandable and distinct to a person having ordinary skill in the art who can read and comprehend U.S. English.

Regrettably, not all examiners have such capabilities. Fortunately, such issues often can be overcome by involving the examiner's supervisor, who almost always does have sufficient technical and language skills to grasp the meaning of the claims. On a few occasions, an appeal of the rejection must be pursued to resolve the issue.

Sometimes, an indefiniteness rejection is reasonable, due to the use of a vague, relative, or subjective phrase in a claim, such as "high viscosity", "smooth surface", or "aesthetically pleasing". Thus, I avoid the use of such phrases in my claims, and consequently tend to avoid such rejections.

Also, by providing definitions of the phrases used in my claims, I tend to prevent indefiniteness rejections, since my definitions clarify and add distinctness to the subject matter of those claims.

In summary, I have found that most indefiniteness rejections are relatively easy to overcome, and often can be avoided by using best practices for application drafting.

4. *Written Description*

Section 112 of the patent statute also requires that each U.S. non-provisional patent application provide some indication that the named inventors had "mental possession" of the claimed subject matter at the time the application was filed. That means that the application must not present a claim to subject matter that was not contemplated by the inventors, as evidenced by the "written description" portion of the application (i.e., the "Detailed Description", drawing figures, and usually, the originally-filed claims).

Perhaps more simply stated, although the application can be viewed as a sort of "well" from which words (and their synonyms) can be drawn to form a claim, most possible combinations of those words will not even remotely define the concepts the inventors actually invented.

Generally, written description only becomes a potential concern for claims that were amended or added after the application was filed. That is, usually accidentally, a claim is amended to recite a concept that is not actually described by the application, although the claim contains phrases that appear or are synonymous with those presented in the descriptive portion of the application.

With this background in mind, I note that a written description rejection typically arises for one of two primary reasons: the claim is misdirected, or the claim is misunderstood.

In the first case, where the claim doesn't define a concept that the application describes, I simply amend or cancel the claim and the issue is promptly resolved.

But the second situation, where the examiner plainly does not understand the claimed subject matter or the descriptive "support" that is provided for it in the application, sometimes can be a bit more challenging to overcome. Frequently, simply pointing the examiner to those portions of the application that provide descriptive support for the claimed concept is sufficient to cause the examiner to withdraw the rejection. On occasion, however, the examiner lacks adequate technical or linguistic capability to comprehend the claimed and/or described subject matter, forcing me to either involve the examiner's supervisor, or to appeal the rejection, thereby involving an administrative law judge, who typically is much better-skilled.

To summarize, I generally avoid written description rejections using best practices for application drafting. And for those few written description rejections that do arise, I typically can vanquish them rather easily.

5. Enablement

In addition to requiring that claims not be "indefinite" and that they be supported by an adequate "written description", section 112 of the patent statute also requires that the claimed subject matter be "enabled".

This "enablement" requirement demands that each claimed concept be described in a manner sufficient to "enable" or "empower" a person having ordinary skill in the art to at least barely operably implement that concept, without substantial experimentation.

Again, this requirement reflects the basic exchange of patenting. Generally, you teach the world how to implement your claimed concept, and in exchange, receive the right to exclude the world from doing so for a limited period of time (roughly 20 years from your application's filing date). Fulfilling this teaching or enablement requirement is the role of the descriptive portion of the patent application, which can be presented via text and/or via graphical illustrations. Note that the descriptive portion of a patent application can not be substantially amended after the application is filed. Thus, it is imperative that the descriptive portion properly fulfill its enablement role at the time the application is filed.

Rejections based on lack of enablement generally arise for one of two reasons.

First, sometimes an application simply does not adequately describe how to implement a claimed concept. To avoid this failure, I generally encourage inventors to go a bit overboard, making sure to provide sufficient detail that _no_ experimentation is required for a person of ordinary skill to arrive at a functioning (at least barely) implementation of each claimed concept.

Second, because not every examiner is truly skilled in the art of the claimed concept, sometimes the examiner does not recognize that the application adequately describes how to implement a claimed concept. The preventative to this issue is the same as the first. Provide more detail, and explain it clearly.

It should be apparent that avoiding enablement rejections is largely within the control of the inventor. During the application drafting phase, provide me with a clear, detailed, and thorough explanation of how to implement all of the claimed concepts, and problematic enablement rejections are unlikely to arise.

6. Novelty

As mentioned above, to be patentable, a concept must be at least useful, new, and non-obvious. The novelty requirement focuses on whether a claimed concept is truly new to the world, measured as of the effective filing date of the patent application that enablingly describes it.

Novelty is primarily determined with respect to single "prior art" references. A "prior art" reference is a document (paper or electronic) that was published, or in the case of U.S. patent documents, filed in the USPTO, before your effective filing date.

Generally, a claimed concept fails the novelty requirement if a single "prior art" publication teaches that concept. Yet to "teach" means more than to simply describe. Teaching requires describing to a person having ordinary skill in the art how to operatively implement the claimed concept in the precise manner and arrangement claimed and without substantial experimentation.

So assume, for example, that you claim a "left-handed smoke-shifting sky hook", and the examiner rejects that claim based on a single prior art reference. Assume also that the cited reference describes both right-handed and left-handed sky hooks, and separately describes smoke-shifting using widgets (but not sky hooks). In this case, that cited reference fails to teach your claimed arrangement (or how to operatively implement it) and thus does not defeat the novelty of your claimed concept. Therefore, this example's novelty rejection is improper, and I would cordially explain that fact to the examiner until either the examiner understands and withdraws the rejection or until you and I decide to appeal the rejection so that a different examiner (or supervisor) gets involved who will convince the original examiner to withdraw the rejection.

Often, novelty rejections can be avoided by performing a thorough patentability search shortly before filing the patent application. The results of such searches can help better focus the claims on truly novel concepts, or convince the inventors to enhance their concepts before attempting to patent them. Thus, I encourage my clients to engage me to perform a thorough pre-filing patentability search.

But, for two primary reasons, even the best patentability search can miss certain novelty-defeating prior art, and thus a certain degree of risk remains that the patentability of your concept will eventually be defeated. First (and somewhat illogically), patent applications filed before, but published after, your effective filing date, can still be used to defeat the novelty of your claimed concept. To avoid this issue, I have encouraged many of my clients to claim and describe as many details that are closely related their core concept as reasonably possible.

Second, sometimes prior art references use unusual, strange, or obtuse language to describe what amounts to your concept. Thus, standard search techniques, such as keyword searching, typically will fail to locate these prior art references. When this is a concern, I can employ more advanced search techniques that sometimes will overcome this issue. Nevertheless, this is a risk that is difficult to completely eliminate, and thus I again have encouraged many of my clients to claim and describe as many details around their core concept as reasonably possible.

7. Obviousness

Even if a claimed concept is novel, to be patentable, it also must be sufficiently "inventive", which is also referred to as "non-obvious".

Although most of patent law is relatively well-developed and clear, as many court opinions have demonstrated, obviousness often seems to be in the eye of the beholder. And because examiners are discouraged only for allowing claims they should not have allowed, this is the most common type of claim rejection, and typically the most contentious (surprisingly, examiners are not penalized for disallowing claims that they should have granted).

Obviousness rejections often involve the examiner linking the descriptions of two, three, four or more prior art references in an attempt at arriving at the entirety of the content of a given claim.

Quite frequently, such rejections fail, for one of three primary reasons.

First, just as with a failed novelty rejection, if the cited references fail to teach all of the claimed "limitations" (phrases), arranged as in the claim, the obviousness rejection also fails. When this deficiency is evident, once I cordially explain it to the examiner, the examiner will typically issue a new Office Action that withdraws the improper obviousness rejection (although sometimes replacing it with a better one).

Second, unlike a novelty rejection, the reference(s) used for an obviousness rejection must be "analogous" prior art. This means that the reference must be either "from the same field of endeavor, regardless of the problem addressed" or if not from that field of endeavor, must be "reasonably pertinent to the particular problem" that concerned the inventor. The Supreme Court further cautions that "[I]t is necessary to consider the reality of the circumstances – in other words, common sense – in deciding in which fields a person of ordinary skill would reasonably be expected to look for a solution to the problem facing the inventor".

Third, an obviousness rejection often will fail because a person having ordinary skill in the art, faced with the same problem as the inventor on the effective filing date of the application, reasonably could not and/or would not have combined the teachings of the cited prior art references to solve the problem in the same way as the claimed concept. I often can show this deficiency in any of a number of manners, such as by the combination being inoperative, the combination defeating a purpose of one of the combined references, at least one of the references discouraging the combination, etc.

Sometimes, the obviousness rejection is proper. In that case, I sometimes overcome the rejection by presenting any available evidence of non-obviousness, which can include facts that tend to establish:

1.   recognition of a problem not recognized by others;

2.   a long-felt but unsolved problem;

3.   a prolonged period of research preceding solution of the problem;

4.   failed attempts to solve the problem by others;

5.   skepticism of experts in the solution;

6.   praise by infringers or others for the solution;

7.   teaching away from the solution by others;

8.   discovery of unexpected results or benefits of the solution;

9.   synergistic benefits of the solution;

10. near-simultaneous discovery of the solution by others;

11. failed attempts to design around by others;

12. copying of the solution by others;

13. licensing of the patent application;

14. rapid adoption of the solution by others; and/or

15. commercial success of products covered by the patent claims or made by a process covered by the patent claims.

If such facts are unavailable and the obviousness rejection seems difficult to overcome otherwise, I often can amend the claims to define a somewhat different concept that is of adequate value to my client and sufficiently distinguished from the cited prior art to obtain allowance.

Obviousness rejections currently are one of the most complex, contentious, and challenging aspects of patent prosecution, so I work hard with the inventors during the application drafting stage to avoid and minimize the impact of these rejections. I also employ any of a number of advanced techniques during prosecution to overcome obviousness rejections.

What is "secret" prior art?

As discussed earlier, under current U.S. law, a patent application can function as prior art as of its effective filing date. Yet, that patent application typically will not be published until at least 18 months after that effective filing date, meaning that it is kept in confidence throughout those 18 months, and possibly much longer (especially in cases where the applicant has requested non-publication of the application). Upon publication, the patent application is available for the USPTO to cite to defeat the patentability of other pending applications, and/or it can serve as invalidating prior art for the claims of an issued patent.

This type of prior art is considered to be, at least temporarily, secret.

Additionally, for new utility patent applications filed before 16 March 2013, the U.S. allows a one-year grace period from the date of an offer for sale, commercialization, or non-confidential disclosure of a concept until that patent application describing that concept must be filed if a U.S. utility patent is desired that is permitted to claim that concept.

That one-year grace period creates the potential for other types of secret prior art, including "prior secret invention by another inventor" and "prior knowledge transferred from another to the patent applicant". As you can imagine, trying to evaluate patentability in the face of these factors can be an enormous and extremely costly task, not to mention that it creates the potential for those who would do so to manufacture fraudulent evidence and/or destroy legitimate evidence of secret prior art.

The implementation of the America Invents Act ("AIA"), which changes the U.S. from a "first-to-invent" to a "first-to-file" system, removes these types of secret prior art for patent applications having an effective filing date of 16 March 2013 or later.

Due to some unclear language in the new law, however, it remains to be seen how secret sales, secret offers-to-sell, and secret commercialization by patentees will be interpreted in the first-to-file environment created by the AIA. It's been argued that it is reasonable to expect that in these situations, the sale, offer-to-sell, and/or commercialization must also be available to the public to qualify as prior art, but time (and potentially a significant amount of it) will tell how these issues are clarified by the courts and/or follow-on legislation.

So while the AIA does attempt to make the U.S. patent system more transparent in terms of identifying prior art, the fact remains that regardless of the quality of any patentability search performed prior to filing, there remains a significant possibility that secret prior art eventually will emerge that can be used to defeat the patentability of an application's claim(s), but simply could not have been found during the patentability search.

What is the patent appeal process?

Sometimes, a patent examiner just doesn't get it. Despite my best efforts to help the examiner understand why the claimed subject matter is patentable, the examiner disagrees, and just won't budge.

When this situation arises, I occasionally can arrange an interview with the examiner, along with the examiner's supervisor, that results in convincing the examiner to allow the application. Typically, interviews occur via telephone, but sometimes a client is willing to incur the costs needed for me to travel to Alexandria, Virginia to attend the interview in person. Generally, however, examiners don't seem to like in-person interviews, perhaps because examiners must leave their home office and commute (sometimes long distances) to the USPTO, they must arrange for a conference room (and sometimes attendance by their supervisor), and/ or they must talk face-to-face with attorneys and/or inventors. In any event, most applicant-requested interviews don't budge most examiners.

So the examiner still won't relent. What then?

If the applicant is inclined to modify the claims in the hopes of appeasing the examiner, or is willing to submit an expert's declaration that explains why the examiner's assertions are factually incorrect, then along with filing a "Request for Continued Examination" ("RCE"), I can file a Response containing those claim amendments, presenting the expert declaration, and/or providing accompanying arguments.

But if the applicant really wants a patent to issue that includes claims having precisely the same language as that of the (at least twice) rejected claims, the next step is to appeal the examiner's rejections of those claims to the Patent Trial and Appeal Board.

But before diving deeper into the details of the appeal process, let me share a few general observations about the USPTO, its patent examiners, and its appeal board:

- U.S. patent law is incredibly complex, and grows substantially more so nearly every year.

- The vast majority of U.S. examiners are not patent lawyers, and tend to lack extensive legal training. In my experience, the training provided to its examiners by the USPTO is grossly insufficient.

- It seems that for far too many examiners, English is their second (or third or fourth) language, which tends to be reflected in their communication skills and their ability to learn U.S. patent law.

- The metropolitan DC area is one of the most expensive areas in the country to live. Yet most examiners earn relatively modest compensation for a very challenging job, making the USPTO somewhat of an employer of last resort. Those with sufficient talent and motivation are nearly always attracted to better-paying jobs outside the USPTO.

- The Patent Trial and Appeal Board is made up of a relatively small number of patent attorneys and former examiners (a few of whom are patent attorneys) who have proven themselves to be superior performers. Because they generally dislike being "overturned" (told they are wrong) by the Court of Appeals for the Federal Circuit (which is the next step in the appeals process), the Board usually follows the law carefully, and thereby typically "reverses" (shoots down) improper claim rejection.

The bottom line: examiners are highly unpredictable, yet the Board is rather predictable. Hopefully, there will be no need to involve the Board, but it has become an increasingly frequent step to obtaining a strong patent.

A patent appeal essentially seeks to have some different folks evaluate the examiner's rejections versus the applicant's evidence and arguments seeking to overcome those rejections, and decide which should prevail. With that background, let's briefly explore the appeal process.

1.   File Notice of Appeal.

To initiate the appeals process, I must file on my client's behalf a "Notice of Appeal" and pay the associated USPTO fee within the time period provided by the current Office Action.

Perhaps the best news about appeals is that examiners are upheld completely only about 50% of the time. In another 35% of the appeals, all of the examiner's rejections are shot down. For the remaining appeals, a portion of the examiner's rejections are overturned, and some rejections are maintained. So the odds are roughly 50/50 that at least some ground will be gained by appealing. On the other hand, perhaps the worst part about appeals is that they take too darned long, averaging about 2 years at this point. They also cost a good bit (much less than a new application, but a bit more than a typical Office Action Reply).

2.   File Request for Review.

Fortunately, I can sometimes greatly reduce that delay and cost by asking the USPTO to take a quick look at the situation before I fully initiate the appeal process. This quick look is formally called a "Pre-Appeal Brief Conference". To request it, I must file a "Request for Review" with the "Notice of Appeal".

3.   *Decision on Request.*

At the Conference, the assigned examiner, his/her supervisor, and at least one other senior examiner will review the Request for Review and decide whether the appeal should proceed. About 40% of the time, the Pre-Appeal Brief Conference results in the examiner withdrawing one or more rejections and re-opening prosecution (and sometimes, allowing the application to issue as a patent).

4.   *File Appeal Brief.*

When the examiner still won't withdraw any rejections, I next prepare and file an Appeal Brief (along with the associated USPTO fee), explaining the applicant's position in detail.

5.   *Receive Examiner's Answer.*

Within a few months, the examiner typically will either capitulate and allow the claims, or issue an Examiner's Answer, setting out in detail (sometimes for the first time) the precise reasons why the examiner continues to reject the claims.

6.   *File Reply Brief.*

If the applicant wants to maintain the appeal after reviewing the Examiner's Answer, I then prepare and file a Reply Brief, rebutting the examiner's reasons for rejecting the claims.

7.   *Receive Board Decision.*

After a delay of roughly 2 years (while they work through their backlog of previously filed appeals), a panel made up of three (3) administrative law judges from the Patent Trial and Appeal Board (the "Board" or PTAB) will review all the briefs and make a decision. Note that if desired, I can travel to the USPTO and verbally "argue" new legal developments that support my client's position to the Board, but this is rather expensive and rarely done. Generally, the Board prefers to decide each appeal based only on the briefs.

When the Board's decision is finally issued, if it overturns all the examiner's rejections, the examiner often simply will issue a Notice of Allowance and Issue Fee(s) Due. Typically within 3 to 10 weeks after I pay that Issue Fee, the patent will issue. If any of the examiner's claim rejections are upheld, I can re-open prosecution, amend the corresponding claims to overcome those rejections, and continue trying to convince the examiner to allow all the claims.

Alternatively, I can ask the Board to reconsider its position, and can even appeal the Board's decision if my client feels particularly strongly that the Board erred. In either case, if the USPTO realizes it has made a mistake, it will then relent, otherwise the appeal will move forward.

8.   *File Appeal in District Court.*

If appeal is desired, and there is a need to submit new evidence, then the appeal should be directed to the District Court for the District of Columbia.

9.   *File Appeal in Federal Circuit.*

If appeal is desired based solely on the record of the proceedings before the USPTO, the appeal should be directed to the Court of Appeals for the Federal Circuit. For perspective, only roughly 100 appeals from the USPTO are actually considered by the Federal Circuit each year.

10.   *Resume Prosecution.*

Once prosecution is re-opened at any point in the process, the examiner will again eventually examine the then-pending claims in light of the prior art of which the examiner is aware or discovers.

That's a brief overview of the appeal process. The process is also depicted in the flowchart on the following page. No matter how it turns out, unless the application is abandoned, at some point, the patent application should be allowed.

APPEALING A USPTO PATENT APPLICATION REJECTION

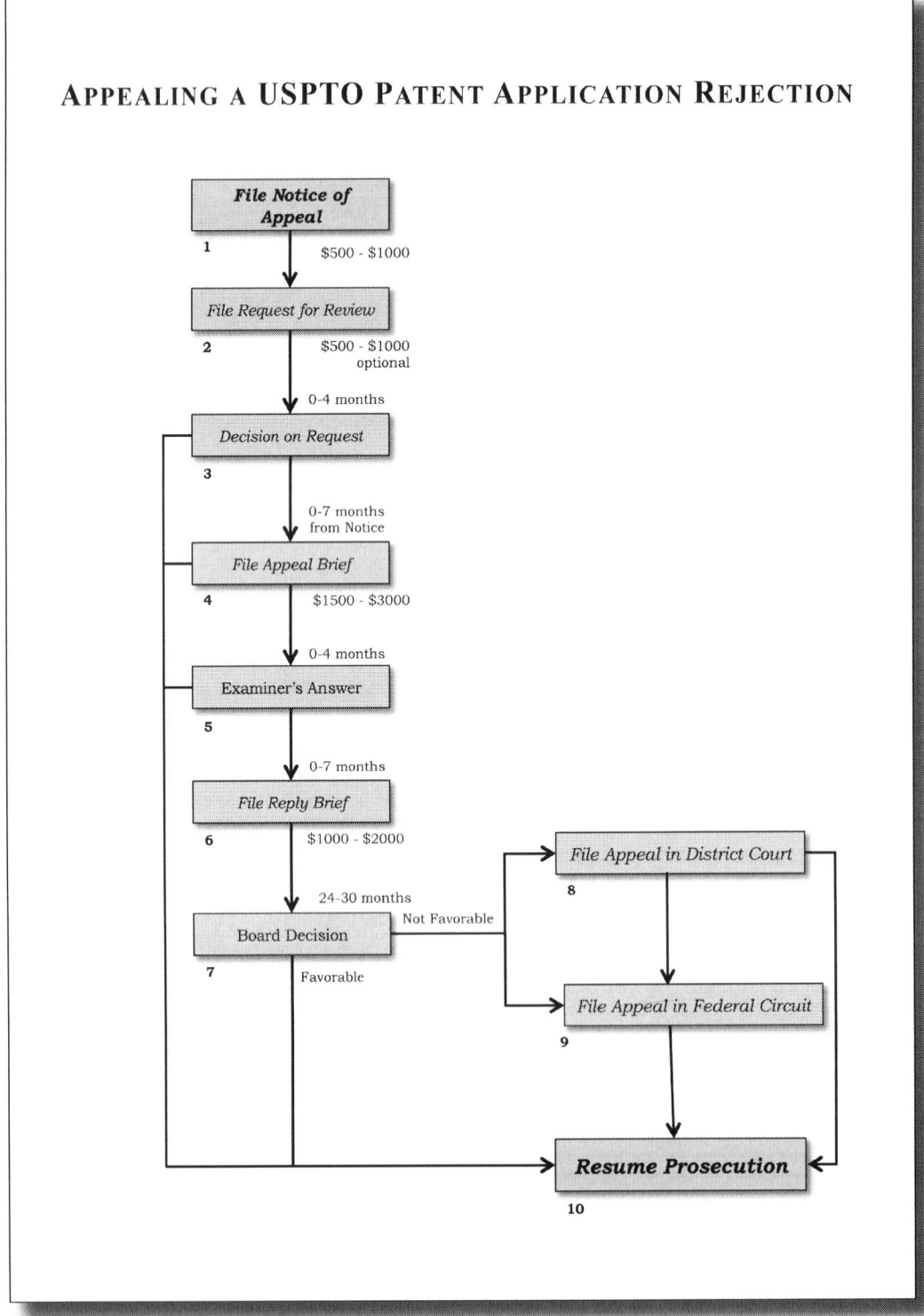

What happens after a patent application is allowed?

When the examiner agrees that the pending claims of a patent application fulfill the requirements for patentability, the examiner signals that the claims are "allowed" by issuing a Notice of Allowability, along with a Notice of Allowance and Issue Fee(s) Due. This notice "closes" prosecution, that is, at least temporarily suspends the ability of the applicant to amend the claims or other portions of the application.

Yet at this stage, issuance of a patent is not a sure thing, as either the applicant or the USPTO can withdraw the application from issuance. But why might that happen?

Although rarely done, the USPTO always has the power to withdraw an application from issuance, initiate re-examination of an issued patent, and even cancel an issued patent. They tend to exercise this power only in response to media-inflamed political pressure or court order, either of which might arise regarding a controversial claimed concept.

Much more commonly, the patent applicant withdraws their own patent application from issuance. The primary reason for doing so is that the applicant discovers that the duty of disclosure has not been fulfilled, and an Information Disclosure Statement ("IDS") must be submitted to fulfill that duty. Since an IDS can only be submitted when prosecution of the application is "open", the applicant must file a "Request for Continued Examination" (RCE), which "re-opens" prosecution, along with the IDS. Although rare, sometimes upon receiving an RCE, an examiner will withdraw the Notice of Allowability and issue a new Office Action rejecting the claims. Usually however, the examiner will simply review and sign-off on the IDS, and issue a new Notice of Allowability, along with a new Notice of Allowance and Issue Fee(s) Due.

Assuming the duty of disclosure has been fulfilled, the issue fee must be paid within 3 months of the date of the Notice of Allowance and Issue Fee(s) Due, otherwise the application will be deemed abandoned.

Sometimes, after payment of the issue fee, the USPTO, in preparing to publish the granted patent, discovers that it considers the drawings submitted by the applicant to somehow be faulty, and requires the applicant to submit corrected drawings. This requirement can be disputed if it seems way off-base, but usually the applicant bites the bullet and prepares and submits drawings that address whatever deficiency the USPTO alleges.

Usually however, within 2 to 8 weeks after paying the issue fee, the USPTO issues an Issue Notification, which specifies the precise date on which the patent is projected to issue, and the patent number the USPTO expects to assign to the issued, granted, published patent.

This issue date is significant for several reasons. First, it marks the date that the patent applicant gains the right to exclude others from infringing the claims of the patent.

Second, a patent application's issue date is the date on which all subject matter described but not claimed in that application will be dedicated to the public, unless one of three things happens before that issue date:

1. issuance is cancelled and claims to that subject matter are added to the allowed application (via an RCE that re-opens prosecution);

2. claims to that subject matter, which were previously presented but withdrawn, are presented in a divisional patent application filed before the issue date; or

3. claims to that subject matter are presented in a new patent application referred to as a "continuation" (or "CON") application.

I have already described RCEs and divisional applications, so let's focus now on the CON, which is identical to the allowed application, except that its claims differ. Since only claims must be prepared, the cost of preparing a CON is typically much less than the cost of preparing an original application. Like a divisional, a CON also receives the same

186

effective filing date as the original application. So essentially, the job of a CON is to claim subject matter that could have been claimed in the original application but was not.

But even though its job seems simple, the value of a CON can be tremendous. In particular, by filing a CON (and potentially a series of CONs), your company can preserve its ability to file claims that precisely target a competitor's product or process (or those of your future licensees or even a future owner of your patent) that implements an innovative concept described in your company's patent application. This tactic can be particularly useful when the claims of your original patent application do not clearly cover that competitor's implementation. Thus, this tactic can prevent your competitor from exploiting the innovative teachings of your company's patent applications.

Also, via a CON, you preserve the option to obtain relevant valid claims even when unexpected prior art emerges to invalidate the broadest claims of your original patent. That is, assume that as you are preparing to enforce your original patent against an infringer, you discover prior art that kills its most valuable claims. Because you have a pending CON, you have an opportunity to add claims to that CON that have the broadest reasonable and valid scope with respect to the known prior art (including the new prior art), and also snare the infringer's activities. Thus, once your CON issues as a patent, you can resume pursuing that infringer with much improved odds of successfully proving infringement, and avoiding invalidity, of at least some claims.

In short, CONs can be extremely valuable.

At times, the USPTO has expedited examination of CONs, and at other times deferred it in favor of original applications, so it can be difficult to predict how much time will pass before a given CON is examined. When possible, the USPTO tends to assign CONs to the same examiner who examined the original application, but this is not guaranteed. Thus, sometimes CONs receive the benefit of quick examination, the learning curve the previous examiner climbed, and any goodwill the applicant has earned with that examiner, but again, no guarantees.

Returning to the issuance of the allowed patent application as a patent, assuming that all Maintenance Fees are paid and the patent stays in force for its entire term, that term is expected to expire typically by no later than 20 years from the original application's effective filing date (possibly extended due to regulatory delays, such as delays in prosecution caused by the USPTO).

How can invalid claims be prevented from issuing?

On occasion, someone will notice that a recently published U.S. patent application includes claims that seem to be far too broad in scope, and knows of prior art that potentially invalidates those claims. Preventing such ostensibly invalid claims from issuing in a patent might be beneficial, not only to the public, but to the patent owner as well, since attempting to enforce invalid claims often can prove very costly and fruitless. Historically however, although the USPTO has allowed third parties to submit such prior art, the USPTO has not permitted them to provide any commentary explaining how the submitted prior art is believed to invalidate the claimed subject matter.

However, as of 16 September 2012, while a patent application is pending, third parties are permitted to submit potentially claim-invalidating prior art along with a concise description of the asserted relevance of each submitted document.

From a third party's perspective, the value of this new option is that, via its submission, the third party can attempt to prevent or slow the issuance of patent claims that the third party views as detrimental to its interests.

From the patent applicant's perspective, the value of this new option is that, if the patent examiner does not agree with the third party, the resulting patent claims likely will be strengthened with respect to the submitted prior art.

To avoid potentially damaging pre-issuance submissions, I generally advise patent applicants to work closely with me to:

1. perform a thorough prior art search before preparing and filing any patent application;

2. determine appropriate approaches for pursuing the most desired subject matter, potentially by filing one or more follow-on continuation patent applications after most or all "hidden" prior art has been revealed;

3. carefully craft claims that clearly avoid, via multiple distinctions, any relevant found prior art; and

4. submit all known relevant prior art, both to fulfill the duty of disclosure, and so that the examiner potentially can consider and commit to a perspective on that prior art before a challenger attempts to adjust the examiner's perspective.

How are mistakes in issued patents corrected?

Your company might want to correct an issued patent for any of several reasons.

First, sometimes the USPTO introduces typographical errors when publishing an issued patent. Upon the patent owner's request, the USPTO will issue a Certificate of Correction identifying and correcting such errors. Similarly, by paying a fee, the patent owner can request the USPTO to issue a Certificate of Correction for typographical errors in the patent that were caused by the applicant.

Second, if the patent owner wants the USPTO to correct substantive mistakes in the scope or language of the claims, the patent owner can request "reissue" of the patent. If a reissue request seeks to broaden the scope of the claims, it must be submitted within 2 years of the patent's issue date. A reissue request that seeks only to narrow the claims, however, can be filed at any time before the patent expires.

Finally, sometimes new prior art is discovered that might impact the patentability of one or more claims of an issued patent. In this situation, either the patent owner or a third party can file with the USPTO a request for "re-examination" of those claims for which the prior art raises a substantial new question of patentability. There are several advantages and disadvantages of "re-exam", particularly for patent owners considering or engaging in litigation. I discuss some of these considerations in *Step 7 – Harness.*

How can an issued patent be invalidated?

Patent litigation can be a very expensive and time-consuming mechanism to challenge the validity of an issued U.S. patent. Historically, the USPTO has offered several somewhat less expensive approaches, but each has been loaded with issues. The America Invents Act offers several new approaches that promise to be quicker and much less expensive than litigation, and much improved over previous USPTO approaches.

Beginning 16 March 2013, any patent having any claim with an effective filing date of 16 March 2013 or later can be challenged on any validity ground via a Post Grant Review ("PGR"). Very generally, within 9 months of a patent issuing, any party other than the patent owner will be able to petition the USPTO to cancel one or more claims of the patent for being invalid. If the USPTO determines that at least one challenged claim is more likely than not to be unpatentable, then the Patent Trial and Appeal Board must review the case and make a decision within a year (extendable by 6 months with good cause).

The first patent subject to PGR likely will be a continuing application that issues after 16 March 2013 and includes at least one claim that does not have an effective filing date before that date.

But, assuming a typical patent issues roughly 3–4 years after being filed, the first large set of patents that can be challenged via PGR will not issue until roughly 2016.

I generally advise patent owners to consider working with me to protect their patents against the eventual emergence of PGRs, such as by:

1. performing a thorough prior art search prior to filing any patent application, and potentially several years after filing it;

2. determining appropriate approaches for pursuing the most desired subject matter, potentially by filing one or more follow-on continuation patent applications after most or all "hidden" prior art has been revealed;

3. carefully crafting claims that clearly avoid, via multiple distinctions, any relevant found prior art;

4. thoroughly describing lots of different implementations (embodiments) of any broad claimed subject matter;

5. filing an enabling patent application (even if only a U.S. provisional application) before offering for sale (even confidentially), publicly disclosing, or secretly commercially using the valuable innovative subject matter of that application anywhere in the world;

6. seeking re-examination of issued claims in light of difficult prior art or other validity issues;

7. amending or disclaiming particularly vulnerable claims; and/or

8. filing one or more continuation applications that safely avoid potential validity issues.

A special kind of PGR was also created by the AIA that allows (only) parties sued or charged with infringement of certain kinds of business method patents to petition the USPTO for post grant review. These PGRs must be filed between 16 September 2012 and 16 September 2020, can be retroactively applied to existing patents, and can be used to stay a civil action.

What happens when a patent expires?

Effectively, the power of a U.S. patent can be extinguished if:

1. its maintenance fees are not paid;

2. its full term expires, that full term typically being 20 years from the effective filing date of the application from which the patent issued, as extended to account for any patent term adjustment granted by the USPTO to account for prosecution delays caused by the USPTO, and/or as shorted to reflect any disclaimer of that term;

3. the USPTO decides to cancel the patent, which although quite rare, can occur at any time during the patent's term;

4. if no claims of the patent survive re-examination;

5. all of the claims of the patent are found invalid by a court whose decision is not overturned on appeal; or

6. the patent is found unenforceable by a court whose decision is not overturned on appeal.

Once any of these events occurs, the patent's owner loses its right to prospectively exclude others from making, using, offering for sale, or selling in the U.S., or importing into the U.S., anything that falls within the scope of any claim of that patent.

Nevertheless, because the statute of limitations for filing a suit for patent infringement is 6 years, a patent owner generally can sue for damages for infringement that occurred at the very end of the life of the patent for up to 6 years after expiration of that patent.

What are maintenance fees, and when are they due?

To keep a U.S. utility patent in force, "Maintenance Fees" must be paid by roughly the 4th, 8th, and 12th year anniversary of that patent's issue date. A Maintenance Fee can be paid up to 6 months late upon payment of a surcharge with the Maintenance Fee. Although the patent will expire if its Maintenance Fees are not timely filed, in limited situations an expired patent can be revived.

Speaking of USPTO fees, now is a good time to talk about reduced USPTO fees, who is eligible for them, and why they need to be handled with care.

What is Small Entity status?

The USPTO allows patent applicants and patent owners to self-classify as either a "Large Entity" or a "Small Entity". Being classified as a "Small Entity" entitles patent applicants and owners to pay 50% of the standard USPTO fees for many filing, prosecution, and maintenance charges.

The USPTO rules define a "Small Entity" as an independent inventor, a non-profit organization, or a "small business concern." A "Large Entity" is defined as any entity that does not qualify as a "Small Entity".

A "small business concern" is any business that, together with its affiliates, has no more than 500 employees and has not assigned, granted, conveyed or licensed, and is not obligated to assign, grant, convey, or license, any rights in any claimed invention to any Large Entity.

For these purposes, an "independent inventor" is an inventor (or other individual to whom the inventor has transferred some rights in the innovation) who has not assigned, granted, conveyed, or licensed, and is under no obligation under contract or law to assign, grant, convey, or license, any rights in any claimed invention to any Large Entity.

Finally, a "nonprofit organization" means any nonprofit organization that has not assigned, granted, conveyed, or licensed, and is under no obligation under contract or law to assign, grant, convey, or license, any rights in any claimed invention to any Large Entity, and is either:

1. A university or other institution of higher education located in any country;

2. An organization of the type described in section 501(c)(3) of the Internal Revenue Code and exempt from federal income taxation;

3. Any IRS-qualified U.S. nonprofit scientific or educational organization; or

4. Any nonprofit organization located in a foreign country that would qualify as a nonprofit organization if it were located in the U.S.

A false claim of Small Entity status can result in the related patent being adjudged unenforceable. That means the patent can not be enforced against anyone, making the patent effectively worthless.

To protect the patent from a judgment of unenforceability, a patent applicant or owner must not incorrectly represent to the USPTO that it is a Small Entity at a time it is not. To avoid such a misrepresentation, whenever Small Entity status is claimed, the patent applicant or owner must first conduct a thorough investigation into whether claiming such status is correct. Specifically, the patent applicant or owner must investigate whether there has been, or is an obligation to make, an assignment, grant, conveyance, or license of any rights in the patent in question to any Large Entity. Also, the patent applicant or patentee must verify that it has not grown too large to continue to qualify for Small Entity status. Failure to investigate before making any claim for Small Entity status could form the basis for a finding that the patent is unenforceable if the patent is ever challenged in court.

Thus, a patent applicant or owner should report to its patent attorney any transactions involving the licensing, conveyance, granting, or assignment of the patent, so the attorney can review the transaction and determine if Small Entity status should be changed. Also, with respect to small business concerns, the patent applicant or owner should thoroughly investigate all affiliate relationships, including investor relationships and obligations, because these relationships can influence the Small Entity determination. Finally, the patent applicant or owner should remain mindful of its employee head count.

Importantly, any loss in Small Entity status must be promptly disclosed to the USPTO. If a patent applicant or owner makes an improper attempt to claim Small Entity status with the intent to deceive, the USPTO or courts might interpret that attempt as fraud, which can expose the patent applicant or owner to sanctions and/or place the enforceability of the patent at substantial risk.

What is Micro Entity status?

As of 19 March 2013, the USPTO has rules in place for certain patent applicants and patent owners to claim "Micro Entity" status, which allows those applicants and owners to pay many standard USPTO fees at a 75% discount.

To qualify as a Micro Entity, the patent applicant or owner must:

- qualify as a Small Entity;

- be a named inventor on no more than 4 previously-filed U.S. non-provisional patent applications (not counting PCTs or applications assigned to former employers);

- have a gross personal income of less than three times the median household income (which at the time of this writing totaled $150,162); and

195

- have not assigned (or be obligated to assign) the application to any entity that would have a gross personal or company income of above three times the median household income.

Alternatively, a patent applicant can qualify as a Micro Entity if:

- most of the applicant's income is derived from employment by a "Institution of Higher Education" (a "public or non-profit accredited institution that admits post-secondary students for programs of not less than 2 years"); or

- the applicant is obligated to assign, or has assigned, the application to such an Institution of Higher Education.

As noted in the discussion above concerning Small Entity status, a false claim of Micro Entity status can have serious implications. To avoid such a misrepresentation, whenever Micro Entity status is claimed, the patent applicant or owner must first conduct a thorough investigation into whether claiming such status is correct. The patent applicant or owner also must continually verify that it has not lost its eligibility for Micro Entity status each time a fee is paid to the USPTO.

Plant Patents

What do plant patents protect?

Generally speaking, plant patents protect asexually reproduced plant variety innovations.

More particularly, plant patents are limited to distinct, new, living, cultivated plant varieties, including sports (shoots), mutants, hybrids, transformed plants, seedlings, algae, and macro fungi, but excluding plants propagated from tubers, plants found in an uncultivated state, and bacteria (which can sometimes be protected via utility patents).

Although there is no requirement to submit a specimen of the plant variety to obtain a plant patent, the applicant must submit a complete botanical description of the variety, including one or more faithful photographic representations of it.

Once the plant patent is granted, its owner may exclude others from asexually reproducing, selling, or using the claimed plant variety in the U.S.. Note however, that plant patent owners cannot exclude others from using their patented varieties in breeding programs.

Plant patents typically expire 20 years from their application's effective filing date.

Like utility patents, provisional (informal) patent applications can be filed for plant varieties that qualify for a plant patent.

Throughout my publications, I use the term "patent" to generally mean "utility patent", since utility patents represent about 96% of the issued U.S. patents. In distinction, I use the phrase "plant patent" to be abundantly clear when I'm talking about this relatively rare and special type of patent, which represents less than 0.5% of all issued U.S. patents.

What are some differences between plant and utility patents?

Plant patents have only one claim.

Because they are typically simpler to draft than utility patent applications and tend to issue without lengthy prosecution (negotiations with the USPTO trying to convince them to issue the patent) plant patents are usually much less expensive to obtain than utility patents.

Plant patents also do not require the payment of maintenance fees.

Aug. 18, 1931.   H. F. BOSENBERG   Plant Pat.   1

CLIMBING OR TRAILING ROSE

Filed Aug. 6, 1930

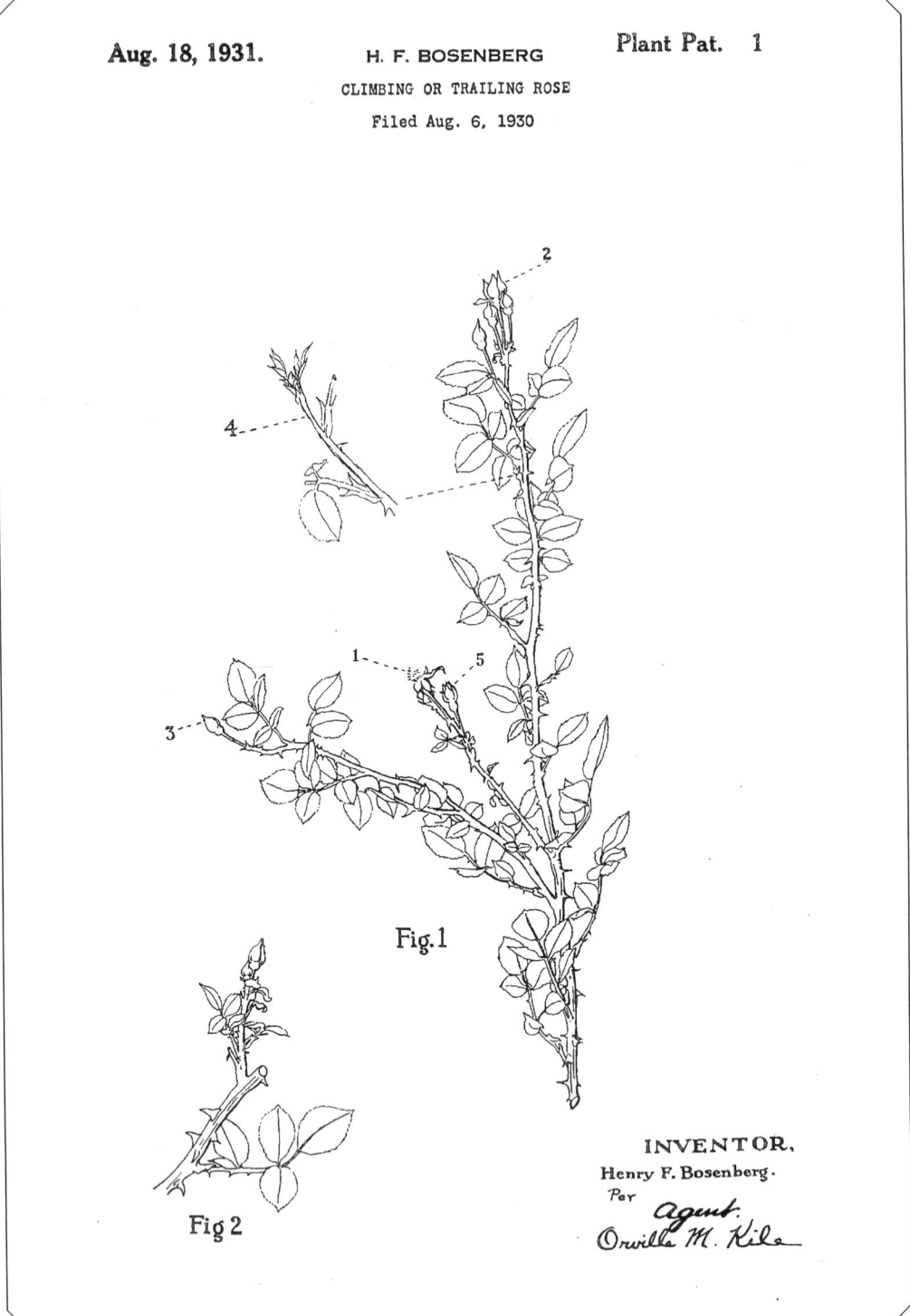

Fig. 1

Fig 2

INVENTOR,

Henry F. Bosenberg.

Per   *agent.*

Orville M. Kile

Design Patents

What do design patents protect?

Generally speaking, design patents protect aesthetic (i.e., ornamental and non-functional), novel, non-obvious subject matter as applied to a product and as graphically described in an enabling manner (that is, sufficient to describe to a person having ordinary skill in the field what that aesthetic subject matter looks like).

Well-known examples of aesthetic features that have been protected via design patents include:

1.   the classic Coca-Cola bottle,

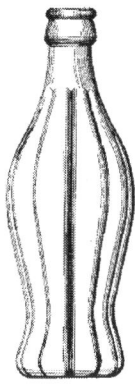

2.   Croc's footware, and,

3.   as I'll discuss in more detail later in this section, various geometric aspects of Apple's iPhone, including its graphical user interface and some of its icons, such as this icon for Apple's Siri voice recognition feature.

Note that throughout my publications, I use the term "patent" to generally mean "utility patent", since utility patents represent about 96% of issued U.S. patents. In distinction, I use the phrase "design patent" to be abundantly clear when I'm talking about this special type of patent. Although design patents represents only about 3% of issued U.S. patents, they are rapidly growing in importance for many patent owners.

Just as with a utility patent application, a design patent application is examined in the USPTO, and that examination includes a prior-art search.

To qualify for a design patent, the design claimed in the application must be:

1. ornamental;

2. visible at any time when the product is in normal use;

3. novel, meaning that no single, identical design exists in the prior art;

4. original to the inventors seeking protection; and

5. non-obvious with respect to any previously existing design or combination of designs from the perspective of a person having ordinary skill in the art.

Regarding the ornamental requirement, a design patent can be issued for:

    a. an ornamental configuration and/or surface decoration of a product, provided that the design is repeatable by others (so that the specific design itself, rather than the method of creating it, is protected by the design patent); and

b. a utilitarian product, but only if the ornamental features of that product dominate its functional features (thus, if a design is mostly utilitarian, it is not protectable by a U.S. design patent).

When evaluating obviousness, the question is whether a designer having ordinary skill who designs products of the type involved would (not could) have combined teachings of the prior art to create the same overall visual appearance as the claimed design. Answering this question requires that one must find a single prior art reference, the design characteristics of which are basically the same as the claimed design. Once the primary reference is found, other secondary references can be used to modify it to create a design that has the same overall visual appearance as the claimed design. For the claimed design to be obvious, these secondary references must be so related to the primary reference that the appearance of certain ornamental features in one would suggest (provide a good reason for) the application of those features to the other.

Any design patent application must show the specific ornamental feature for which patent protection is sought.

The iPhone is a great example. Apple does not directly protect the overall look and feel of its iPhone via patents. Instead, it protects a bunch of specific ornamental features via design patents (and lots of functional features via utility patents). That can be seen in U.S. Design Patent D636,392 (available from www.freepatentsonline.com), which was issued to Apple in April 2011, and covers the iPhone (probably the iPod Touch, and possibly the iPad).

In this design patent, the figures define the claimed ornamental subject matter. In each figure, solid lines define the claimed ornamental feature(s). In particular, the solid lines define the generally rectangular shape of the phone, along with its curved corners, exposed front and back glass layers, and the slightly protruding bezel (central band) linking those two glass layers. The dotted lines indicate features that are not claimed, and thus not protected by this design patent.

Here, whatever utility the glass layers might have does not dictate that their edges be exposed, that they define a rectangle with rounded corners, or that the dimensions of that rectangle be slightly smaller than the rectangle defined by the bezel. So all of those features likely escape challenges of invalidity based on functionality.

The preparer of each design patent application must determine, illustrate, and thereby define its novel ornamental features in much the same way.

U.S. courts only recently decided the first case of infringement of a design patent for a graphical user interface (GUI), but many believe that case (Apple v. Samsung) may spur many more such design patent infringement suits. According to the USPTO, applications for GUIs and on-screen icons are the fastest growing among filed design applications. [31]

To obtain a patent for a GUI design (including on-screen icons), the design or surface ornamentation must be shown with some portion of a display or other article of manufacture (typically a computer screen).

The number of design applications filed at the USPTO is on the rise and applicants' strategic use of them increasingly sophisticated. For example, instead of filing one application claiming all of the design features of a product, some savvy applicants file multiple applications, each claiming a small piece of the total design. How does this benefit the patent owner? Any copiers stealing just a small feature of the product's overall design will still infringe. And if the patentee's own product design changes slightly (often due to market feedback), the overall design will still retain patent coverage assuming that at least some of the patented design features are retained. In this situation the applicant is splitting various aspects of the original design across multiple applications so that some protection remains even after a re-design.

Another strategic use for design patents is to file the desired design application(s) and also file additional applications claiming features that are similar to the applicant's product design. This strategy tends to be most effective when the patent owner needs to protect against competitors who might attempt to approach, but not slavishly copy, the patent owner's novel design features.

Recent high-profile litigations like Apple v. Samsung have emphasized the importance that design patents can have in an IP portfolio. Design patents have historically been somewhat underestimated, but there is a growing recognition of the impact that design has on consumer choice, the potential competitive advantage it can provide through brand image and product differentiation, and the power that design patents can have when fully exploited.

What are some differences between design and utility patents?

Unlike utility patents, which generally have a term of 20 years from their application's effective filing date, design patents expire 14 years after they are issued (to be extended to 15 years beginning 19 December 2013), and do not require the payment of maintenance fees.

Also, provisional patent applications (described on page 114) are not available for design patents.

In addition, design patents can be invalidated if the design has a substantial non-aesthetic function or a practical utility.

Nevertheless, design patents tend to issue without lengthy prosecution (negotiations with the USPTO trying to convince them to issue the patent). Thus, design patents usually are much less expensive to obtain than utility patents.

Consequently, design patents can fill a vital role in the IP portfolio of certain companies. For example, because design patents tend to issue much more quickly than utility patents, design patents can be helpful for expediting your company's ability to challenge slavish copiers. Although design patents typically issue in under 12 months from their filing date, it's not unheard of for a design patent to issue in as little as three months from the date of filing. Also, because infringement of a design patent tends to be simpler to analyze, pursuing an infringement action, and obtaining an infringement verdict against blatant pirates, can be much simpler, quicker, and cheaper than pursuing infringers of a utility patent.

How is design patent protection obtained outside the U.S.?

Recently, the U.S. implemented two patent law treaties that will enable U.S. applicants to file international design applications (IDAs) either directly with the World Intellectual Property Organization (WIPO), or indirectly with the USPTO beginning 19 December 2013. An IDA is somewhat similar to an international or "PCT" application for utility patent applications (see page 119 for more about PCT applications). When an IDA is deemed allowable, the resulting International Design Registration provides design protection in the participating jurisdictions selected by the applicant. IDAs can help save applicants some of the fees (and time) associated with having to file separate design applications in desired markets.

Unlike regular U.S. design applications, IDAs are published after filing, which can provide certain provisional rights, like the right to claim pre-issuance damages from infringers that have knowledge of the pending application. IDAs may (but aren't required to) claim priority to an earlier application, so long as the IDA is filed within six months of the first filing. Once granted, IDAs have an initial term of five years, must be renewed by payment of maintenance fees, and will expire based on the term granted in each selected jurisdiction. As with PCT and foreign utility patent applications, thoughtful consideration of the risk-adjusted return on investment values, such as those described in *Step 6 - Enhance*, should be used to decide among the filing options for design applications.

Patent Considerations

What is the typical role of a patent attorney?

U.S. patent attorneys are required to be state-licensed, USPTO-registered, and to hold at least an approved bachelor's degree from an accredited university in a technically-oriented field (e.g., engineering, science, etc.). Yet regardless of their technical training and/or experience, most patent attorneys work with a wide range of technical subject matters.

Education and/or experience might provide the patent attorney with a general understanding of the basic technical concepts and/or jargon of an innovation's field, might allow the patent attorney to ask certain relevant technical questions, and/or might empower the patent attorney to understand and communicate certain meaningful technical aspects during the patenting process.

In some cases, the patent attorney might hold a business degree and/or might have accumulated substantial business experience, and thus be qualified to provide limited business expertise.

But rather than serving as the primary technical or business expert for a client, the fundamental role of most U.S. patent attorneys is to provide outstanding legal services. Thus, the role of the patent attorney typically does not include serving as the client's innovator, primary technical expert, or senior business consultant.

For example, because each true innovation is new and unique, only the actual innovators should be viewed as being the primary technical experts regarding that innovation.

As needed, additional technical experts, such as highly credentialed academics and/or deeply experienced industry experts, can be sought and engaged. Submitting the written opinion of such an expert often can be particularly helpful when a patent examiner is not correctly interpreting the claims, the specification, and/or the prior art.

Similarly, in general, only the principals of the business and those who have sufficient business expertise should be thought of as sufficiently qualified to provide thorough business guidance or direction for a particular enterprise.

Must a patent attorney be used to obtain a patent?

In other words, can you "patent it yourself"?

Well yes, you can. It is permissible for anyone to write, file, and prosecute a patent application for their innovation with no professional assistance.

But just as with performing your own brain surgery or flying your own space shuttle, rarely is it advisable to enter such difficult waters without relying on substantial help from a well-trained and deeply experienced professional.

What makes patenting so difficult? For starters, there are the labyrinthine federal statutes and rules, along with thousands of court cases interpreting those laws, as well as a roughly 6 inch thick set of administrative procedures promulgated by the USPTO.

Moreover, the courts, and particularly the United States Court of Appeals for the Federal Circuit, which hears all patent appeals (and for nearly all practical purposes decides which litigated patents have teeth and which are toothless), have changed directions repeatedly over the last few years in their interpretation of the patent laws, to such an extreme degree that even many patent attorneys have trouble keeping up.

Finally, if they give you any attention at all, those who might otherwise be appropriate candidates to license your patent will lick their chops at the thought of taking advantage of you when they realize you obtained your patent without competent legal representation.

But if your budget leaves no other options, then at least read and heed *"Patent It Yourself"* by David Pressman, which its publisher, Nolo Press, declares to be the "world's bestselling patent book". And finally, good luck. You really will need lots of it.

What is an invention promoter?

"Invention Promoters", are also sometimes known as "Invention Marketers", or "Invention Brokers". In addition to preparing and filing patent applications, typically having extremely narrow and valueless claims, Invention Promoters typically offer to:

- tell an innovator if an innovation is patentable;

- evaluate the innovation's market "potential";

- develop a product based on the innovation; and/or

- market the innovation and/or its implementations.

Too often, however, customers of numerous unscrupulous Invention Promoters have reported paying substantial sums while receiving remarkably little service in exchange. These rogue Invention Promoters are generally known for high-pressure sales techniques, repeated misrepresentations, and even downright fraud.

Because so many innovators had endured so many ugly experiences at the hands of Invention Promoters, in 1999 Congress enacted section 297 of the Patent Act (35 U.S. C. 1 et seq.), which provides substantial legal remedies for customers found by a court to have been injured by an Invention Promoter.

The USPTO provides warning signs and suggestions for dealing with Invention Promoters, and publishes complaints about Invention Promoters. See: http://www.uspto.gov/inventors/scam_prevention/index.jsp

The Federal Trade Commission also provides alerts and tips for avoiding problems with Invention Promoters. For a list of allegedly suspect Invention Promoters, see for example, www.InventorEd.org, which identifies invention promotion firms against which complaints have been filed with the FTC.

Typically, Invention Promoters are not Patent Attorneys, who must be both licensed to practice by the state in which their primary office is located and registered with the USPTO.

As an established and registered patent attorney, I have been and remain legally permitted to perform patentability searches, prepare and prosecute patent applications, draft agreements, and provide legal advice. Although my primary focus has not been raising capital, developing products, marketing innovations, etc., I have provided basic guidance in these areas, and have identified reputable professionals and resources to assist with my clients' most advanced needs.

How can the power of a patent be harnessed?

I identify 70+ tactics for harnessing the power of intellectual assets in *Step 7 – Harness*. As a brief preview of that section (see page 331), some of the most common tactics to utilize a patent include:

Distinguishing its inventors and owners, such as by:

- publishing and promoting their technical prowess, innovativeness, and skill;

- creating an aura of innovativeness, intelligence, and skill;

- attracting investors, customers, licensees, and alliances;

Creating and enhancing revenue, such as by:

- requiring competitors to pay licensing fees and royalties for the right to use or sell the innovation;

- landing related deals;

- carving out exclusivity in the marketplace;

- enabling enhanced downstream pricing & terms (sole seller); and/or

- empowering enhanced upstream pricing & terms (sole buyer).

Discouraging competitors from entering or staying in a market, such as via obtaining:

- injunctions

  – e.g., shutting down competitor's research, production, marketing, website, etc.

  – e.g., seizing and destroying imported knock-offs

- damages

  – at least a reasonable royalty

  – possibly the patent owner's lost profits

  – possibly treble damages for willful infringement

- costs & attorneys fees (in exceptional cases)

Of course, patent rights only arise upon issuance of a patent. No patent means no patent rights. Thus, only an issued patent can be legally enforced against potential and/or actual competitors to prevent the making, using, offering for sale, and/or selling in, and/or importing into, the country in which the patent is in force, anything that falls within the scope of one or more valid unexpired claims of that patent.

For example, enforcement often can be achieved inexpensively outside the judicial system, such as via providing a simple patent notice on the patent owner's goods that fall within the scope of one or more claims of an unexpired in-force patent.

On the other hand, occasionally enforcement can require the threat and/or filing of a lawsuit alleging infringement of the patent. If the parties are unable to settle their differences early in the suit, the litigation costs can become very expensive and time-consuming for both parties. Fortunately, the vast majority of patent infringement suits settle rather quickly.

Those who do not have the financial means to enforce a patent often can much more affordably purchase patent assertion insurance that will provide the financial muscle to litigate all the way to an enforceable judgment, even after being upheld on appeal, if necessary.

Often, the patent owner is willing to allow competitors to make, use, and/or sell the innovation, provided that the competitors pay the patent owner fairly for the right to do so. A document that provides for the grant of such rights and the associated payments is typically called a "Licensing Agreement".

Sometimes, a patent publication can serve as an advertisement of the technical capabilities of its inventors and/or owner. The audience for that message can be potential investors, customers, employees, competitors, and/or suppliers, etc.

What is a "Patent Troll"?

The phrase "patent troll" has been used pejoratively to describe a patent owner that does not manufacture or market the subject matter claimed in its patent and that attempts to enforce that patent against an alleged infringer in a manner considered to be overly aggressive or opportunistic. Microsoft's former Chief Technology Officer, Nathan Myhrvold, argued that the expression "patent troll" is primarily used as a public relations tactic by large corporations seeking to intimidate such patent owners.

A less inflammatory phrase is "non-practicing entity", w emphasis to the fact that the owner of the patent does not compete ɪɪ. market for the claimed subject matter. Yet even the urge to use this phrase sometimes reflects a failure to recognize that for centuries, patents have been enforced by non-practicing owners, including Thomas Edison, many universities, and numerous large established companies who enforce patents outside the realms in which those companies compete. The ability for anyone to own and enforce patents, regardless of what goods and services they sell, allows patent markets to function more liquidly, and thus efficiently, thereby serving to encourage R&D, innovation, and disclosure.

So perhaps a better definition of "troll" is a patent owner who asserts their patent knowing that it is invalid and/or its claims do not cover the accused product and/or service. Such a definition can apply to both "practicing entities" and non-practicing entities, and focuses more on the known or knowable quality and scope of the patent and its claims.

Using the phrase "non-practicing entity" can be helpful when the emphasis is on the asymmetries and differences in legal tactics and rules that tend to apply to non-practicing versus practicing entities. For example, certain techniques that are often used by accused infringers to defend against practicing entities are ineffective against non-practicing entities who sue for patent infringement. Such techniques include: patent infringement counterclaims; "scorched earth" litigation tactics; patent misuse and antitrust defenses; and settlement offers for cross-licensing and/or patent pooling.

Yet practicing entities still can protect themselves from the potentially exorbitant expenses of infringement suits using any of the following remaining tactics:

1. Monitoring new patents and published applications to spot those that might be relevant to their company;

2. Performing clearance searches before bringing products to market;

3. Buying critical patents to prevent others from doing so;

4. Purchasing patent infringement defense insurance;

5. Initiating re-examination or opposition proceedings to challenge the validity of overly broad patent claims;

6. Designing-around patent claims of concern;

7. Locating invalidating prior art and asserting it via litigation; and

8. Settling early to minimize litigation costs.

On the other hand, unlike "practicing entities", non-practicing entities are not entitled to collect "lost profit" damages when patent infringement liability has been proven. Moreover, due to relatively recent changes in the law, non-practicing entities generally encounter more difficulty than practicing entities in obtaining an injunction to halt infringing activities. The net effect of this dramatic legal change has yet to be fully determined, but it does seem to have made it more difficult for non-practicing entities to scare an accused infringer into a large early settlement.

How can patent infringement be avoided or mitigated?

Although litigation is often a fact of life for bigger companies, companies of all sizes tend to shudder at the idea of being threatened with a patent infringement lawsuit. And nearly all companies would prefer to never have to fight such a suit.

Avoiding patent infringement suits starts with avoiding infringement. And fortunately, there are many paths to avoiding infringement, including:

- identifying others' patent rights that might cover your products or services;

- determining what those rights actually cover;

- assessing the validity of the patent rights;

- initially designing your product and/or services to avoid patent rights of potential concern;

- re-designing your product and/or services to fall outside such patent rights;

- explaining why your product and/or service doesn't infringe, or why the rights are invalid, to the owner of the rights; and/or

- obtaining the owner's authorization to practice the patent rights.

I have assisted my clients with each of these activities, which also can apply to other types of intellectual property, such as trade secrets, marks, and copyrights.

In the patent realm, professional searches can lay the groundwork for avoiding and/or resolving many potential infringement disputes. For example, identifying what patent rights are owned by others is the objective of a patent clearance search and opinion. Determining what another's patent rights cover, and whether those rights are infringed is the goal of a non-infringement search and opinion. And assessing the validity of another's potentially infringed patent rights is the aim of a validity search and opinion.

Once you have obtained an appropriate and professional search and opinion, you might want to negotiate with the owner of the IP rights. Yet negotiating why another's IP rights are invalid or not infringed can be a delicate exercise, which might evaporate the litigation threat, transform it into a lucrative business deal, or escalate hostilities substantially.

So sometimes, it simply can be easier to avoid another's IP rights altogether, possibly by initially designing around, or later re-designing the potentially infringing product or service. Based on my legal understanding of the potentially infringed rights and my technical capabilities, I often can guide my clients to successful design-arounds and re-designs.

In other situations, it can make good business sense to obtain authorization to practice another's IP rights, such as via obtaining an assignment of, or license to, those rights.

How can potential patent infringers be discouraged?

Just as it is important for potential defendants to avoid or mitigate liability for patent infringement, it can be very worthwhile for patent owners to prevent and/or discourage infringement, so that there is no need for them to take legal action against suspected infringers.

U.S. patent law provides that patent applicants and their licensees may notify the public that their products are subject to a pending patent application by marking the word "patent pending" on the product (or its packaging when the product itself can not be marked).

Similarly, patent owners are permitted to mark their patent number (e.g., "U.S. Patent 7,777,777") on their products that fall within the scope of one or more unexpired claims of that patent. Additionally, the 16 September 2011 America Invents Act ("AIA") revised the marking laws to allow "virtual marking", that is, marking with "Patent" and a publicly accessible web address, the identified web page associating patent numbers with the products covered by those patent numbers. Virtual marking can allow any patent owner to easily notify the public of potential patent coverage, and to easily change that notification to avoid false marking.

It is important to begin properly marking all products subject to a patent application as soon as possible after that application is filed to avoid limiting the patent owner's monetary relief in case of infringement of the resulting patent.

On the other hand, please note that U.S. patent law prohibits and mandates fines for marking, labeling, or advertising a product as "patent applied for", "patent pending", "patented", or the like, when a patent application is not pending or a patent is not in force.

How should patent infringers be addressed?

As discussed above, the owner of a patent has the legal right to exclude others from making, using, offering for sale, or selling within, or importing into, the jurisdiction that issued their patent, anything that falls within the scope of any valid unexpired claim of that patent.

The "legal right to exclude" means the right to sue in federal court to force the infringer to halt their infringing activities and pay damages to your company for their past infringement.

With ownership of such powerful exclusive rights, when it's your patent that seems to be infringed, the first impulse might be to boldly tell the suspected infringer, Rambo-style, to knock it off, or take a license, *right now*. Yet telling anyone any such thing is more than sufficient grounds for them to haul *you* into federal court *right now*, in the jurisdiction *most convenient to them*.

That is, once threatened, the suspected infringer may very well file a lawsuit seeking a "declaratory judgment" (commonly referred to as a "DJ") where the court declares that the suspected infringer does not infringe your patent(s) and/or that your patent(s) are invalid and/or unenforceable. And don't think that only a formal "cease-and-desist" letter sent to a suspected infringer will incite a declaratory judgment. Though decided on a case-by-case basis, there is ample precedence for far less formal communications conveying what seems to be only a benign invitation to license to be deemed adequate grounds for the issuance of a DJ. Clearly, a suspected infringer can turn the tables quite suddenly on even a mildly assertive patent owner who doesn't handle the matter very carefully.

Now tell me, what is the benefit to your company or its IP strategy of being forced to defend its patent in a suspected infringer's home court, especially when you haven't fully prepared to litigate, and might not even have the necessary funds yet? That's right. None!

So when infringement is suspected, a prudent patent owner will proceed extremely carefully by:

1. recognizing the time limits for enforcing their patent rights:

   • The patent owner must not delay filing suit for an unreasonable and inexcusable period of time from the date it knew or reasonably should have known of the potential infringement, particularly if that delay causes the alleged infringer to be placed in a worse position than if the suit had been filed earlier.

   • A delay likely will be considered to be unreasonable when it results in evidentiary or economic prejudice to the alleged infringer. Courts have found delays of as little as 5 years to be unreasonable.

   • Per the applicable statute of limitations, damages for patent infringement *must* be sought within 6 years of the infringing activity.

2. verifying that adequate financial resources are available to finance enforcement of the patent owner's legal rights by:

   • budgeting funds based on the company's expected revenues, royalties, and profits;

   • borrowing from an appropriate lender;

   • soliciting investments from desired investors; and/or

   • purchasing patent assertion insurance from a reputable carrier.

3. fully verifying that their patent rights have indeed been meaningfully infringed by:

- seeking a competent patent attorney to review the situation;

- providing all available evidence of the alleged infringement to that patent attorney;

- assisting the patent attorney in determining the economic value of the alleged infringement.

4. thoroughly considering the patent attorney's:

- factual and legal analysis of the alleged infringement;

- assessment of the legal and economic strengths and weaknesses of the patent owner's position; and

- suggested tactics for enforcing the patent rights.

5. with the patent attorney's assistance, potentially initiating a catious and calm dialog with the alleged infringer, such as by:

- providing to the alleged infringer a properly written infringement analysis;

- discussing the infringement concerns with the alleged infringer;

- listening carefully to all issues, vulnerabilities, and potential defenses raised by the alleged infringer;

- negotiating a satisfactory settlement; and/or

- suing the infringer for patent infringement (but not necessarily in this order).

6. properly seeking an appropriate and desired measure of respect for the patent rights, such as:

- a purchase of the patent by the alleged infringer;

- payments of monetary royalties to the patent owner;

- removal of the allegedly infringing products from the market; and/or

- exit of the alleged infringer from the market.

7. wisely avoiding overly emotional reactions, which can:

  - sour negotiations;

  - undermine the patent owner's position;

  - raise the need or likelihood for a costly, untimely and/or inconvenient litigation; and/or

  - incur liability for false accusations of infringement.

If you have concerns about patent infringement, talk with competent patent counsel. They can help you properly evaluate your situation and take the right steps to resolve your concerns, while guiding you away from some potentially very serious and expensive pitfalls.

Marks

What is a mark?

A mark is an identifier of the unique source of a good or service. What kind of identifier? Well, a mark can be nearly anything (e.g., one or more words, logos, and/or design details) that is used in commerce with the good or service and that indicates the single source of that good or service, and thereby distinguishing one source from another.

For example, any of the following can serve as marks:

- Logos, e.g., McDonald's golden arches, the CBS eye, Nike swoosh

- Words and alphanumeric combinations, e.g., APPLE, ABC, V-8

- Slogans, e.g., INTEL INSIDE, JUST DO IT, HAVE IT YOUR WAY

- Colors, e.g., Pink (for insulation), yellow and black for Cliff's Notes

- Musical notes, e.g., NBC's chimes, Law and Order theme music

- Cartoon characters, e.g., Mickey Mouse, Twitter's bird

- Product configuration, e.g., hour-glass shaped Coca-Cola bottle

Below is another example, which is a label for horseradish (of all things), that, while it also mentions the source explicitly, illustrates the use of at least 3 distinct marks at once:

- a logo (the kicking mule)

- a word mark (KICK)

- a slogan ("with a kick like a Missouri mule")

Trademark law protects such distinctive source identifiers that are used on goods or services. In other words, trademarks do not directly protect a good or service, but instead protect the brand or identity of a good or service.

What are the categories of marks?

There are several categories of Marks, including:

- Trademarks, such as EXXON for gasoline products

- Service marks, such as HERTZ for car rental services

- Certification marks, such as UL for electrical product certification

- Collective marks, such as Boys and Girls Clubs of America

Although these categories are sometimes collectively referred to as "trademarks", to avoid confusion, I refer to all of these categories generically as "marks", and to marks associated with products only as "trademarks".

How can marks distinguish?

Identify the Source

Without even mentioning the actual name of a source, a mark can identify that source. For example, the "golden arches" can identify the location of a McDonald's fast-food restaurant, without ever using that word.

Guarantee Quality

A mark can serve as a guarantee that your experience with the goods and/or services with which that mark is used will be of an expected quality. For example, consumers have grown to expect an outstanding user interface with Apple's products, excellent customer services from Zappos.com, and hot french fries at McDonald's.

Facilitate Advertising

By communicating certain values, a mark can function as an advertisement all by itself. Think Coach, Gucci, and Rolex. Or the Apple logo, Nike swoosh, or golden arches.

Reinforce Image

Once a good and/or service and its accompanying mark have been connected with certain values, the mark can then reinforce the associated image. This is particularly true for certain slogans, such as Nike's "Just Do It", which reinforces the image of a committed athlete, and the values of dedication, hard work, and accomplishment.

Align Aesthetics

Choosing a "look" for a product or its advertising, including its website, can allow consistency and alignment of many of its aesthetic aspects. For example, Apple has currently aligned the look of its products around a brushed aluminum material, color, and feel, those products having rectangular shapes with rounded corners, sharp edges, and minimalistic design flourishes. This consistency across products allows the source of an Apple product to be instantly recognized. The same can be said for Campbell's soup can labels, the interior decor of Wendy's and Taco Bell's restaurants, and the shape of the Volkswagen Beetle.

Extend Brand

Once a source is well established in one market, it can apply its brand to goods/services in related markets, thereby facilitating extension of that brand. For example, after Jello was well-established in the instant pudding category, it extended its brand to frozen desserts (Jello Pudding Pops). Similarly, Richard Branson has leveraged his Virgin brand into music, air travel, cell phones, and more, creating over 300 Virgin branded companies along the way.

Monetize Reputation

As a company builds goodwill with its customers, much of that goodwill is carried by the company's marks. If the company were to abruptly discontinue use of a mark, their customers could easily be lost to competitors. Similarly, if a company allowed its mark to be pirated by the makers of cheap knock-offs, the company could suffer a tremendous negative impact on its sales, profits, and reputation. Sometimes, customers are willing to pay a premium for products or services associated with a particular brand (e.g., Tiffany jewelry, Mercedes-Benz automobiles, a stay at the Waldorf Astoria). Thus, marks can be extremely valuable. For example, the Coca-Cola mark is estimated to be worth hundreds of billions of dollars, and is perhaps the most valuable piece of intellectual property in the world.

How can marks create revenue?

Recognition in the marketplace

A well-developed mark can allow customers to easily recognize and pick out your products, stores, website, etc. from amongst all the marketing "noise" generated by competitors. Whether you are a patron/customer/fan or not, think of how easy it is to spot a McDonald's restaurant while driving down the interstate, or how readily Duracell's "CopperTop" batteries can be found in a store.

Premium pricing

By careful branding, some companies have positioned their products as "luxury goods", such that consumers are willing to pay a substantial premium to own a product that carries that brand's mark. Similarly, certain services are associated with a premium image, and premium pricing. Examples include Rolex watches, Coach leather goods, and Ritz Carlton hotels.

Licensing fees and royalties

Many marks earn considerable revenues from licensing. Disney earns billions yearly from royalties earned by licensing its cartoon characters. Ferrari licenses its valuable logo for use on products ranging from boots to lighters to colognes to sunglasses. And of course, professional and college sports teams rake in amazing profits from licensing their marks for use on scores of products.

How can marks discourage piracy?

The first user of a mark within a given state can prohibit use of confusingly similar marks by others on related goods or services in that same state.

The owner of a federally registered mark can prohibit use of confusingly similar marks by others on related goods or services anywhere in the U.S.

Infringement of federally registered marks can result in award of:

- injunctions & seizures,

- compensatory damages,

- punitive damages, and/or

- attorneys fees.

How do rights in marks arise?

One can obtain rights in a mark in any of several ways:

- obtaining previously established rights in the mark by purchasing the mark and the goodwill it represents from the mark's rightful owner;

- obtaining local, common law rights in the mark by being the first to continuously use the mark with particular goods or services within a particular state; or

- obtaining national, federal rights in the mark by being the first to continuously use the mark in association with particular goods and/or services in interstate commerce AND registering the mark for the appropriate class of goods and/or services with the USPTO.

Rights in a mark:

- are maintained by continuing to use the mark properly;

- potentially can last forever; but

- can be lost if, e.g., assigned improperly, used generically, or not enforced.

What are the types of marks?

A mark that is either:

- fanciful (Exxon for gasoline, Kodak for film, and Colgate for toothpaste);

- arbitrary (Apple for computers, Starkist for tuna, and Dutch Boy for paint); or

- suggestive (Greyhound for buses, Pepsi for soda, and Windex for glass cleaner)

typically is considered to be distinctive and thus is protected upon its first use in interstate commerce.

A descriptive mark (Apple for a fruit grower, and Puppy Chow for dog food) of a product or service requires established secondary meaning to gain distinctiveness.

A generic mark is never protected, and a mark can become generic through common use as a noun or verb. Examples include Aspirin for acetylsalicylic acid, Cellophane for plastic film, Dry Ice for solidified carbon dioxide, Kerosene for light fuel oil, Laundromat for a coin-operated laundry shop, Thermos for a vacuum flask, and Zipper for a closure mechanism.

Why is it so important to use my mark "properly"?

To create and maintain rights in a mark, it is vitally important to use the mark properly. As discussed above, marks are unique indicators of the source of goods or services. Proper use means presenting a mark, such as a term or logo, as a source identifier, as opposed to as a company name or as a generic descriptor. Proper use also means presenting the mark prominently, consistently, and in a way that helps consumers distinguish your goods or services from those of a competitor. The USPTO or a court will look for proper use before accepting your claim of ownership of a mark.

Moreover, proper use builds value, develops broader and stronger legal rights, and protects against the possibility that your mark will lose its distinctiveness and become a generic term, in which case you could lose your rights to the mark.

I have identified over <u>40</u> serious, common, and easily avoided vulnerabilities that could allow hostile licensees, crafty infringers, and blatant pirates to legally steal your marks. At least half of those vulnerabilities are related to how a mark is used, regardless of whether that mark is federally registered.

Precisely how should I use my marks?

Know what type of mark you have

Trademarks are brands of goods. Service Marks are brands of services. A company name is not a mark, unless also used as a brand of goods or services. Trademarks and Service Marks are used differently.

Examples:

- "Ford Motor Company" is a company name.

- FORD is both a Trademark for cars and a Service Mark for car repair services.

Pointers:

- You "use" a Service Mark by presenting it in advertising and promotional material.

- While Trademarks can and often do appear in ads, they are not considered properly used until they are applied to the goods themselves, to packaging for the goods, to tags or labels applied to the goods or their packaging, or (if nothing else is practical) to displays associated with the goods. To register a Trademark successfully, you must apply the mark in one of these ways. Below, I provide some guidelines for creating acceptable specimens of use.

Present your mark properly

When presenting a term as a mark, at least in text, always use it as an adjective followed by a generic term. By presenting a mark as an adjective modifying the generic type of good or service you sell, you enable your mark to do its job: distinguishing your version of a generic item from a competitor's brand of that same generic item. Using your mark as an adjective (and even reminding customers and the press to do so) also reduces the risk your mark will become a generic term for the generic item with which it is used.

Examples:

- INTEL™ microprocessors.

- AMAZON℠ on-line book and music retail services.

Pointers:

- Logos and stylized presentations of marks often are presented alone, at the beginning and ends of promotional literature. In this circumstance, it is desirable but not always necessary that the logo be followed by a generic term.

- It is perfectly fine if promotional literature sometimes uses a term as a noun to identify the company (e.g., "Ford introduces its new models.") and at other times as a mark (e.g., "FORD™ TAURUS™ sedans are equipped with ...."), so long as there is some conspicuous Trademark or Service Mark presentation.

- Use of a mark as a noun, or even allowing others to do so, can cause you to lose your rights in the mark. ASPIRIN and ESCALATOR were once marks that became generic because people used the brands to define the generic good. Companies like Xerox take pains to remind people to refer to XEROX copiers, and not talk of "making a XEROX" of, or "XEROXING" a document. The risk of a mark becoming generic exists even for less well-known brands.

Use proper notice to let people know you are claiming exclusive rights to your mark

Proper notice, such as ™ or ®, tells competitors and customers that you claim exclusive rights in your mark. Generally speaking, notice should always be presented in logo marks or stylized presentations set apart from text. In text, give notice as often as is practicable, at least with the first appearance of a mark. It is not necessary to give notice every time a mark appears in text.

Pointers:

- Use "TM" as notice for unregistered Trademarks and "SM" as notice for unregistered Service Marks.

- Use "®" for marks registered with the PTO. Note however that: (1) you should not use this symbol if you filed an application that has not yet resulted in an issued registration; and (2) your registration of a mark for one good does not necessarily mean you can use the "®" symbol when that same mark is used with other goods that are outside the scope (class and/or description) of that registration. Intentionally using the registered trademark symbol with an unregistered mark might give rise to claims for false advertising or trademark fraud, or possibly provide an infringer with a defense against otherwise legitimate infringement claims.

- Some documents may use the same word as both a company name (usually using the term as a noun) and a mark (usually presented as an adjective). Give notice only when the term is being used as a mark.

- There is no strict rule governing where notice appears, its size, or how often it should appear. Notice usually is placed as a superscript or subscript of a mark, but some companies use footnotes to give notice descriptively. Notice should be used prominently and often enough so that it attracts the attention of the ordinary consumer.

Present marks prominently and consistently

To build recognition and to distinguish your brand from other brands or descriptive terms, it is important to give your mark special prominence. Consider adopting a unique typographical treatment for your mark. Some good examples are a unique font, a considerable larger size, Italics, Bold, ALL CAPS, Initial Caps, etc. Be consistent with the special typographical treatment given to a particular mark. Similarly, if you adopt your mark in logo or stylized form, present it in the same way in all publications.

Pointers:

- Attorneys with expertise in marks usually present word marks in BLOCK CAPITAL LETTERS. This is only a convention, not a legal requirement. You may present your mark however you like, but do so conspicuously and prominently.

- Mark owners often combine their word marks with a logo. It is preferable that you adopt a single presentation (relation of words to logo; color scheme, etc.), although minor variations are permissible.

- Occasional variations in presentation will not destroy your rights.

- For a mark registered in a particular color scheme, consistently present the mark in only that color scheme.

Do not permit unauthorized uses of your mark

By definition, a mark identifies your unique brand of a generic type of good or service sold in associated with that mark. If the mark is not unique to you, or if you do not control the use of the mark by others, then the mark is not performing its function. If you allow others to use your mark, or any mark that is so similar to your mark that it is likely to cause confusion among an appreciable segment of consumers, you may lose your exclusive rights in the mark, and the investment and goodwill that you have developed in it among customers.

Precautions:

- If you wish to authorize others to use your mark (e.g., a distributor or franchisee), ask legal counsel to assist you in preparing a license defining how the other party can use your mark. Such licenses must require the other party to comply with your specified standards for the quality of goods and services sold under the mark by the licensee.

- You need not specify any particular level of quality (e.g., MERCEDES-BENZ and KIA both have valid marks, and each imposes quality control requirements (on dealer-franchisees), but it is likely that each requires somewhat different quality levels. You must actually monitor and enforce compliance with your quality control requirements.

- Well-written licenses also contain provisions requiring the licensee to present the mark in manners acceptable to you.

- Generally speaking, no license is needed if another is simply re-selling your goods without any alteration. Nordstrom's does not need a license to sell CHANEL cosmetics, because it simply resells those goods as it receives them. By contrast, each McDONALD'S franchisee needs a license to operate a restaurant, because it is independently implementing the franchisor's business systems and standards.

- Do not allow another, even a licensee, to use your mark as part of its name, or in combination with another mark.

- Do not delay if you discover a possible infringing use of your mark. Inaction for a period of, in some cases, even a few months can cause you to lose your ability to prevent use of the infringing mark. Instead, consult competent legal counsel promptly.

What does it cost to register a mark, and how long does it take?

I provide below some typical cost and timing ranges for various activities that arise in registering a mark. When considering these ranges, please keep in mind the following caveats:

- These ranges apply to U.S. marks and applications only.

- I have tapped my network of foreign IP professionals to obtain estimates for similar registration-related activities in the foreign countries of interest to my clients.

- Although registrability searches are generally recommended, only a very quick search, or no search at all, might be advised in certain situations.

- These ranges cover only the most common activities for a single mark and class.

- These ranges do not include counseling, opinions, exceptional needs, or certain potential expenses, such as translation costs, specimen creation, express mail, travel, or additional government fees.

- Keep in mind that expenses, the amount of attorney time required, and provider availability can vary widely depending on the specifics of a particular situation, and thus total costs and durations could differ significantly from these ranges.

- Consequently, rather than *relying* on these figures, talk to legal counsel to obtain cost and timing ranges that reflect your particular situation.

Registrability Search and Opinion:

- Cost: $0 - $1500+

- Timing: within a few hours to 21 days

Application Preparation:

- Cost: $350 - $800+

- Timing: within a few hours to 7 days

USPTO Filing Fees:

- Cost: $275 - $350+

Application Prosecution:

- Cost: $400 - $1500+

- Timing: within 9 to 24+ months, averaging roughly 12 months if no objection or opposition is raised

USPTO Registration Fees:

- Cost: $100 - $500+

Total:

- Cost: $1125 - $4650+

- Timing: 9 to 24+ months

How are marks federally registered?

Once a mark appears to be registrable, there are two common processes to federally registering that mark:

    a. Via an "Intent to Use" application, which involves:

        1. determining the required filing information;

        2. filing the application;

        3. avoiding rejection by the examiner;

        4. surviving the opposition phase;

        5. receiving a notice of allowance;

        6. providing satisfactory evidence of use; and

        7. obtaining federal registration.

    b. Via a "Use-based" application, which involves:

        1. gathering satisfactory evidence of use;

        2. determining the required filing information;

        3. filing the application AND evidence of use;

        4. avoiding rejection by the examiner;

        5. surviving the opposition phase;

        6. receiving a notice of allowance; and

        7. obtaining federal registration.

As mentioned elsewhere in this book, the facts of any given situation will determine what legal approach is best for that situation. Yet generally speaking, when the guidelines outlined in this book were followed, most U.S. trademark registration applications I have prosecuted tended to advance very smoothly to registration according to the process laid out below, depicted in the flowchart on page 238, and described in more detail in the upcoming sections.

1. *Identify mark.*

Broadly, a "mark" (whether a trademark, service mark, collective mark, or certification mark) is an identifier of the unique source of a good or service. A mark can be nearly anything (e.g., one or more words, logos, and/or design details) that is used in interstate commerce with the good or service and that indicates the single source of that good or service, and thereby distinguishing one source from another. Rights in marks do not directly protect a good or service, but instead protect the brand or identity of that good or service. As you weigh your choices, remember that the world will know your goods and/or services (and maybe even you) by the identity you create for them. The more distinctive that identity, the easier it will be for the world to remember your goods and/or services, for you to obtain federal rights in that identity, and for you to exercise those rights to exclude pirates and thieves from attempting to cash in on them.

2. *Evaluate registrability.*

To determine whether a mark is federally registrable, I first typically consider whether the mark is improperly descriptive of the goods and/or services with which it is (or will be) used. If not improperly descriptive, I usually perform a registrability search, or sometimes obtain it from a professional mark searcher. I evaluate the results of the registrability search to determine whether the mark is distinctive and unique enough to likely qualify for registration.

To be "unique enough", use of the mark must not create a "likelihood of confusion" with another's mark regarding the origin of the goods/ services. If it does, I might recommend any of several approaches, including purchasing the other mark, obtaining a consent agreement from the owner of the other mark, and/or adopting a different mark to avoid the potential for an infringement challenge or suit.

3. *Prepare and file application.*

As noted above, of the two, the Intent to Use application is very frequently preferred and is the focus here, because it typically provides more flexibility in providing proper evidence of use of the mark.

4. *Examining Attorney objects to application.*

After an application is filed, at least 6 months typically pass before the USPTO's assigned Examiner reviews the application and provides feedback. When that feedback is provided, sometimes the Examiner will express "objections" to the application that must be overcome by filing a properly evidenced and/or argued Reply.

5. *File reply.*

To overcome the Examiner's objections, I will prepare and file a Reply that might adjust the application (e.g., by amending the identification of the goods/services or by submitting a disclaimer of some presumed generic portion of the mark) so that the Examiner will be comfortable with letting the process move forward.

6. *Examining Attorney approves application.*

Assuming the Examiner is comfortable that the application fulfills all legal requirements, the process will move forward. Otherwise, one or more additional rounds of objections, replies, and possibly appeals might be required. The corresponding expenses and delays often can be avoided by carefully following our Guidelines.

7. *USPTO publishes mark for opposition.*

Typically, within 4 months after the Examiner approves the application, the USPTO will publish it for "opposition", which is a proceeding within the USPTO via which an opposing party tries to prevent registration of the mark by presenting satisfactory evidence and arguments that registration will damage that opposing party. The opposition process is rather complex and infrequently invoked, so I won't dwell on it here, other than to note that I have helped my clients navigate opposition when the arose.

8.   USPTO allows mark.

Assuming no opposition is filed within the 30 day period following the publication date, it is very likely the USPTO will issue a Notice of Allowance sometime in the following 2 months.

9.   File specimens of use.

The USPTO provides 6 months in which to file acceptable specimens of use after it issues a Notice of Allowance. Upon submission of a satisfactory reason for delay and payment of a USPTO fee, this deadline can be extended in 6 month intervals, up to a final deadline of 36 months from the date of the Notice of Allowance. If acceptable specimens of use have not been filed by the 36 month deadline, the application will be deemed abandoned, meaning you will have to start the process over again by filing a new application. The guidelines outlined in this book explain how to prepare proper specimens of use that very likely will be promptly accepted by the USPTO.

10.   USPTO registers mark.

After submitting acceptable specimens of use, within a few months the USPTO typically will grant registration of your mark for the goods and/ or services identified in the application and will shortly thereafter issue a paper "Certificate of Registration". At this point, you have federally enforceable rights in the mark, and can and should continue to use the mark per the guidelines outlined in this book, including labeling the goods and/or services identified in the registration with the registered trademark ® symbol.

11.   File affidavits during years 6, 10, 20, 30, etc.

Other than policing your mark and using it properly, the most important steps following registration involve periodically telling the USPTO that you are still using your mark (as it was registered), by filing certain required "Declarations" during years 6, 10, 20, 30, 40, etc. after registering your mark. The long duration between these mandatory Declaration submissions can be problematic for many companies, if merely because employees come and go, are promoted to new duties, forget the requirements, etc. Fortunately, good legal counsel can take care of keeping track of the due dates, give clients a heads up well beforehand, and provide the necessary forms and explanations to make the task easy.

PROSECUTING A U.S. TRADEMARK APPLICATION

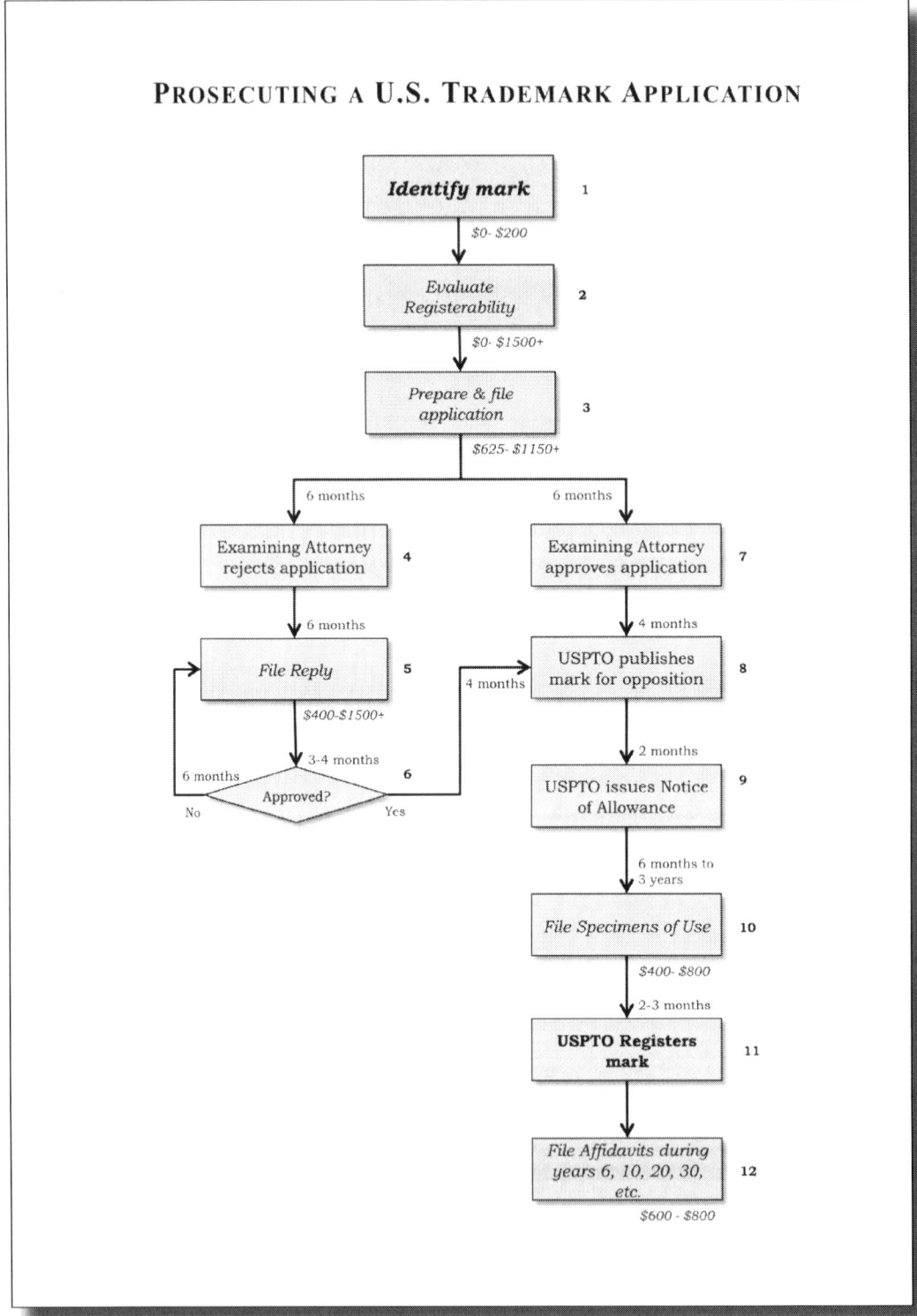

Why do examiners object to marks?

In 1947, the U.S. Congress implemented federal protection of marks via a statute called the Lanham Act, which can be found at Chapter 15 of the United States Code. To determine what marks are worthy of federal protection, the Lanham Act requires that the U.S. Trademark Office examine each registration application's mark to verify that it complies with the legal requirements of that Act. Those legal requirements revolve around several core notions.

First, registration will proceed only if the applicant dots all the i's and crosses all the t's. That is, the USPTO is a stickler for administrative detail, and minor errors can create substantial delays and costs.

Second, to be entitled to register your mark, it must be "distinctive". That means your mark must not include "generic" content (e.g., words that nearly everyone tends to call the goods or services with which your mark is used) or be "merely descriptive" (e.g., PET SUPPLIES CENTRAL for a pet supply store).

Third, for the USPTO to agree to register your mark, when used on the identified goods or services, your mark must not create a "likelihood of confusion" with a currently registered mark. Whimsical examples of marks that probably would be found to create a likelihood of confusion with registered marks include: MAVIS rental cars, GOOGOO search software, and POPSI cola beverages.

Finally, marks are not eligible for federal registration unless they have been properly used with their associated goods and/or services in interstate commerce, and proper evidence of that use has been timely submitted to the USPTO. What qualifies as a proper use and a proper specimen can depend on whether the mark is used with a good or with a service. Thus, I provide my clients with detailed guidelines explaining how to properly use their marks and how to generate proper "specimens" of that use.

These four notions serve as the basis for the most common objections that examiners raise against federal registration applications. I now will briefly explain those common objections, and how I typically overcome each of them.

Unacceptable Identification of Goods/Services

The goods and/or services with which the mark is used must be identified "acceptably". That is, the goods/services should be described in a satisfactory manner, which is typically by the generic name that the relevant trade calls them. For example, although you might prefer to identify your brand of car antennas as BULL™ "whips", if the relevant trade would call them BULL™ "car antennas", then the examiner will probably require that you identify them in that manner.

Also, the identification must not be overly vague or generic. For example, for your EVERGREEN™ mark for shrub fertilizers, "chemicals" might be considered by the examiner to be too generic if another identifier, such as "fertilizers" better describes the goods with which your mark is used.

Fortunately, the USPTO offers an "Acceptable Identification of Goods and Services Manual", which lists identifications that the USPTO will automatically accept, and will result in lower fees if utilized in your registration application.

Also, the law does not require that the identifier used in a registration application perfectly describe the goods/services used with the mark. Instead, so long as the goods/services described are sufficiently close to the actual goods/services that they fall within each other's "likelihood of confusion" umbrella, the selected identification is probably adequate.

Thus, I am nearly always able to find an identifier in this manual that my client agrees adequately describes the goods and/or services with which their mark is or will be used.

Generic Content

Let's assume you refer to your company's brand of dog toys as ROVER TOYS™. While that mark might seem distinctive enough, the examiner might take issue with the inclusion of TOYS in the mark. That is, the examiner might find TOYS to be a generic descriptor of dog toys.

Thus, the examiner might require that you "disclaim" TOYS unless it appears with ROVER.

The examiner might have a solid objection if:

- TOYS does not contribute to the overall distinctiveness of the mark as a whole in the context of the associated good/service, i.e., dog toys; and

- over time (at least 5 years), consumers have not come to associate the mark, ROVER TOYS™, with the associated good/service, which in this case is dog toys.

If the examiner's objection is solid, I usually encourage clients to go along with the examiner and "disclaim" the allegedly generic content.

Otherwise, with the client's help, I will gather evidence and/or fashion a well-written argument explaining why the examiner's position is incorrect.

Descriptive Mark

Objections based on descriptiveness can be tough, but sometimes can be overcome. The greatest immunity from such objections is carried by marks that are fanciful, followed by arbitrary marks, and then suggestive marks.

Fanciful marks include terms that were created solely to function as a mark. Examples include EXXON, PEPSI, and KODAK.

Arbitrary marks include terms that are known, but do not suggest or describe any significant ingredient, quality, or characteristic of the goods/services (e.g., MONSOON for a restaurant; APPLE for computers; UNICORN for printing services).

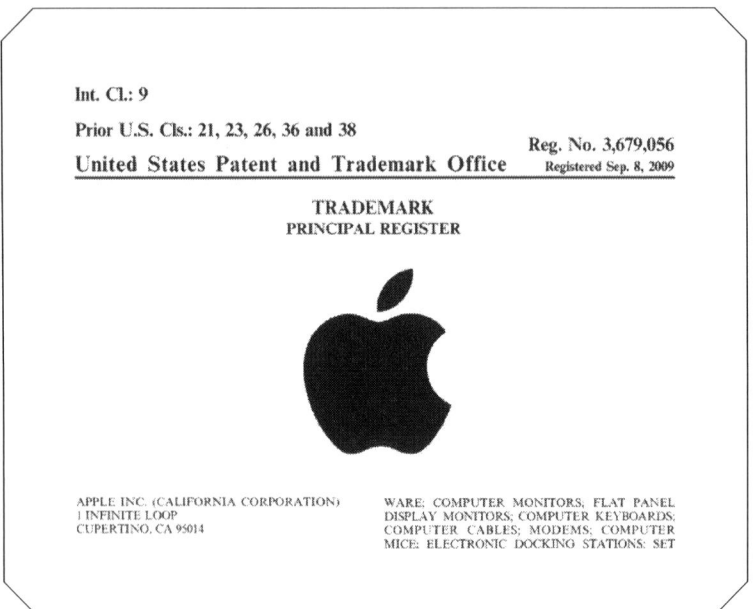

Suggestive marks hint at the goods/services or one of their attributes, but also hint at lots of other goods/services or an obvious non-attribute, or require a bit of imagination to make the connection. Generally, a mark is not descriptive when it is only suggestive of its goods/services.

Similarly, some marks have a "double entendre", that is, two clear meanings. The law will not consider such a mark to be descriptive when at least one of its meanings does not describe the goods/services with which the mark is used. But for a double entendre argument to carry the day, both meanings must be readily apparent, to the consumers in the relevant market, from the mark itself.

Often, I assess descriptiveness prior to filing a registration application, and by doing so, typically avoid descriptiveness objections for my clients.

So when a descriptiveness objection does arise, my client and I usually find it easy to provide a reason, such as one of those above, that will help convince the examiner why my client's mark simply is not descriptive.

Likelihood of Confusion

As with descriptiveness objections, likelihood of confusion objections can be quite challenging, but sometimes can be overcome. There are a number of types of facts, which clients can help me gather, that can help me convince the examiner (or an appeals board if necessary) that there is no reasonable likelihood of confusion with another registered mark.

But first, recognize that the best way to avoid a likelihood of confusion objection is by performing a good search before seeking registration. Searches focussed on registrability will likely identify many, if not all, registered marks for which a likelihood of confusion objection might arise.

Even broader searches that cover unregistered marks also can be beneficial, potentially helping you avoid a "seniority" or "priority" fight. This can be of vital importance, because the loser of such fights (the party who is found not to be the first user of the mark for the goods/services in the relevant market) might be forced to change their mark, and possibly pay damages to the winner.

Your mark fails the likelihood of confusion test when it is more likely than not that a reasonable consumer of the associated goods/services, upon encountering your mark and exercising ordinary care, would be confused. That confusion can be manifested by either the consumer buying your good/service when that is not what they intended, or the consumer wrongly believing that your good/service is sponsored by a source other than you.

Factors that are often considered when evaluating likelihood of confusion include:

    a. The similarity or dissimilarity of the marks, considered in their entireties, from the perspective of appearance, sound, meaning, and commercial impression.

b. The similarity or dissimilarity and nature of the goods/services as identified in the application or registration in comparison to those for which a prior mark is in use.

c. The similarity or dissimilarity of established, likely-to-continue trade channels for each mark.

d. The likely carefulness and/or sophistication of the consumer, prior to purchasing the goods/services. More expensive goods/services, and more sophisticated buyers, tend to be more discriminating, and less likely to be easily confused.

e. The strength and/or fame of the prior mark (based on, e.g., sales, advertising, length of use, public recognition, etc.).

f. The number and nature of similar marks in use on similar goods.

g. The length of time during which, and conditions under which, there has been concurrent use without evidence of actual confusion.

h. The variety of goods on which the mark is or is not used (i.e., house mark vs. "family" mark vs. single product mark).

i. The nature and extent of any actual confusion.

When faced with an objection that alleges likelihood of confusion, I typically work closely with my client to evaluate these and similar factors, to determine whether I can advance a solid argument explaining why the objection is factually incorrect and should be withdrawn.

When a strong argument is not available, I help my client find the optimal work-around. That is, when it makes sense and to the greatest extent possible, I seek a solution that preserves the client's investment in the mark and any resulting goodwill that investment has generated.

What if there are no objections?

If the examiner does not raise any objections to registering your mark for the identified goods and/or services, then the USPTO will publish your mark for opposition. An opposition is a proceeding within the USPTO via which the opposing party tries to prevent registration of the applicant's mark by presenting satisfactory evidence and arguments that registration will damage the opposing party. The opposition process is rather complex and infrequently invoked, so I won't dwell on it here, other than to say that I have helped clients navigate opposition when the need arose.

Assuming no opposition to the registration of your mark is filed within the 30 day period following the publication date, it is very likely the USPTO will issue a Notice of Allowance sometime in the following 2 months. At the time the Notice of Allowance is issued, if acceptable specimens of use have been submitted, the USPTO will grant registration of your mark. Otherwise, you will have to submit specimens of use to obtain registration.

What are "specimens of use"?

Before it will issue a Trademark or Service Mark registration, the USPTO requires submission of one or more "specimens of use" as evidence that the applicant is actually "using" the relevant mark "in (interstate) commerce." Based on the submitted specimen(s) of use, the examiner will verify that the mark is actually being used with the genuine sale of the specific goods or services listed in the application.

The USPTO has very particular rules governing what it will accept as a specimen. Submission of a specimen that does not meet USPTO requirements can result in abandonment of the application.

Thus, I urge clients to consult with me before gathering specimens of actual packaging, labeling, advertising, etc., for submission to the USPTO.

How should acceptable specimens of use be created?

Specimens should not be gathered or submitted until you actually are using the mark in "interstate commerce" involving the good or service listed in your application. In this context, "interstate commerce" means an actual, arms-length, interstate sale of the good or service. Generally you can meet this requirement by: (1) in the case of Trademarks, making only a few genuine sales to customers across state lines or to foreign countries; or (2) in the case of Service Marks, via rendering the service, even within only one state, if at least a few genuine sales are made to customers from other states, or via advertising the service via a web page.

Examples of acceptable use in commerce:

a. Exports or interstate sales of goods to genuine customers.

b. Interstate sales to an independent distributor, so long as they are open, "arms-length" transactions.

c. A restaurant's sales of meals, when at least some consumers are tourists from other states.

Examples of what is not considered use in commerce:

a. Sales between divisions of a company, or sales to family members.

b. Shipping a good for testing, unless testing is part of the service.

c. In most cases, pre-sales promotion and publicity. For example, a restaurant sign is not a suitable specimen until the restaurant actually opens to the general public.

d. Company and investor promotion. For example, use of a mark in business plans or investor presentations is not use in commerce because the mark is promoting the sale of stock, not a good, and because the actual good is not yet being sold to customers.

You must tell the USPTO when you first used the mark anywhere and when you first used it in interstate commerce, even though the specimens do not need to be from the first use. Thus, keep records of your first use of a mark with sales in interstate commerce. And if possible, keep records evidencing your first use of a mark in any manner.

Know whether you have applied to register your mark as a Trademark or as a Service Mark, and create specimens for that type of mark. Trademarks are brands of goods. Service Marks are brands of services. Sometimes a mark is both a Trademark and a Service Mark (e.g., XEROX for copiers and XEROX for document management services). To create suitable specimens, you must know how you applied to register the mark. This is because the PTO has different rules for evaluating specimens for Trademarks versus specimens for Service Marks.

If you are applying to register a Trademark, the specimen must show the mark affixed to the goods themselves, on packaging or labeling for the goods, on boxes or containers for the goods, or (only where no other means is practical), on displays associated with the goods.

Examples of acceptable Trademark specimens:

  a. A picture of a good clearly showing the mark stamped onto the good.

  b. Hang tags, labels as applied to goods or packaging, or packaging with the mark printed on.

  c. The goods need not be stated if it is obvious what they are (e.g., a photo of a computer chip with INTEL appearing on it). By contrast, if the goods are not obvious from the specimen, they should be stated (e.g., a clothing hang tag, that could be separated from the garment, should say "LEVI'S blue jeans," not just 'LEVI'S").

  d. Since it is not practical to place a mark on bulk goods like textiles, and since those goods are not typically sold in packages, use of the mark in POS displays might be accepted.

Examples of unacceptable Trademark specimens:

  a. Advertisements bearing marks for goods.

b. Instructions, invoices, bills of lading or other shipping documents, or price lists.

c. Press releases, letterhead, and business cards.

A web page can be an appropriate specimen for goods, if it displays a photograph of the goods, displays the mark in proximity to the photo, and provides a means of ordering the goods and all information necessary to order the goods. A telephone number, mailing address, e-mail, "Add to Cart" button, or a link to an ordering page can be sufficient means for ordering the goods.

If you are applying to register a Service Mark, specimens may consist of any advertising or promotional material used for ordering, or used for providing, the service(s) recited in the application. With services, there is no tangible good on which to apply the mark, so use in promotional materials is accepted. The specimens must show use of the mark in a manner that would be perceived by potential purchasers as identifying the applicant's services and indicating their source, as recited in the registration application.

Examples of acceptable Service Mark specimens:

a. Newspaper, magazine, or other ads; signs, billboards, point-of-sale displays, menus, etc.

b. Web pages and web banner advertisements.

c. A logo appearing on Powerpoint presentations used in educational or training services.

Examples of unacceptable Service Mark specimens:

a. Internet hyperlinks that are not part of larger Internet advertisements.

b. Letterhead and business cards.

c. Advertisements that use the mark only to identify the company, not the brand of service.

d. A simple telephone book listing (although a larger yellow pages ad would be acceptable).

A web page can be an ideal specimen for Service Marks, provided that it is publicly-available, displays the mark as an indicator of source (i.e., prominently, somewhat apart from other text, and with the Service Mark (SM) indicator), and, preferably, lists all the services precisely as identified in the application. Typically, this sort of web page is accessed via a link on the "main" page, perhaps attached to the mark, the Service Mark indicator, or a "Legal" page.

Specimens must show the mark as used with the specific goods or services identified in the application. Each application identifies certain goods or services with which the mark will be used, and with which it will be registered. These goods and services are organized by "classes." You must submit specimens for each class, but not for each specific good or service within each class. However, if your application lists several types of items within a class, you should not declare use of the mark for that class until you are using the mark with each of the items.

Examples of proper specimens by class:

a. An application to register GREEN GIANT for canned corn, beans, and peas, all in Class 29, requires only one set of specimens, and it suffices if the specimens show use of the mark only with canned corn. However, the applicant should be using the mark with all of the identified goods when it claims use and submits specimens.

b. An application to register VIRGINIA TECH as a Trademark for publications (Class 16) and as a Service Mark for educational services (Class 41), requires two sets of specimens. Class

16 specimens might be copies of a magazine, and Class 41 specimens might be copies of a web page promoting the school.

As an interesting aside, a 2012 report prepared by the Economic and Statistics Administration and the USPTO revealed that most trademarks are registered in just a single class. [32]

Examples where specimens do not show use with the goods or services of the application:

a. In an application to register a mark for hats, a specimen showing the mark on blouses.

b. An application to register a mark for website development services is not supported by an advertisement showing the same mark to promote website hosting services.

c. A classified ad soliciting new employees, or a specimen promoting the company's stock.

The specimen must reasonably show that it is actually being used with the sale of the goods or services described in the application. The specimens must show that the mark really is being used with the sale of the identified goods or services, not just a sample of a mark that might be used. The USPTO might reject a specimen if it simply is a sample of the mark and does not reasonably show actual use in sales or, where allowed, advertisement.

Examples of specimens that may not adequately show actual use:

a. Printer's proofs of advertisements (because the ads may not have run).

b. Published articles about a good, even with the mark attached to the good (a third-party article does not show use of the mark by the Applicant).

> c. Computer printouts of gummed labels not identifying the good or not applied to package.

The specimen must show the mark exactly as it appears in the application. A specimen that depicts a mark differently than it appears in the "drawing page" of the application will be rejected. Only minor differences that do not create a different commercial impression are tolerated. If an application claims a logo in a particular color scheme, the specimen must show the same color scheme. However, if a logo is registered simply in black and white, the applicant may submit specimens presenting the logo in any color scheme.

Specimens must show the mark being used "properly." A mark should be presented consistently and prominently enough that consumers will recognize it as a mark. In text, marks should be presented in bolder, larger text, as adjectives modifying the generic type of goods or services being sold. Ideally, "TM" or "SM" should appear in proximity to the mark, as notice of your claim to the mark. Note: do not use the ® symbol with a mark until you have received the federal registration for that mark.

Service mark specimens should be formatted as a JPEG file of no larger than 5 megabytes presenting a highly legible image of the mark that is no larger than 8-1/2 x 11 inches.

Initially, the USPTO grants you 6 months in which to file acceptable specimens of use after it issues a Notice of Allowance. This deadline can be extended in 6 month intervals, up to a total of 36 months from the date of the Notice of Allowance. If acceptable specimens of use have not been filed by the 36 month date, the application will be deemed abandoned, meaning you will have to start the process over again by filing a new application.

Otherwise, within a few months after submitting acceptable specimens of use, the USPTO typically will grant registration of your mark for the goods and/or services identified in the application.

At this point, you can and should mark the goods and/or services identified in the registration with the registered trademark ® symbol.

What happens after a mark is registered?

Once your mark is registered, expect to receive any number of unsolicited notices, offers, and/or "invoices" from companies offering mark-related services (i.e., monitoring, international registration, and/or online database publication, etc.). At first glance, some of these communications may look legitimate. However, the USPTO and World Intellectual Property Organization (WIPO) have both issued warnings about such communications. For more information, visit the USPTO website at http://www.uspto.gov/trademarks/notices/warning_uspto_customers. jsp. To see examples of such solicitations, visit WIPO's growing collection at http://www.wipo.int/pct/en/warning/pct_warning.html. I have encouraged my clients to have me review any suspicious communications they received when in doubt.

Other than policing your mark and using it properly (which is explained below), the most important steps following registration involve periodically telling the USPTO that your company is still using its mark.

What makes this task somewhat challenging is its timing. You must inform the USPTO, by filing certain required "Declarations", at each of roughly 5, 10, 20, 30, 40, etc. years after registering your mark.

The long duration between these mandatory Declaration submissions can be problematic for many companies, if merely because employees come and go, are promoted to new duties, forget the requirements, etc. Fortunately, good legal counsel can take care of keeping track of the due dates, give clients a heads up well beforehand, and provide the necessary forms and explanations to make the task easy.

Worth noting is that, if your mark has been in continuous use since it was registered, you also can file with the USPTO a special Declaration of

Continuous Use. Filing this Declaration can allow your mark to become "incontestable", which actually means that your mark is harder, rather than impossible, to contest.

The significant benefit of "incontestable" status is that an infringer can not challenge your mark on the grounds that it lacks distinctiveness, thereby making your mark relatively strong from a legal perspective.

On the other hand, an accused infringer can always defend on any of the following grounds:

1. the infringer's mark is descriptive of the infringer's goods and/or services;

2. the infringer's mark is descriptive of the infringer's geographic location;

3. the infringer's mark was used in interstate commerce before your mark;

4. the infringer's mark was registered before your mark;

5. you fraudulently obtained your registration or its incontestability status;

6. you abandoned use of your mark;

7. you are using your mark to misrepresent the source of your goods and/or services;

8. your mark is being used to violate antitrust laws.

What if I need protection outside the U.S. for my mark?

For companies seeking protection for their marks in countries outside the U.S., trademark registration applications can be filed with the corresponding foreign trademark offices. Those foreign applications will be considered based on that country's requirements for filing, examination, registration, and maintenance/renewal.

When warranted, however, there is a potentially very attractive alternative to filing trademark registration applications with each desired country's trademark office.

Administered by the International Bureau of the World Intellectual Property Organization ("WIPO"), the Madrid System (so named because it implements the Madrid Agreement of 1891 and Madrid Protocol of 1989), allows trademark registration applicants a way to seek registration in multiple countries by filing one international application with their own participating national (or regional) trademark office. The applicant designates the countries desired from the list of contracting states (totaling 89 as of January 2013). If a designated country's trademark office doesn't refuse registration within the applicable time limit (varies by country), the mark will be registered in that country.

For U.S. applicants, filing a Madrid international application requires at least one U.S. trademark registration or pending U.S. trademark registration application, though the international application can be based on multiple registrations/applications if desired. The list of goods and/or services for the international application must be the same or narrower than the U.S. registration/application.

The fees paid to the USPTO upon filing is relatively modest: $100 per class of goods/services, or $150 per class if the application is based on more than one U.S. regular registration/application. Fees paid to the International Bureau upon filing vary considerably, and are dependent on the countries designated, number of classes, whether color is a feature of the mark, and whether the mark is of the collective or certification type. For example, assuming a single class, no color, and a typical trademark or service mark, with registration sought in the UK, Germany, and France, the fees charged by the International Bureau currently would be about $1200.

International trademark registrations are maintained by payment of a renewal fee to the International Bureau every ten years. Currently, a renewal fee based on the same example would be about $1240.

With the payment of a fee (currently about $425 plus each country's own fee), additional countries can be added after the international registration date.

Of course, reliance on foreign trademark registrations implies reliance on policing and enforcing the mark in the corresponding foreign countries. Depending on the nature of the registrant's (and/or its licensees') business, this task might be relatively easy or relatively hard.

Also, as with other IP protections, thoughtful consideration of the risk-adjusted return on investment values, such as those described in *Step 6 - Enhance*, should be used to decide among the various filing options for trademark registration applications.

What are some pitfalls involving marks, and how are they avoided?

Selecting an improper mark

- avoid descriptive marks

- avoid misdescriptive marks

Losing full scope of rights

- apply for federal registration of your valuable marks

- register for sufficient classes and descriptions

- be the first to use your marks in desired foreign countries

- be the first to obtain rights to your marks in desired foreign countries

Obtaining an invalid registration

- describe only goods/services you have actually brought to market

Killing your mark

- use you marks consistently, prominently, and properly in your advertising materials

- use your marks as adjectives (e.g., KLEENEX facial tissue) only

- publish "guidelines" to help outsiders properly use your marks

- don't allow improper or unauthorized use of your marks

- don't allow your marks to be used generically

- enforce your marks

Failing to notify potential infringers

- use ™, ℠, and ® notices properly

- use the ® symbol for all your registered marks, but only for those goods and/or services actually covered by the registration(s)

- use the ™ or ℠ symbol for all your unregistered marks

Failing to exploit your mark

- grow the goodwill associated with your mark

- extend and build your brands

Infringing mark of another

- perform a clearance search

- federally register your mark

Must an attorney be used to obtain a federally registered mark?

In other words, can you "register it yourself"?

Well yes, you can. It is permissible for anyone to file and prosecute a federal trademark registration application with the USPTO with no professional assistance.

On the surface, filing an application to federally register a mark and seeing that application through to registration (and beyond!) may seem simple when compared to filing and prosecuting a patent application. Hopefully however, the discussions in the previous sections shed some light on the complexities and intricacies of the process, as well as how the application can "crash and burn" with improper handling.

As with anything else, you tend to get what you pay for.

In the end, hiring a well-trained attorney with deep experience in trademark matters will very often be well worth the (relatively small) amount that might be saved by working on your own.

What is "trade dress"?

The trade dress of a product can be its source-indicating packaging, materials, configuration, design, decor, colors, and/or shape.

For example, a soda bottle having certain hour-glass-like curves will be instantly recognized by most consumers as a Coca-Cola bottle. Likewise, the shapes, materials, and colors of certain smart phones instantly identifies them as iPhones from Apple. And recently, courts have begun treating as trade dress the "look and feel" of certain user interfaces, such as websites.

Because trade dress can serve as a source identifier, it can be protectable as a form of intellectual property under federal law, much like a trademark. The legal protections provided to trade dress law are intended to protect consumers from unwanted imitations, that is, to help consumers avoid mistakenly buying a product that is mimicking what the consumer really wanted to buy.

Just as with trademarks, although not required, there are many advantages to registering a product's trade dress with the USPTO. And just as with trademarks, one of the significant registration requirements is that the trade dress be distinctive, that is, not improperly descriptive.

But trade dress law requires something more. To be registerable, trade dress must be non-functional. That is, even if the packaging, materials, configuration, design, decor, colors, and/or shape of a product are distinctive, they must not provide any substantial function other than to indicate the source of that product.

Domain Names

Sometimes considered to be a type of mark, a Domain Name is a portion of an internet "address", or more precisely, a portion of a Uniform Resource Location ("URL") that is unique to a website. As an example, for the URL "www.MichaelHaynes.com", the Domain Name is "MichaelHaynes.com".

Each Domain Name is registered to only one owner via a Domain Name registrar, each of whom typically charges a fee for their registration services. Registrations expire after a pre-specified period of time, and must be re-registered beforehand (with any desired registrar), otherwise another party could register that same Domain Name, and thereby obtain rights in that Domain Name.

According to the World Intellectual Property Organization (WIPO):

> Domain name disputes arise largely from the practice of cybersquatting, which involves the pre-emptive registration of trademarks by third parties as domain names. Cybersquatters exploit the first-come, first-served nature of the domain name registration system to register names of trademarks, famous people or businesses with which they have no connection. Since registration of domain names is relatively simple and inexpensive - less than US$100 in most cases - cybersquatters often register hundreds of such names as domain names. As the holders of these registrations, cybersquatters often then put the domain names up for auction, or offer them for sale directly to the company or person involved, at prices far beyond the cost of registration. Alternatively, they often keep the registration and use the good name of the person or business associated with that domain name to attract business for their own sites.

More information is available from WIPO at: http://www.wipo.int/about-ip/en/studies/publications/domain_names.htm

The Internet Corporation for Assigned Names and Numbers (ICANN) has promulgated a Uniform Domain Name Dispute Resolution Policy with which most registrars comply, and WIPO touts itself as the leading ICANN-accredited domain name dispute resolution service provider.

Although domain names qualify as a form of intellectual asset, issues involving them are not often brought to the attention of IP attorneys, except, for example, when litigation is needed to protect a mark.

Copyrights

What is a copyright?

A copyright arises, by federal statute, at the moment an original work of authorship is fixed in a tangible medium of expression.

A copyright provides exclusive rights to control who can:

- reproduce the work;

- prepare derivative works;

- distribute copies to the public by sale, rental, lease, or lending;

- perform the work publicly; and

- display the work publicly.

These rights are divisible, and each one can be allocated for different uses, territories, times, mediums, etc.

More information is available from the U.S. Copyright Office at www.copyright.gov.

What is protectable via copyright?

Copyrightable works of authorship can include:

- literary works, such as books, training manuals, software, print ads;

- musical works, such as songs, ad jingles;

- pictorial and graphic works, such as photos, website content, graphical interfaces; and/or

- audiovisual works, such as movies, videos, television ads.

Pictorial, graphic, and sculptural works can include two-dimensional and three-dimensional works of fine, graphic, and applied art, photographs, prints and art reproductions, maps, globes, charts, diagrams, models, and technical drawings, including architectural plans.

Copyright law only protects fixed and original works of authorship.

A work can be fixed in a number of ways, including being painted on a canvas, written on a piece of paper, stored on a hard drive, or recorded on a tape, video cassette, CD, or DVD.

Originality requires some amount of creativity from an original author.

Copyright protection is generally available for the life of the author plus 70 years for individuals, or the shorter of 95 years from the date of publication or 120 years from creation for corporations or works for hire.

Copyright protection is not available for de minimis (inconsequential) contributions (words, titles, short phrases, and ornamentation), facts (including research and history), forms (format, layout, and style), color, typeface, photographic subjects, athletic events, scenes a faire (common themes and plots), ideas, procedures, processes, systems, methods of operation, concepts, principles, discoveries, and government works.

What is a copyright notice?

A copyright notice should be applied to a work to put others on legal notice that the work is subject to copyright.

A proper copyright notice includes the copyright symbol © or the word "copyright", the year of first publication, and the legal owner (e.g., © 2007 Joe Smith or Copyright 2011 Jane Jones).

Copyright notice generally should be provided regardless of whether the copyright has been registered.

Copyrights can be lost if a work is published without proper notice.

What are some benefits of registering a copyright?

Proper registration of a copyright can provide many benefits, including:

- a public record of the copyrighted work and its registration;

- proof of ownership and validity (when a certificate of registration issues within five years of first publication, the certificate becomes evidence of validity and ownership);

- ability to record registration with US Customs to prevent importation of infringing goods;

- the right to file an infringement suit against a substantially similar work; and

- a potential award of statutory damages & attorneys fees for infringement.

Secondary benefits of registering the copyright can include:

- notification of rights;

- deterrent of potential pirates/infringers;

- recognition in a crowded market (e.g., John Grisham, Stephen King);

- premium pricing (e.g., Apple);

- enhanced ability to exploit the work via licensing (e.g., Pixar); and

- improved opportunities to build a protectable "product" identity, e.g.:

    - the Bond films

    - the Disney characters

    - The Beatles' lyrics and tunes

    - Thomas Kincaid's impressionist paintings

What is the process for registering a copyright?

Generally, the steps for preparing a copyright application are:

1. Identify the copyrightable work;

2. Obtain a copy of the work for submission with the application;

3. Complete the appropriate copyright application form;

4. File the application with the required fee.

5. Wait about 6 to 26 months to receive notice that the work has been registered.

What does it cost to register a copyright, and how long does it take?

I provide below some typical cost and timing ranges for various activities that arise in registering a copyright. When considering these ranges, please keep in mind the following caveats:

• The ranges apply to U.S. works and applications only.

• I have typically tapped my network of foreign IP professionals to obtain estimates for similar registration-related activities in the foreign countries that were of interest to my clients.

• These ranges cover only the most common activities for a single work and form.

• These ranges do not include counseling, opinions, exceptional needs, or certain potential expenses, such as translation costs, express mail, travel, or additional government fees.

• Keep in mind that expenses, the amount of attorney time required, and provider availability can vary widely depending on the specifics of a particular situation, and thus total costs and durations could differ significantly from these ranges.

- Consequently, rather than *relying* on these figures, please talk with legal counsel to obtain cost and timing ranges that reflect your particular situation.

  Application Preparation:

  - Cost: $250 - $600+

  - Timing: 1 hour to 14 days

  Copyright Office Fees:

  - Cost: $35 - $65+

  Total:

  - Cost: $285 - $665+

  - Timing: 1 hour to 14 days

  Copyright Office processing:

  - Timing: within 6 months for electronically-filed applications

  - Timing: within 26 months for paper-filed applications

Compared to protecting other intellectual assets, registering a copyright is relatively easy. Often, you can successfully register your copyright without any help at all from an attorney.

More information is available from The U.S. Copyright Office at www.copyright.gov/help/faq/.

What are some copyright pitfalls?

Registration: necessary for instituting infringement suits, and for obtaining statutory damages and attorneys fees.

Delays in registering a work may make obtaining statutory damages and attorney fees impossible (it's best to register within 90 days of first publication).

Term: copyrights have a long duration, e.g., life of author plus 70 years.

Assignment: requires a written agreement.

Ownership: paying for a material object (such as a painting, book, CD, etc.) does not necessarily mean the copyright to the work embodied by that object has been purchased. That is, very generally, even if under contract to create a work for your company, a written assignment of copyright typically is needed from any independent contractor, and from any employee working outside the scope of their employment, if the copyright is to be transferred from the creator to your company.

Agreements

The variety of potential business agreements is simply astounding. Nevertheless, certain business scenarios appear with such frequency that tools and rules of thumb have emerged for smoothing the way and avoiding many potential pitfalls.

Perhaps the most common scenario is the need to disclose a trade secret, know-how, or other confidential information to someone outside the control of your company. In this situation, a Confidentiality or Non-Disclosure Agreement (NDA) is frequently utilized. Key to many such agreements can be a clear identification of what must be kept secret, and what uses are allowable for the secret information.

Closely related is the Employment Agreement (and its cousin, the Consulting Agreement). These agreements typically include confidentiality provisions, as well as requirements for assignment of intellectual property rights, assistance with obtaining and protecting intellectual property rights, and possibly, a non-compete and/or non-solicitation clause.

Assignment clauses can require that employees, contractors, and/or business partners assign their intellectual property rights to your company. Yet difficulties can emerge when, for example, the resulting assignment documents are drafted incorrectly, sought at the wrong time, or recorded improperly.

When entities agree to work together to research and/or develop technologies, products, and/or services, they typically enter a Joint Development Agreement, which usually spells-out how jointly created innovations, discoveries, and knowledge will be owned and handled.

Once an entity obtains intellectual property rights, it can retain those rights, yet authorize others to exploit some of them, via a Licensing Agreement. The terms of such agreements can vary substantially depending on, for example, business needs, the type of intellectual property involved, the specific rights licensed, and/or the industry.

Disputes can arise, for example, in the process of seeking to license intellectual property rights, or after such a license is in place. Yet careful license agreement drafting, and reliance on professional dispute resolution techniques, can avoid litigation while preserving the business relationship and maximizing the value of the intellectual property rights.

Recap

Over the preceding sections, we have explored the importance of not only innovating, and the intellectual assets that result, but also why owning property rights to your company's intellectual assets can be so critical to achieving sustained profitability. We also have reviewed best practices for taking stock of your company's existing intellectual assets, discovered how best to generate market-needed innovations, and learned how to strongly secure your company's intellectual assets. Next, I explain how to enhance your company's intellectual assets and properties, thereby optimizing their value and power, and ripening them for harvest.

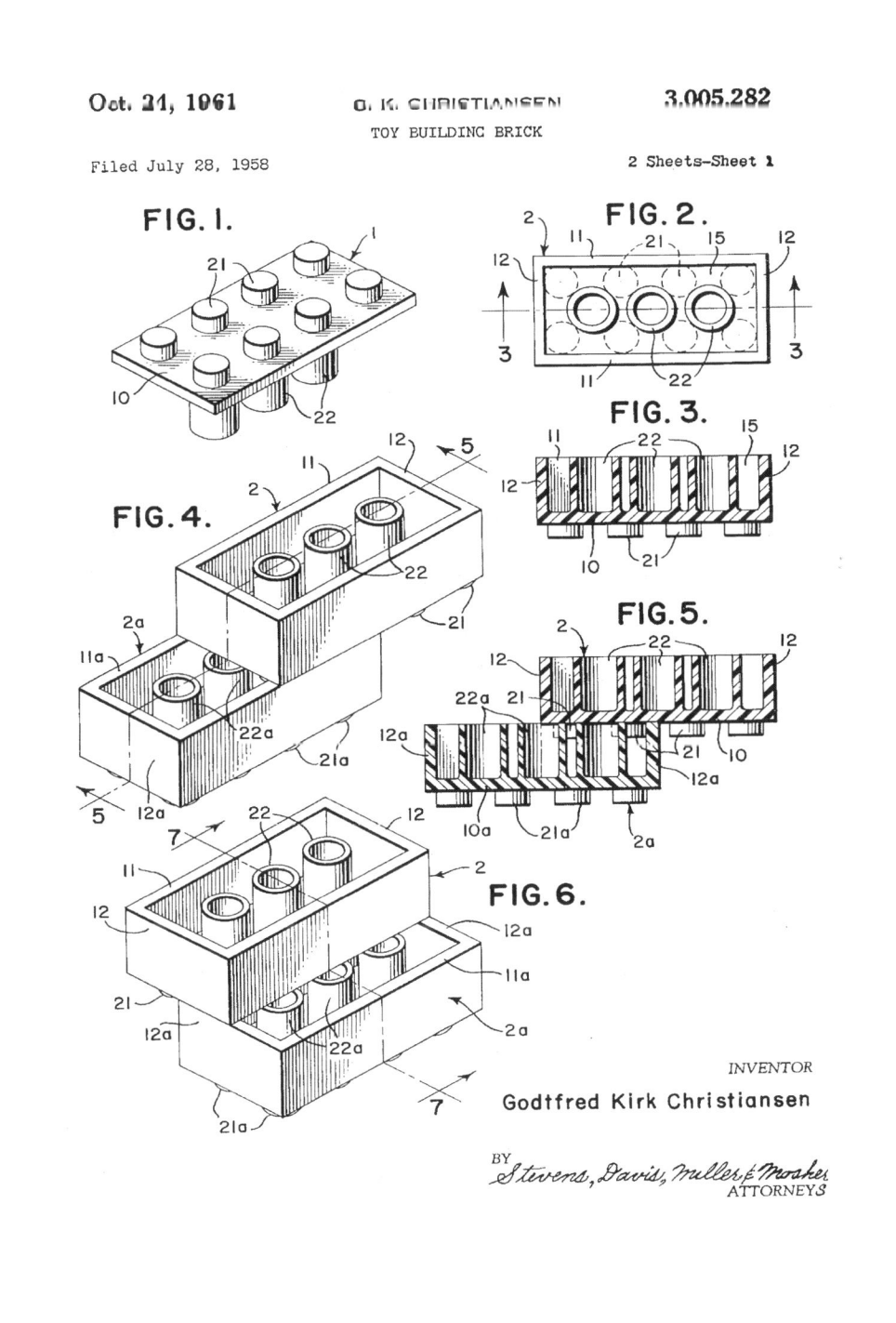

Oct. 21, 1961   G. K. CHRISTIANSEN   3,005,282

TOY BUILDING BRICK

Filed July 28, 1958   2 Sheets—Sheet 1

FIG. 1.

FIG. 2.

FIG. 3.

FIG. 4.

FIG. 5.

FIG. 6.

INVENTOR

Godtfred Kirk Christiansen

BY Stevens, Davis, Miller & Mosher
ATTORNEYS

269

J. F. GLIDDEN.
Wire-Fences.

No. 157,124.

Patented Nov. 24, 1874.

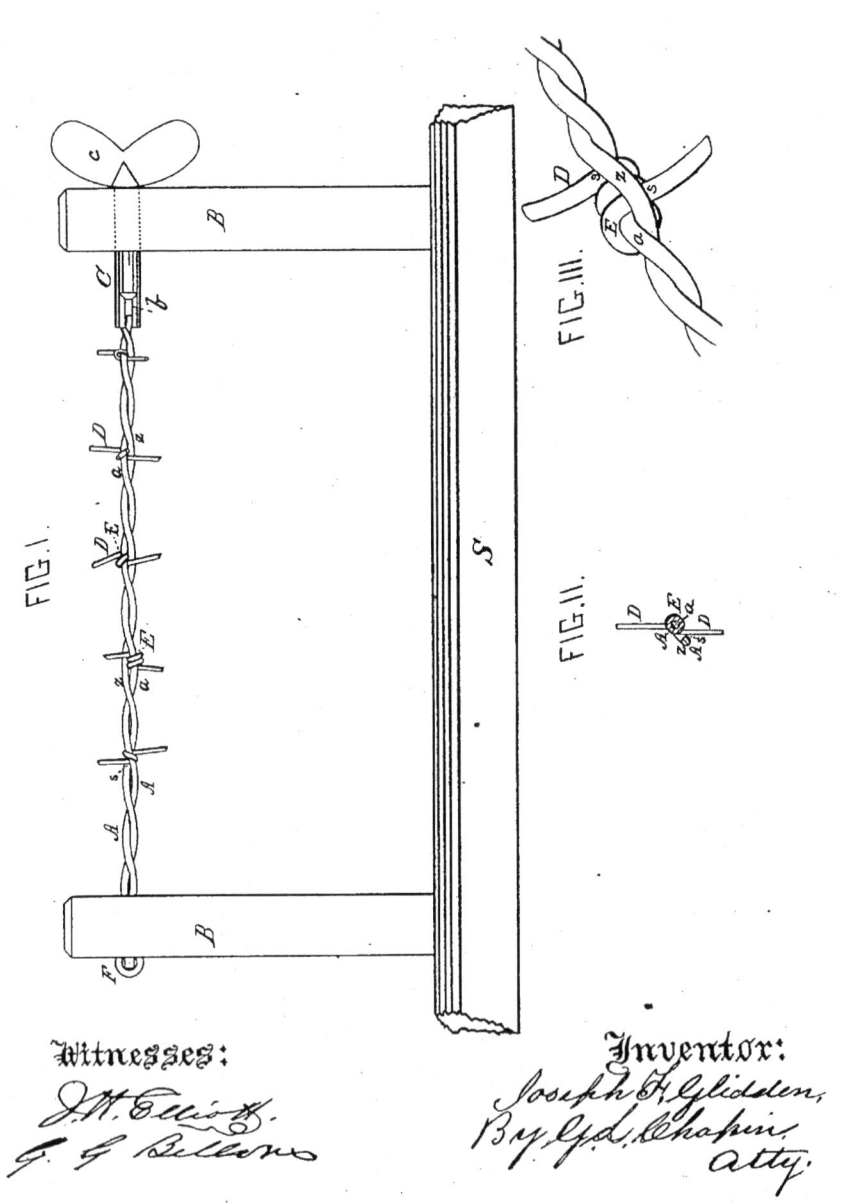

Witnesses:
J. W. Elliott.
J. G. Bellows

Inventor:
Joseph F. Glidden,
By G. H. Chapin,
Atty.

STEP 6
ENHANCE

If you really want to **enhance** your company's intellectual assets, so that you can optimize their full value, then implement the best practices described in this section for their protection, risk avoidance, and valuation.

What you'll learn

▸ When does enhanced IP (such as patents, mark registrations, copyright registrations, etc.) make strong business sense?

▸ Which common IP risks can be easily avoided, which are usually correctable, and which tend to destroy value?

▸ What value-added legal practices should your company demand for its patents and marks?

▸ What techniques can be used to valuate intellectual assets?

▸ How should likely returns be adjusted to account for IP risks?

▸ What factors can strongly influence likely returns, investments, and risks for different types of intellectual assets?

▸ How should your company prepare for successfully harnessing the value of its intellectual assets?

Even if your company already has an arsenal of IP, there are a number of reasonable steps it can take to enhance that IP prior to attempting to harness its value and power. Equally importantly, the likelihood is high that your company has overlooked the potential, and even the existence, of many of its valuable intellectual assets. This section will introduce best practices for determining and optimizing the full value of all your company's intellectual assets and properties, so it will be well-positioned to harness and exploit that value.

Choosing Your Weapons

Get Instant Protection

A few simple adjustments to its practices can allow any company to inexpensively protect its intellectual assets immediately upon their creation.

Protect your company's know-how and trade secrets now!

At a minimum, always immediately label each item that includes or embodies know-how or a trade secret with your company's name and the phrase "Proprietary and/or Confidential". Doing so puts everyone who encounters that item on notice of your company's rights in those intellectual assets.

Next, verify that anyone who potentially encounters your company's know-how or trade secrets is under a clear written obligation to treat those intellectual assets with respect (e.g., don't steal them, maintain their confidentiality, etc.). Ask experienced legal counsel to briefly review those written agreements for any major vulnerabilities that might leave you, and your valuable intellectual assets, exposed.

As resources allow, verify and improve your company's physical and digital security, to slow "leakage" of your know-how and trade secrets. For example, I have consulted with clients and performed a brief audit to help them determine the company's current secrecy vulnerabilities and how to correct them. In some cases, I have performed more extensive audits, helping the client identify and resolve both tactical issues and more important strategic issues related to their know-how and trade secrets.

Promptly secure your marks!

At a minimum, always immediately include a trademark indicator (TM) or service mark indicator (SM) with at least the first use of any of your company's mark on a given page, product, etc.

Next, verify that your company uses its marks correctly. This is not trivial. I have identified over 40 serious, common, yet easily avoided vulnerabilities that could allow hostile licensees, crafty infringers, and blatant pirates to legally steal your company's marks and the expensive goodwill you have built up around them. At least half of those vulnerabilities are related to how a mark is used, regardless of whether that mark is registered.

Protect your creative works instantly!

At a minimum, always immediately include a copyright notice on each of your company's copyrightable works (artistic creations), including every article, training manual, software program, photo, video, product brochure, web page, and advertisement, etc.

If the work seems to have at least moderate commercial value, register the work so that it qualifies for statutory damages if infringed.

Explore Enhanced Protections

For many intellectual assets, providing inexpensive instant protections is adequate. Some assets, however, really need much stronger protection, such as patents or federal registration. Although these enhanced protections are discussed in considerable detail in *Step 5 – Secure*, I provide a few additional insights on them here.

Research Patentability

Before your company obtains a patent, it will spend many thousands of dollars preparing and filing a patent application that describes and claims the innovative concept, and after waiting several years for examination, at least several more thousands of dollars prosecuting that patent application to issuance. So doesn't it make sense to verify that your company's odds of actually receiving a patent on that concept are reasonably good?

Of course, I write patent applications in a manner that reduces or eliminates all of the legal risks that I can control. But regrettably, I can't actually *control* whether or not an innovative concept is truly patentable. What I can do, however, is help a company, via one or more patentability searches, substantially lower the risk that it will discover rather belatedly (after spending tons of money) that others invented your company's concept first, thus preventing your company from earning a patent on it.

The primary value of a patentability search is that it typically:

- identifies what features of the innovation likely are not patentable

- clarifies what features remain to pursue

- informs patent application drafting so that only likely patentable features are claimed

A patentability search usually begins with brief communications between me and one or more of the innovators to develop a clear understanding of:

- the problem the innovation is believed to uniquely solve;

- the innovation's believed unique functions, ranked by innovator-perceived value;

- the significant parts or steps for accomplishing those valuable unique functions, the inter-relationships between those parts or steps, and how they solve the problem;

- the most significant difference(s) between the innovation and any innovator-known previous solutions to the problem and/or closely related problems.

Based on this information, I determine the best search strategy, including identifying the search's relevant concepts, terms, and queries.

My basic patentability search typically includes searching for relevant U.S. patents, U.S. applications, and PCT applications. By relevant, I mean published documents that describe how to implement the concept your company wants to claim (and therefore own).

I also can provide various degrees of advanced patentability searches, which can include searching even more publications, such as websites, newsgroups, English-language non-patent literature, and/or foreign-language patents, applications, and literature.

Occasionally, during my search, I identify a publication that appears to be a "direct hit", such that it "kills" a company's concept (describes all of its major features). When that happens, I pause the search, inform my client of my findings, and work with my client to determine whether it is worthwhile to continue the patentability search or to halt it right away and possibly save the company some money.

Typically, my patentability search results in a report that explains:

- the scope of the search;

- the search criteria;

- a list of potentially relevant found documents; and

- selected excerpts from the found documents.

After reviewing the patentability search report, my client and I have typically discussed differences between their innovation and what is described in the found documents. If the differences are not substantial from a patentability perspective, I often will recommend abandoning the pursuit of a patent for that innovation, or enhancing the innovation sufficiently that it extends to a patentable and valuable concept. If there are substantial differences, such that my client's company's original concept (or possibly a somewhat revised version of that concept) does appear to be patentable and sufficiently valuable, I typically will recommend that we work together to prepare a patent application that claims and describes how to implement that concept. With a reasonable idea of the extent of the found prior art, I typically have been able to draft those claims to define my client's innovative concept to avoid that prior art.

Hopefully, the above explanation clarifies why it makes great sense to try to determine whether a concept will be patentable before investing substantial sums chasing a patent. But innovative concepts are not the only type of intellectual asset that can benefit from searching before filing an application for enhanced protection.

Research Registrability

Just as with innovative concepts, plenty of money and time can be saved by an early registrability search that seeks to eliminate from consideration those marks that very likely are not appropriate for federal registration.

The primary value of a registrability search is that it typically:

- evaluates the potential strength of the mark

- identifies whether the mark is likely to be registrable

- informs brand development and marketing decisions

Determining whether your company's desired mark is registrable typically starts by evaluating the descriptiveness of the mark, followed by determining whether the mark (or one that is confusing similar to it) has already been registered and/or is already in use.

A basic registrability analysis typically begins with brief communications to help me develop a clear understanding of:

• the mark;

• what aspects of the mark to search (e.g., word, logo, combination, etc.);

• the nature of the goods and services with which the mark is and/or will be used; and

• whether and to what extent your company is already using the mark.

Then, I evaluate whether a company's desired mark is improperly descriptive of the goods and/or services. My basic descriptiveness analysis typically considers whether a mark seems to be:

• primarily merely descriptive of the goods/services;

• deceptively misdescriptive of the goods/services;

• primarily geographically descriptive of the goods/services;

• primarily geographically deceptively misdescriptive of the goods/ services;

• primarily merely a surname; or

• distinctive.

If the desired mark does not seem to be improperly descriptive, I next review existing U.S. Trademark Office federal trademark registrations to see whether the desired mark already has been registered by someone else. If it has, the Trademark Office's assigned examining attorney likely will not allow you to register the desired mark.

If requested, I also will research whether certain similar marks to the desired mark have been registered, such that use of the desired mark likely would cause confusion in the relevant market, and thus be both unregistrable, and a potential infringement.

When a considerable investment will be made in a company's desired mark and/or where RARE values justify it (see below), I will coordinate an advanced search, which can include searching state and/or foreign registrations, web-based uses of the mark, and/or use of the mark in periodicals or other literature.

Just as with patentability searches, occasionally, during my search, I identify a registration or use of a mark that appears to be a "direct hit", such that it "kills" a company's ability to register and/or use its desired mark. When that happens, I pause the search, inform my client of my findings, and work with them to determine whether it is worthwhile to continue the registrability search or to halt it right away and possibly save the company some money.

But more typically, my registrability searches result in a written report that explains:

- the scope of the search;

- the search criteria; and

- potentially relevant found information.

After reviewing my report, we typically discuss differences between the company's desired mark and the found marks, potential difficulties with registering or using the desired mark, and appropriate and/or desired action items.

Early, and sometimes repeated, evaluations of the registrability of marks, and likewise, the patentability of innovative concepts, can help to avoid several risks, especially the risk of spending time and money pursuing mark registrations and patents that simply will not be issued. Of course, there are many other risks that can negatively impact not only whether a patent or mark registration will issue, but also your company's ability to successfully enforce those protections and harness their value. So we turn next to better understanding those risks and how to reduce or eliminate them.

Avoiding Unnecessary Risks

If you really want to know whether your company's IP portfolio is at risk, and perhaps ruined, via any of over 120 serious, common, and easily avoided vulnerabilities that could allow hostile licensees, crafty infringers, and blatant pirates to legally steal your markets, then I certainly can help.

Here's a summary of what you'll learn next:

1. What types of flaws can be identified via an IP risk analysis?

2. What types of benefits can a risk analysis reveal?

3. What are the potential outcomes of these flaws and benefits?

4. How common are these flaws and benefits?

5. Why do the flaws continue to be produced and the benefits ignored?

6. Which flaws can be corrected, and which can't?

7. Which flaws can be avoided, and how?

Patent Risks

Are your company's patents crippled by any of over 50 serious, common, and easily avoided vulnerabilities that could allow hostile licensees, crafty infringers, and blatant pirates to legally steal the market for your company's mission-critical innovations?

Risky Business – A Widespread Culture of Value Destruction

Over **99%** of recently surveyed U.S. patent *applications* had fundamental ***drafting*** flaws that could have been easily avoided at essentially no cost at all to the patent applicants.

Similarly, over **99%** of recently surveyed issued U.S. *patents* had at least one fundamental ***prosecution*** flaw that could have been easily prevented with effectively no additional expenditure.

What I find astonishing is that courts have repeatedly warned patent attorneys to avoid these flaws, in some cases for over 10 years!

In the meanwhile, the presence of these unnecessary flaws infects the resulting patents with substantial legal risks, in many cases so severe that potential licensees likely will devalue, ignore, or challenge the patents, competitors easily will avoid liability for infringing those patents, and the patent owners will lose the ability to maximize the value and power of their innovations.

I have studiously cataloged the vast majority of these flaws and created powerful, proprietary, and *patent-pending* software that can automatically analyze any published U.S. patent application or patent for their presence and potential impact.

Senseless Risks – A Closer Look

I have been fortunate in that I have systemized and leveraged my litigation background and extensive knowledge on relevant patent law to create a powerful document analysis tool (patent-pending of course!). My innovative software tracks over 100 patent metrics, including numerous risks and benefits springing from how a patent application is drafted and/or prosecuted. Many of those metrics can have substantial impact on the value of the resulting patent. To show their impact, I have linked these metrics to some of the court cases that expose risky practices and punish the patents that take those risks. My ground-breaking tool includes a powerful search engine that can analyze nearly any patent document, such as a patent application or issued patent, for evidence of these metrics, and grade that document accordingly, thereby providing a meaningful quantitative measure of just how severely the value of the corresponding patent has been compromised (or possibly enhanced) by how it was written and/or prosecuted.

My research conclusively proves that the vast majority of patent applications are written and prosecuted in a manner that is simply oblivious to their impact on patent licensing and litigation outcomes. In contrast, thus far, my patent drafting and prosecution work has consistently and substantially outperformed the norms, based on dozens of objective statistical measures.

How do I know? Using my unique custom-designed software tools, I have surveyed tens of thousands of patent applications and patents. I have statistically analyzed the found patent documents according to over 100 metrics of relevant risks and benefits. I link each of those risks and benefits to the relevant court decisions. And those court decisions provide patent-opposing lawyers with the tools they need to help their otherwise apparently infringing clients avoid liability for infringement, or worse yet, invalidate the resulting patents so that they can't be enforced against anyone. So I have the survey data, and its appropriate analysis, that undeniably prove my points.

The results of my surveys and analysis are simply astounding, even to me, and I already knew that most of what passes for good patent work is in fact filled with serious errors, risky practices, and downright ignorance of the law. For example, over 93% of 8000+ recently surveyed patent applications needlessly included a single legal risk that has been repeatedly explained, harshly criticized, and loudly discouraged by the top federal patent court for unquestionably the past 14 years, and arguably for over 30 years. Yet even today, typical patent applications keep on taking that risk, simply mindless of the potential harm. And that is only the tip of the iceberg. My analysis proves that the problem is much, much worse.

Consider those 8000+ patent applications I studied, which included every utility patent application published by the USPTO for a particular week in April 2010. Less than **1%** avoided 4 basic drafting risks that are very well-known among patent litigators, and would have cost the drafters of those applications essentially nothing to bypass. Even worse, these easily-avoided risks have substantial potential to inflict severe penalties on the patents that eventually result from those patent applications, as conclusively proven by what has happened to other patents having the same risks when their owners tried to assert those patents against competitors in the federal courts. In particular, some of the patents that have taken these risks have been invalidated, meaning that with the stroke of a judge's pen, they became completely worthless, and could not be asserted against anyone. In other lawsuits, the patent's claims were interpreted so that the competitor was found not to infringe, thereby completely avoiding liability, and allowing the competitor to continue profiting from the patent holder's market with impunity.

Building Quality Patents by Adding Real Value

Obviously, the patent applications I have drafted and prosecuted carefully avoided these risks, at essentially no additional cost to my clients. And sometimes I even have been able to fix the risks earlier patent attorneys created. But I actually have gone much, much further. In addition to avoiding and sometimes correcting value-destroying risks, I have built value-enhancing benefits into each patent application I drafted and prosecuted. In a moment, I will describe one of those benefits, but first, a little background.

No reasonable expert will dispute that, as a group, U.S. patents issued for pharmaceuticals are by far the most highly valued patents in the world. Some of these "pharma" patents are responsible for protecting literally billions of dollars in profits each year. Given that value, you would expect the owners of these patents to demand quality that goes well above and beyond that of the garden-variety patent. And in general, the pharmaceutical industry "gets it." Upon analyzing typical pharma patents, one of the most striking things that distinguishes them is that, compared to the average patent, the pharma patents tend to define over twice as many of their claim terms.

Why is defining claim terms a good thing? Because although a patent provides its owner with the legal rights to exclude others from making, using, importing, or selling the patent's inventive concepts, it is only the claims of that patent that define the scope of those concepts. That is, the claims define what infringes and what does not. And because words are almost always open to different interpretations, defining the words used in the claims tends to narrow those interpretations, thereby removing many opportunities to define an inventive concept such that it is invalid or not infringed. Simply put, definitions add substantial value to patents.

Patent case law proves this point again and again and again. The failure to define claim terms has repeatedly led the courts to interpret patent claims so that they are found legally invalid or not infringed, thereby undermining or destroying the patent owner's case, along with the value of their cherished patent.

The pharmaceutical companies apparently have learned this lesson reasonably well. Simply stated, appropriately defining claim terms tends to produce substantial benefits when asserting a patent, whether via licensing or litigation. But why should only mega-billion dollar pharma patents be entitled to this benefit?

I firmly believe that every patent should be written to take advantage of the benefits of defining its claim terms. So while the typical patent application only defines an average of 3 of its claim terms, with the help of my powerful, patent-pending software, I have been able to go the extra mile, and have defined an average of over 111 claim terms in my previous patent applications. That's right. An average of over 111 versus 3. Given the demonstrated legal importance of defining claim terms, it doesn't take a rocket scientist to see the value.

So while others have continued to weaken their client's patent applications by ridiculously building in huge unnecessary risks, I have meticulously avoided those risks, and instead have added proven benefits that tended to greatly enhance the value to my clients of their resulting patents.

With that background, let's next take a brief look at reducing risks and adding value to your company's marks.

Marks at Risk

Are your company's marks undermined by any of over 40 serious, common, and easily avoided vulnerabilities that could allow hostile licensees, crafty infringers, and blatant pirates to legally steal your company's brands and the valuable goodwill you have painstakingly built-up in those brands?

Over 66% of U.S. mark registrations that I recently surveyed suggested fundamental vulnerabilities that could have been easily avoided at little to no cost. Below I describe some of the most commonly-occurring flaws.

Descriptive marks

The law of marks generally requires that a mark be distinctive to be registrable. Thus, the U.S. Trademark Office will refuse to register any mark it considers to be merely descriptive of the identified goods/services with which it is or will be used.

For example, although wannabe entrepreneur Jo would love to call her pizza shop JO'S PIZZA, such a mark doesn't qualify for federal registration, because it is overly descriptive, and thus not sufficiently distinctive. On the other hand, JO'S ZA, or better yet, JOZZA just might work, since the word "za" might not yet be (and perhaps never will be) widely recognized as slang for "pizza".

From a registrability standpoint, marks that only hint about the underlying product or service are good, and marks that leave you clueless are even better (think EXXON, CENTRUM, XEROX, VIAGRA, VERIZON, etc.). By the way, the attorneys at the USPTO who are responsible for examining marks typically do not rely on the spelling of a "word" mark (i.e., a "brand name", alphanumeric mark, and/or textual mark that is not limited to any particular font, style, etc.). Instead, the primary focus of the examination is on how that text sounds (i.e., the audible impression it creates when spoken). For logos (even if they include text), the primarily focus is on the visual impression of the mark.

Indefinite descriptions of goods/services

The USPTO permits trademark owners to provide a customized identification the goods and/or services with which their mark is and/or will be used. But doing so can result in an indefiniteness objection if the USPTO is not familiar with that customized identification. To avoid this issue, the USPTO maintains a manual that lists identifications of goods/ services that the USPTO considers to be "acceptable" without the need for the USPTO's further inquiry (provided the selected identification is supported by the submitted specimen of use). Submitting identification language selected directly from the manual typically enables trademark owners to completely avoid objections by the Trademark Office concerning indefinite identifications of goods or services.

Sub-optimal filing bases

From the perspective of the USPTO, there are several types of registration applications. The two most common types of applications are the "intent to use" application and the "use-based" application. Of the two, the first type is frequently preferred, because it typically provides more flexibility in providing proper evidence of use of the mark in interstate commerce.

Inappropriate specimens of use

Achieving registration of a mark requires submission of acceptable evidence (specimens) showing that the mark has been properly used in interstate commerce with the goods and/or services identified in the registration application.

Because I have encountered dozens of different types of errors in specimens of use, I provide my clients with very detailed "Guidelines for Creating Specimens of Use" so they can avoid those errors. You will find those guidelines under the "Marks" heading in *Step 5 – Secure.*

I have developed the ability to analyze each of my clients' marks for any of over 40 serious, common, and easily avoided vulnerabilities, and have helped them correct nearly all of these vulnerabilities.

Or course, correcting errors isn't the ultimate goal. Any reasonable company would rather not have their IP infected with serious errors in the first place. Those are the companies who insist that their IP attorneys follow best practices.

Demanding Best Practices

Although this book is filled with descriptions of best practices for empowering your company's intellectual assets and properties, here are a few more that are worth serious consideration.

Confidential communications

During litigation, unless a communication is privileged or otherwise protected, your company can be compelled via the "discovery" process to provide that communication to its litigation opponent, who then might be able to use that communication against your company.

There are several different types of privilege, but the one that is typically most relevant to companies is the "attorney-client" privilege.

Understanding attorney-client privilege

Attorney-client privilege is a legal doctrine that can prevent litigation opponents from using litigation's discovery process to compel disclosure of certain confidential communications that occurred between a client and that client's attorney. The privilege is based on the U.S. legal system's recognition that by preserving confidentiality of such communications, the privilege encourages clients to engage in full, frank, and uninhibited discourse with their attorneys, who are then better able to provide candid advice and effective representation.

Generally, the privilege arises when a client or potential client confidentially seeks legal assistance from a licensed attorney, and attaches to each related confidential communication that results.

The attorney-client privilege generally will not attach to communications that:

- are not kept confidential;

- do not seek or provide legal assistance; or

- are made to further a crime or fraud.

The privilege also will not attach to any underlying facts that are conveyed to an attorney if those facts can be discovered from a non-privileged source.

For companies, a communication with the company's attorney can be privileged if made by or to a director/officer/employee of the company and it seeks or provides legal assistance regarding an issue that is directly related to his/her responsibilities within the company. U.S. courts generally protect communications between the company's attorney and any company employee when pertaining to information the attorney needs in order to provide legal advice to the company. In these kinds of communications, an attorney must identify him/herself, describe the purpose of the communication, and advise the employee of the confidentiality of the communication. Importantly, courts have applied privilege even to communications to/from former employees and independent contractors that are the "functional equivalents" of employees.

Courts also recognize that the entity that controls a company also controls privilege. This can include the buyer of a company's subsidiary or even bankruptcy trustees.

Privilege can be "waived" (i.e., lost or destroyed) by breaching the confidentiality of the communication. Most courts have ruled that privilege is waived when such communications are shared with outside agents such as financial advisors, consultants, bankers, etc. Attorneys and their clients must protect privileged communications and resist the temptation to breach confidentiality with team member agents outside the company. Note, however, that when these kinds of agents are directly involved in assisting the attorney with giving legal advice, the courts do tend to protect communications between the attorney and client's agent.

Communications that are not privileged, or for which privilege has been waived, can be discovered during litigation, meaning that your company can be forced to provide to your opponent a copy of that communication and/or testimony regarding it. Privilege can be waived intentionally or inadvertently, and once waived the privilege is destroyed forever and for all purposes.

Preserving attorney-client privilege

To protect the attorney-client privilege, your company should maintain the confidentiality of the associated communications.

That means that:

- any privileged communication should not be treated as an ordinary business document;

- no one outside the company should be given a copy, excerpt, or summary of the communication in any form without your attorney's explicit and specific written approval; and

- if there are other people outside the company who you believe need to receive the communication or its substance, contact your attorney and let the attorney determine the best manner to provide the information.

Finally, keep in mind that most foreign countries do not provide as much protection of attorney-client privilege as U.S. courts. If your company has operations overseas, don't assume you'll be afforded the same level of protection as in the U.S. Find out what precautions are necessary to protect attorney-client privilege in each country of operation.

Relying on an attorney's opinion

During any legal representation, your company is likely to ask its attorney to provide to an opinion on a legal question. Normally such opinions (and other information) provided to your company by its attorney are intended for a particular purpose, such as, in the patent context, to enable you to make an informed judgment whether an innovation is likely to be patentable, or whether producing a product is likely to result in patent infringement liability. Unless told otherwise, your attorney typically will assume that only your company will rely on the attorney's opinion and will therefore structure investigations and considerations consistent with that limited expected use of and reliance on the opinion. Therefore, no third party should rely on any opinion your attorney provides to your company unless the opinion was written with such reliance specifically in mind. Also, attorneys usually do not update their opinions unless requested, so any legal opinion eventually can become somewhat stale.

Avoiding risky communications

Because attorney-client privilege can be waived or otherwise breached, best practices suggest minimizing written communication of risky statements that an opponent potentially can use against your company during litigation. That is, if something needs to be communicated that is negative, critical, or otherwise against your company's interests, that communication should be verbal, and written notes should not be kept and/or should be written very thoughtfully, in clear recognition of the risk of their discovery.

With this general guidance in mind, in the IP context, companies and their attorneys generally should be reluctant to clearly communicate in writing that, for example:

- the company's know-how, trade secret, or innovation is surely known in the industry, taught by the prior art, or "obvious";

- the company unquestionably intends to abandon a patent application or a mark registration application;

- the company definitely should not have been awarded a particular patent or registration;

- the company's use of a mark absolutely creates a likelihood of confusion with another's mark; or

- the company certainly infringes someone else's IP rights.

Trade secrecy versus patenting

Patenting is not the best approach in certain situations. For example, sometimes it is more advantageous to maintain an innovation as a trade secret than to seek a patent for that innovation.

This can be particularly true when:

- your company's innovation lends itself to secrecy because it is very difficult for your competitors to arrive at the innovation, such as via independent discovery or reverse engineering from one's marketed products and/or services, and

- your company is willing to take appropriate and substantial measures to maintain the innovation's secrecy, recognizing that the average trade secret loses its secrecy, and thus its trade secret status, within relatively few years.

Sometimes, your company can secure the advantages of both patents and trade secrecy for a given innovation. For example, when an innovative concept is so new that you don't yet know how to implement it, that concept simply is not yet ripe for patenting. Instead, your company should keep it secret until you can describe how to implement it in a manner that will at least barely work.

Yet there is no need to wait until your company has optimized an innovative concept to seek patent protection. In fact, by filing a patent application at the moment your innovator finally can describe how to implement their innovative concept in a manner that will at least barely work, your company can keep secret any later optimization details it discovers.

Worthless provisionals

It is not uncommon to encounter a company that thinks that hastily preparing and filing a provisional patent application, which contains a skimpy disclosure of an innovation, is adequate to "secure" a full year of protection, and then a strong patent if a follow-on non-provisional is filed within that year. Yet there is a serious possibility that, during the year after that provisional was filed, a second company might create the same innovation, file its own provisional followed by a non-provisional, and ultimately is awarded a dominant patent for the innovation. How can that be true?

If the second company's provisional properly fulfills the law's demand to describe how to operably implement the innovation, but the first company's sparse provisional does not, the first company's provisional legally fails its role. That is, the filing date of the meager first provisional does not establish a filing date for the first company, and thus the second company wins the "race" to establish seniority of inventorship.

Whether they originate from provisionals or non-provisionals, all strong patents are based on applications that teach a person having ordinary skill in the art how to at least barely implement the innovative subject matter, and for U.S. patents, how to do so in the best way known to any of the innovators on the original application's filing date.

For guidance in how to disclose an innovation, so that it more than adequately fulfills this teaching requirement, turn to the model Innovation Disclosure Form in the Appendix.

Number of patents

Some companies believe that all they need to sustain profitability is a few patents. In some cases that might be true, but just like baseball, base hits are much easier to come by than grand slams, or even home runs. So, the winningest baseball teams tend to rely on many solid hitters, rather than a lone slugger who can knock the cover off the ball. Consequently, the more patents a company obtains for truly valuable innovations, the more likely it is to earn extraordinary returns on its investments in that patent portfolio.

We have seen this repeatedly recently, when the purchase price paid for large patent portfolios sold by Nortel, Motorola, Novell, AOL, and even Kodak have far exceded expectations.

Taking this diversified approach, your company can and potentially should try to lay a patent minefield against its competitors, with each patent in the portfolio protecting a different aspect of the competitive advantages of your company. To better appreciate this guidance, consider what you would do if accused of infringing hundreds or even thousands of claims spanning perhaps dozens of patents. Given how incredibly expensive it would be to investigate and defend against such a challenge, wouldn't you be agreeable to nearly any reasonable licensing terms?

Occasionally, companies believe that they should minimize the number of patent applications they submit for a given set of innovations because the USPTO charges fees for:

- receiving a newly submitted patent application;

- issuing a new patent; and

- maintaining an existing patent.

Yet sometimes a company can earn an enhanced return on investment by submitting multiple patent applications instead of one (sometimes even for the same concept). This can be particularly true when:

- a given innovative concept can be claimed multiple ways across several applications, each directed to a different art unit at the USPTO, at least one of those art units likely to expedite allowance of its corresponding application;

- there are multiple innovations that can be implemented independently of each other;

- there are alternative, even if somewhat less desirable, ways to implement a given innovation;

- there can be functionally distinct actors who might practice a given innovation; and/or

- the art is rapidly evolving, and thus can not be perfectly known prior to submitting an initial patent application, but will emerge much more clearly after serially submitting several applications.

Geographic scope

Often, companies that are new to patenting believe that they must seek patent protection throughout the industrialized world. Yet this can be a very expensive and ultimately sub-optimal proposition.

Fortunately, owning patent protection in large markets often can help generate profits that are sufficient to, where legally allowed, subsidize competition-discouraging pricing in unpatented markets.

So, prior to deciding where to patent, your company should carefully analyze the geographical distribution of its market.

Once the desired countries are determined, through my network of skilled foreign patent professionals, I assure that proper patent applications are filed, prosecuted to issuance, and maintained in each of those countries.

The name of the game is the claim

It is the claims of a patent that define the patent owner's exclusive rights (i.e., the right to exclude others from making, importing, using, offering for sale, or selling the claimed subject matter). Thus, its claims are a vital component of any patent's value, and I consequently strive to ensure that my clients' claims are aimed very thoughtfully, both initially, and throughout their prosecution.

Securing strong claims often starts by obtaining a clear understanding of the market's structure, how the innovation will be implemented, and the competitive advantages that your company seeks to exploit. Valuable claims typically provide a clear, broad, yet focused definition of your innovative subject matter. Importantly, powerful claims will be aimed at deep-pocketed competitors who are likely to infringe, and sometimes at potential licensees outside of your company's intended markets. Such claims should be written to protect against any single entity that implements the claimed subject matter in the U.S.

To avoid competitors' design-arounds and other non-infringement tactics, the best claims tend to ignore minor implementation details and instead focus on the core function(s) of the innovation.

Patience... is a virtue

Some patent attorneys lead their clients to believe that initially-submitted claims should be as broad as possible within the then-known prior art, and only narrowed in response to invalidating prior art presented by the patent examiner. What they don't explain is that this approach can result in a loss of claim scope that is much more substantial than the literal language of the narrowed claims would suggest.

Thus, I typically encourage my clients to initially submit relatively narrow claims that are clearly distinguished over the known prior art (sometimes in two or more ways), and then later incrementally broaden those claims as previously unknown prior art emerges, and only then to the extent the known prior art reasonably allows.

Although this approach might seem to take longer to arrive at the desired claims, following it avoids wasting lots of time and money prosecuting claims that ultimately prove to be unpatentable. It also results in issued claims that have both the broadest possible scope and a high likelihood of being perceived as valid by competitors, licensees, and courts (if the claims must be litigated). Thus, following this approach tends to economically provide your company with patents of the greatest value.

Knowledge is power

No companies desire toothless patents that are full of vulnerabilities that can allow hostile licensees, crafty infringers, and blatant pirates to legally steal the market for their mission-critical innovations. Instead, they seek patents that will be respected by all competitors, including their licensees. Achieving this goal starts with having the right patenting knowledge and techniques.

For example, rather than being written to blindly follow tradition, conform to optional USPTO aspirations, or attempt to serve as a marketing document, a patent application should be solely written to withstand the legal scrutiny of all hostile audiences (including the USPTO, competitors, and the courts).

All U.S. patent infringement suits are initially heard by one of the Federal District Courts or by the Court of International Trade. But it is the Court of Appeals for the Federal Circuit that is responsible for hearing and deciding all patent-related appeals, including those seeking to overturn patent infringement decisions of a lower court, and all appeals originating from the USPTO, such as refusals to issue a patent. On very rare occasion, the U.S. Supreme Court will weigh-in on a patent case, but for nearly every appealed patent case, the Federal Circuit is the highest court that will get involved, and effectively has the final say on U.S. patent law. Consequently, it is the Federal Circuit who tends to make most U.S. patent law. And as you should expect, the Federal Circuit is the primary audience for well-written patent applications.

Fortunately, I have promptly read and studied every precedential Federal Circuit (and Supreme Court) patent decision for the past 12+ years (which adds up to roughly 3000 patent decisions). So when the Federal Circuit has changed U.S. patent law, I have known it, and adjusted my tactics, as needed, right away.

I have been blessed with the opportunity to integrate my vast experience and knowledge into the preparation of over 950 patent applications, of which over 800 were U.S. applications. To varying extents, I also have prosecuted over 1450 patent applications, at least 1000 of which were

U.S. applications. And my work has been fruitful. Over 1000 patents have issued related to my work, in at least 45 countries.

As too many companies eventually learn to their great dismay, most patent attorneys who prepare and prosecute patent applications have little to no patent or trademark litigation knowledge or experience. Yet in addition to staying current on the relevant case law, I have had the good fortune to have developed a deep, broad, and relevant collection of real-world experience and formal education in IP litigation. For example, I have been heavily involved in 8 U.S. patent litigations, 4 foreign patent suits, and several trade secret and trademark litigations. I also have negotiated and drafted many IP agreements, including dozens of IP licensing agreements, one of which resulted in a 7 figure deal!

In any event, I am grateful that I have been able to deeply learn not only intellectual property law, but also how it has been and can be applied to protect or destroy the value of IP, and particularly, patents.

Knowing Your IP's Value

There are times when you just intuitively know that a given intellectual asset is worth protecting and exploiting. Other times, intuition commands the opposite conclusion. But what about the vast gray middle ground, where the value of securing and capitalizing on a given intellectual asset is somewhat unclear? What should be done with it? How can you be reasonably sure?

Generally, there are 2 basic approaches to determining value, or "valuating". First, *qualitative* approaches tend to rely on relative comparisons of non-numerical attributes. Example attributes can include:

- How necessary are rights to this IP for others to compete?

- What alternatives are available?

- How easily can infringement be detected?

Yet answers to such qualitative questions can leave a hunger for numerical, that is, *quantitative* analysis that considers these answers, but also weighs the answers to other, more easily measurable questions, such as:

- What will it cost to obtain this IP protection?

- How long will it take to obtain that protection?

- What are the odds this IP will be respected by competitors?

- How much would competitors likely pay to license this IP?

- For how long will this IP be relevant to the market?

Fortunately, after studying this issue thoroughly, I have developed a thoughtful analytical technique for quantitatively valuating IP at nearly any desired degree of depth. My powerful technique provides values that can be easily understood, analyzed, and compared, thereby promoting sound decision-making.

Looking closer, based on my extensive study of valuation, it is clear that if you really want to figure out the value of your company's intellectual assets and properties, so you know which to pursue, and which to kill off before wasting thousands of dollars, you first need to learn the Risk-Adjusted REturn on investment (RARE) value of each of those assets.

I am happy to show you the way. Here's what you'll learn next:

1. What factors influence likely returns (profits)?

2. What investments are typically required for IP protections?

3. How does timing impact returns and investments?

4. What risks should be weighed?

5. How do likely returns, investments, risks, and timings vary across different types of IP protections?

6. How are RARE values estimated for IP?

7. What RARE values are reasonable thresholds for various business stages and IP types?

Why the RARE approach?

Nearly every business activity (particularly those involving IP) is motivated by a desire to obtain an acceptable financial profit (or return) on the expenses invested in that activity. Yet every such business activity is also accompanied by one or more risks that, if realized, will financially impact the costs of the activity and/or the return from that activity.

The desired profit can be quantified as a Return on Investment (or ROI), and the accompanying risks can be quantified as a percentage that discounts or adjusts the ROI to reflect the impact of these risks. The result is a risk-adjusted return on investment.

By comparing risk-adjusted return values for different scenarios and/or intellectual properties, your company can determine which scenarios and intellectual properties to pursue.

Although an analysis of other metrics, such as break-even time and free cash flow, is sometimes critical, such metrics are tightly correlated with risk-adjusted return, and easily can be determined from the same fundamentals used to determine risk-adjusted return.

What is a RARE valuation?

Given that costs, returns, and risks can all be quantified, and their approximate timing estimated, relying on my client's input and my legal, technical, and business background, I can determine a range of Risk-Adjusted REturn on investment ("RARE") values associated with implementing and exploiting your company's IP. Comparing these RARE values to ROI thresholds for the corresponding type and/or development stage of the IP and/or business can provide a reasonable quantitative foundation for my client to decide whether to continue or cease investing in that IP. With my client's input, I can periodically update each intellectual property's RARE valuation so that they can easily decide which path optimizes your investment in that IP.

How is a RARE valuation performed?

A RARE valuation is based on an analysis of likely investments, returns, risks, and timings, and is most easily explained by example.

Let's say we are planning a charity golf outing, for which 100 players have paid $50 each to register in advance, and we are expecting another 50 players to register on the day of the event. Advertising the event costs us $1000. Obtaining event T-shirts, refreshments, and engraved trophies costs an average of $25 per player, and totals $3750 for the expected 150 players. Thus, our investment in the event is $4750 ($1000 + $3750), our expected revenue is $7500 (150 players @ $50 each), and thus, our expected return is $2750 ($7500-$4750). Consequently, our return on investment can be calculated as 58% ($2750 ÷ $4750).

Yet the weather report is predicting 50% odds that torrential thunderstorms could pass through the area on the day of our event. Moreover, the golf course is booked for every desired date on either side of our scheduled date, so there would be no rain date to which we can move the event. If we are rained out, our investment stays the same, yet our revenues drop to $5000, leaving us with a return of only $250 and an ROI of only ~5%.

To account for our knowledge (albeit imperfect) of the weather risk, we can apply the accompanying risks to the expected ROIs to obtain a RARE value, as follows:

- No rain-out (50% chance or risk):
  - Revenue: 150 players * $50/player = $7500
  - Return: $7500 - $4750 = $2750

- Investment: $4750

- ROI: $2750 ÷ $4750 = 58%

• Rain-out (50% chance or risk):

- Revenue: 100 players * $50/player = $5000

- Return: $5000 - $4750 = $250

- Investment: $4750

- ROI: $250 ÷ $4750 = 5.3%

• RARE: 29% (50% chance of no rain-out * 58% ROI) + 2.65% (50% chance of rain-out * 5.3% ROI) = roughly 32%

Treating valuation from an income-oriented perspective, we can use RARE valuations to compare different approaches to strategizing an investment.

In the charity golf event example, assume that, because we want to make sure we can contribute a substantial sum to the charity, we have established a threshold ROI of 50% for our efforts in organizing and running any charity benefiting event. Thus, we are unsatisfied with the below-threshold RARE value for the golf outing as currently planned.

To address this issue, we can explore some options. For example, if we were to raise the player entry fee to $75, we see the following impact:

• No rain-out (50% chance or risk):

- Revenue: 150 players * $75/player = $11250

- Return: $11250 - $4750 = $6500

- Investment: $4750

- ROI: $6500 ÷ $4750 = 137% (Wow!)

• Rain-out (50% chance or risk):

- Revenue: 100 players * $75/player = $7500

- Return: $7500 - $4750 = $2750

- Investment: $4750

- ROI: $2750 ÷ $4750 = 58%

• RARE: 68% (50% chance of no rain-out * 137% ROI) + 29% (50% chance of rain-out * 58% ROI) = 97%

Thus, we see that, as we might expect, our RARE value is very sensitive to changes in the player entry fee. We also see that, with a $75 player entry fee, we will surpass our threshold ROI even if the event is rained out (assuming that we can attract the same number of players with no increase in marketing costs).

Although the above examples are greatly simplified, they demonstrate that RARE values can be used to analyze the impact of different strategies and their associated risks on the expected return on investment. Determining and/or comparing a sufficient number of tactics and their associated RARE values can therefore allow us to select an optimal path.

Although not demonstrated in these examples, I typically would apply a time-value analysis to adjust the RARE values for timing effects. Such adjustments can make sense, for example, when revenues are unequally spread across substantial periods of time, expenses are incurred well before revenues are collected, and/or expected interest rates are sufficiently high.

Also, where applicable, I can adjust the RARE values to reflect tax effects, such as ordinary income versus capital gains, amortizing R&D expenses, applicable tax credits, etc.

What are the limitations of a RARE valuation?

Applicability

Because each intellectual property is unique and not directly comparable or replaceable, market-based and cost based valuation approaches tend to be inapplicable. Instead, generally the only valid technique for valuing IP is the income-based approach, which is the approach followed by the RARE valuations described here.

Accuracy

When we create a composite RARE value that attempts to account for all known substantial risks, we must recognize that because some of those risks necessarily will not be realized, the composite RARE value is unlikely to match the ROI actually achieved. Nevertheless, because the composite RARE value *accounts* for all known substantial risks, it can be a very useful analytical tool.

If we instead calculate a range of RARE values, we usually can feel a bit more comfortable that the ROI actually achieved will fall within that range. If the low end of the range is satisfactory, we very likely will have sufficient confidence to recommend the investment.

Dependency

As with most analytical endeavors, garbage in will produce garbage out. In other words, the quality of any RARE valuation is highly dependent on the quality of the numbers used to calculate it. So if an estimated investment amount or an estimated return amount deviates substantially from the real world amount, the RARE value can deviate substantially from the actual ROI.

Similarly, RARE values can be highly dependent on estimates of risks. If an important risk is ignored, or if an accounted-for risk level is substantially minimized or exaggerated, the RARE value can be substantially different than the actual ROI.

Changing circumstances

Because market-based IP valuations depend heavily on necessarily imperfect and/or uncertain forecasts of returns, it is often very beneficial to re-visit such valuations on a periodic basis as actual returns are realized and/or as more information is gathered that can be used to better forecast future returns.

Determining IP returns

Generally

There are a number of qualitative and quantitative factors that can impact the benefits, profits, and/or returns that can be obtained from exploiting a given intellectual property. Below I outline a few categories of such factors, and a few general factors within those categories.

IP scope

The greater the number of territories for which exclusive rights in the IP are owned, the greater the potential return. For example, owning patent rights in the U.S., Canada, and Mexico can provide more licensing revenues than owning rights in only the U.S.

Also, the broader the rights of the IP, e.g., the greater the degree to which those rights can exclude competitive efforts involving similar subject matter, the higher the potential return.

Conversely, the greater the extent to which market-acceptable non-infringing substitutes are or will become available, the lower the potential return on investment.

The extent to which related intellectual properties create synergy with a given intellectual property can be an important consideration. That is, the return generated by a related family of IP can be greater than that of its members considered individually.

Market value

A consideration of the total market revenues, costs, and profits for all of the goods and/or services that do or reasonably could embody the IP can have a significant bearing on its return.

For example, to the extent that multiple parties can be licensed to implement the IP, differences in their revenues, costs, and/or profitability can impact the overall return.

Market demand

The greater the market's current desire for the subject matter embodied by the IP, the higher the potential return. Conversely, the larger the need to educate the market in order to build demand, the lower the potential near-term return. Thus, the speed at which market demand increases and decreases can be an important factor in determining IP returns. And on a related note, how long the IP remains relevant to the market can be a vital concern.

Ability to exploit the property

The nature of the exploitation of the property can impact its valuation. For example, an IP owner might plan to:

1. bring to market goods/services covered by that IP;

2. form a joint venture with someone already in the market; and/or

3. license or sell the IP to others.

Generally, the greater the ability to deliver to the market goods/services embodying the IP, the higher the potential return.

Of course, the stronger the owner's ability to police its rights in that IP, the higher the potential return, so ease of enforcement should be considered.

Timing & trends

The more immediate the demand, the greater the potential near-term return on investment.

The longer the expected life of the IP, the greater its total potential return.

The longer it will take others to bring market-acceptable non-infringing substitutes, the higher the return from a given intellectual property.

The greater the royalty rate paid for similar IP, the greater the likely royalty rate for a given intellectual property.

Finally, the extent to which external economic, technical, social, and/or regulatory factors will influence demand can be a vital consideration.

Determining IP investments

There are a number of potential costs (which are perhaps more accurately viewed as "investments") that can be associated with creating, obtaining, protecting, and exploiting IP. Below, in Tables 6-1 through 6-3, I identify a few categories of such investments, and a few potential cost-generating activities within those categories for trade secrets, patents, and marks. Of course, knowing the details of a particular intellectual property and the expected tactics for exploiting it, I have helped determine estimates of the corresponding range of investments a given company was likely to incur to secure and/or enhance that intellectual property and to fulfill the chosen tactics.

Table 6-1: Potential Investments Associated with Trade Secrets

Learning
- educating employees on what trade secrets are, their importance, and how to maintain them.

Identifying
- recognizing existence and scope of each trade secret
- marking the trade secret
- communicating the trade secret to those with a need to know

Evaluation
- cataloging the trade secret
- determining a relative importance of the trade secret
- valuing each relatively important trade secret
- estimating potential investment costs

Utilization
- exploiting the trade secret, as appropriate

Maintenance
- preventing breaches in physical access
- preventing breaches in information access
- discouraging unintentional leaks (e.g., via education, compensation incentives, etc.)
- discouraging intentional misappropriation (e.g., via contracts & agreements)

Enforcement
- proactively preventing use of a leaked or misappropriated secret
- enjoining use of a misappropriated secret
- establishing liability for misappropriation
- obtaining damages for misappropriation

Loss
- detecting loss of secrecy
- determining extent of loss
- mitigating the loss
- innovating around the loss

Table 6-2: Potential Investments Associated with Patents

Learning
- educating employees on what innovations are potentially patentable, their importance, and how to secure them

Evaluation
- cataloging the innovation
- assessing patentability
- valuing the innovation

Procurement
- preparing patent application
- filing patent application in appropriate jurisdictions
- prosecuting patent application:
  - overcoming close (possibly previously hidden) prior art
  - overcoming improper examination
  - overcoming unexpected changes in the law and/or regulations
- obtaining patent grant

Acquisition
- identifying potential licensors and negotiating terms
- bearing up-front fees
- bearing other fees and royalties

Maintenance
- tracking required maintenance activities
- fulfilling required maintenance activities

Detection
- identifying potential infringers
- identifying potential infringement traps

Utilization
- Commercialization
  - making or having made the innovation
  - advertising inventive features
  - selling and delivering the innovation

- Sale/Licensing Out
  - identifying counter-parties & negotiating terms
  - policing compliance

Assertion
  - Pre-litigation, Discovery, & Pre-Trial
    - determining litigation strategy & tactics
    - gathering pre-litigation evidence
    - preparing discovery requests and disclosure documents
    - responding to discovery requests of opponent
    - preparing expert reports
  - Trial & Post-Trial
    - selecting jury
    - limiting opponent's evidence
    - presenting case
    - asserting motions
    - bearing imposed damages, injunctions, costs, fees
  - Appeal & Post-Appeal
    - developing strategy
    - posting bond
    - preparing and submitting briefs
    - preparing and presenting oral arguments
    - bearing any imposed damages, injunctions, costs, fees

Avoidance
  - discouraging infringement of other's patents
  - designing around potential infringements

Opposition
  - evaluating possible forms of opposition
  - developing strategy and tactics
  - implementing strategy and tactics

Table 6-3: Potential Investments Associated with Marks

Learning
- educating employees on what marks are potentially registrable, their importance, and how to secure them

Evaluation
- cataloging the mark
- valuing the mark

Procurement
- performing registrability search
- assessing likelihood of confusion
- preparing trademark registration application
- filing trademark registration application in appropriate jurisdictions
- prosecuting trademark registration application
  - overcoming close pending or registered marks
  - overcoming improper examination
  - overcoming unexpected changes in the law and/or regulations
- preventing breaches in physical access
- preventing breaches in information access
- discouraging unintentional leaks (e.g., via education, compensation incentives, etc.)
- discouraging intentional misappropriation (e.g., via contracts & agreements)
- obtaining trademark registration

Acquisition
- identifying licensor
- negotiating terms
- bearing up-front fees
- bearing royalties

Maintenance
  – tracking required maintenance activities
  – fulfilling required maintenance activities

Detection
  – identifying potential infringers
  – identifying potential infringement traps

Utilization
  – Commercialization
    • using the mark properly
    • avoiding loss of distinctiveness
    • avoiding abandonment
  – Sale/Licensing Out
    • identifying counter-parties
    • negotiating terms
    • policing agreement
  – Assertion (see Patents, above)

Avoidance
  – Evading infringement of other's marks
  – Mitigating infringement

Opposition
  – Evaluating possible forms of opposition, e.g.:
    • Post-publication opposition
    • Cancellation proceeding
    • Declaratory judgment
  – Developing strategy and tactics
  – Implementing strategy and tactics

Determining IP risks

Risks associated with a given intellectual property can be realized when investment-related activities are not appropriately performed and/or when returns are not appropriately sought and obtained. Below, I outline some examples of general risks that can apply to multiple types of IP, as well as some risks that are typically aligned with specific types of IP.

Exemplary general risks that might apply to some or all of a company's IP can arise based on macro-economic factors, such as:

- inflation or deflation

- credit crunches

- recessions

- asset bubbles and their collapses

Similarly, such general risks can arise based on micro-economic factors, such as:

- enterprise issues, e.g.:

  - *production calamity*

  - *labor strike*

  - *loss of business license*

  - *major change of ownership or management*

  - *loss of key personnel*

- financial issues, e.g.:

  - *bank failure*

  - *embezzlement*

  - *large unexpected financial liability*

- *radical increase in costs of capital, labor, and/or materials*

- market issues, e.g.:

  - *loss of major customer*

  - *loss of major supplier*

  - *radical advance in competing technologies*

  - *emergence of sales-impacting non-infringing substitutes*

  - *regulatory restrictions*

Specific risks involving Trade Secrets

Although a few trade secrets have been maintained for a very long time, e.g., the formula for Coca-Cola allegedly has been kept secret for over 125 years, the vast majority "dissipate in a matter of a few years in view of the high degree of employee mobility and inadvertent or deliberate leakage". [33]

Moreover, even if not outright stolen, a trade secret can be compromised by a competitor who legally reverse engineers your company's innovation, or by a competitor who, without any knowledge of your innovation, independently creates that same innovation.

In fact, there are numerous ways that trade secrecy can be lost or put at risk. I have identified over 50 potential trade secret vulnerabilities that I can investigate and assess to determine their impact on the RARE valuation of a particular trade secret.

Specific risks involving Patents

Prior art

Because the legal value of a patent stems from the ability to enforce its claims to innovative subject matter, it is critical that those claims cover an actual innovation, rather than subject matter that was already in the prior art. Yet at the time the underlying patent application was filed, the precise state of the prior art was not necessarily known, or completely knowable.

Nevertheless, this prior art risk can be substantially mitigated by a modest initial patentability search, and can be further reduced by occasional updates to that search.

Ideally, the patentability search is performed by the patent attorney who drafts the patent application. Doing so allows the attorney to focus the application on those aspects of the innovation that are most likely to distinguish the desired and/or claimed subject matter over the known prior art, thereby shortening prosecution time, lowering costs, and reducing the risk of claim invalidity.

And this ideal is very attainable. As an example, for over 15 years I have been performing such prior art searches, carefully catering each search to my client's desired concepts, search scope, budget, and schedule, and then expertly drafting patent claims to thoughtfully avoid the closest known prior art.

Drafting

Due to drafting flaws, the claims of many patents fail to reach the desired subject matter or are easily designed around, and thus are not actually infringed. Moreover, U.S. courts have created literally dozens of reasons for holding patent claims to be invalid or unenforceable. In fact, I have cataloged over 50 serious, common, and easily avoided patent application drafting vulnerabilities that can allow hostile licensees, crafty infringers, and blatant pirates to legally steal the market for your mission-critical innovations.

I find it fascinating, disappointing, and downright scary that over 99% of recently surveyed U.S. patent applications demonstrated at least one of the 4 most common of these drafting flaws.

The presence of such unnecessary vulnerabilities infects the resulting patents with substantial legal risks. In many cases, those risks are so severe that potential licensees likely will devalue, ignore, or challenge the patents, competitors easily will avoid liability for infringing the patents, and the patent owners will lose the ability to maximize the profitability of their valuable innovations.

To battle this issue, I have developed incredibly powerful, patent-pending software that has allowed me to automatically analyze any desired published U.S. patent application or patent to identify the presence of any of these 50 drafting flaws and assess their potential impact on RARE valuation.

Prosecution

Further vulnerabilities can be introduced during the negotiations between the patent attorney and the patent examiner that seek to convince the examiner to allow a patent application to be granted as a patent. Depending on the experience, expertise, and tools of the patent attorney, most such vulnerabilities can be identified with relatively modest effort, and then can be assessed for their potential impact on the RARE valuation of the patent (even including pending patent applications).

Specific risks involving Marks

The value of a mark can be negatively impacted by any of numerous risks related to, e.g., the selection, use, and/or registration of that mark.

For example, many desired marks are not sufficiently distinctive to properly serve their required function as a source identifier. Of the distinctive marks, many are not properly used by their owners, leaving them vulnerable to legal appropriation by others.

As another example, a mark, even a registered mark, can be abandoned due to as little as a few days of non-use, which often arises due to changes in business and/or product tactics, firm ownership, etc.

I have identified over 40 vulnerabilities that I can investigate and assess, typically rather easily, to determine their impact on the RARE valuation of a particular mark.

Valuation – Pulling it all together

We now have seen the role of valuation in optimizing IP power, a few RARE valuation fundamentals, and some of the many factors that can be thoughtfully considered. I have shown how RARE valuations can be used to reasonably guide investment decisions for IP (and even for intellectual assets that are not protected via property rights).

To arrive at such valuations, I apply my custom-developed and innovative RARE valuation tools. Using those tools, I compile and crunch identified returns, investments, risks, timings, and assumptions, to arrive at an easy-to-understand and well-supported report that provides a reasonable RARE value estimate at nearly any desired level of sophistication for nearly any intellectual property, project, or business. For example, I have developed the ability to provide a simple RARE analysis at a very modest cost, and as my client's needs regarding that IP evolve, follow-up with a more sophisticated analysis that better accounts for even more variables.

With strongly-supported valuations in-hand, you will be well-positioned to determine how best to convince others of the value of your IP, harness the power of that IP, and contribute to your sustained profitability.

Identifying Prospects

To best exploit the value of your company's IP, your company should determine who it wants to target with that IP. A good way to start is by identifying categories of prospects, then narrowing the categories, and finally selecting particular targets within the narrowed categories.

Determine relevant prospect categories

To set the stage for identifying your company's targets, first consider and rank these potentially relevant categories of prospects by how well they fit with your company's chosen IP strategy. Also consider the preferred tactics for exploiting your company's IP (see *Step 7 – Harness*). Keep in mind that some intellectual properties might be more appropriate than others for certain tactics, categories of prospects, and targets.

- competitors

- infringers

- licensees

- joint venturers

- investors

- acquirers

- acquisition targets

Identify possible targets

As explained under the heading "*Discovering Future Relationships*" in *Step 3 – Survey*, patent publications can be analyzed to help identify potential competitors, licensees, and/or infringers. For example, a "watch" service can provide periodic reports of new patent publications that mention a specific keyword, are classified within an identified technical field, and/ or are associated with a particular company, inventor, or earlier patent publication. Comparing such data for different points in time can allow important changes to be identified, such as emergent technical trends, inventors, and/or patent owners.

Also, patent analysis software can be used to identify parties who are very active in a given technical field, as well as those who are recent entrants, those who have fallen behind (and might need your help to get back in the game), and those who have pursued patents on potentially complementary concepts. A careful analysis of patent publications also can suggest potential suppliers, customers, and/or acquisition targets.

Determine each target's needs

Not only are needs often different from one prospect category to another, but individual targets within those categories often have different perceived needs as well. For example, a given potential licensee (or infringer) might only care about maintaining the relatively short-term profitability of only one product that is covered by a single claim of a particular patent in your company's portfolio. Yet a joint venturer might be more concerned with the right to practice several of your company's patents and gaining access to your company's wealth of know-how. And a potential investor's interest might be focused on the long-term value of your entire IP portfolio.

So a target's needs can vary depending on any of many factors, such as its desired:

- market

- geography

- time horizon

- risk sensitivity

- financial resources

- narrow business goals

- broad strategic objectives

As needed, further research can help uncover a potential target's past, current, and/or future products, services, markets, customers, suppliers, competitors, alliances, infringements, licenses, financial resources, beliefs, behaviors, failures, plans, tactics, and/or strategies. For example, a given target's tendency to quickly settle IP disputes might be worth noting. Or a company's heavy involvement in a particular standard-setting committee might suggest future product development aligned with that standard. And investor reports often signal major strategy shifts long before they are fully implemented.

Map needs to strengths

Even roughly determining the likely needs of your company's targets can give you the opportunity to associate those needs to the strengths of various aspects of your company's IP portfolio. For example, your company might have deep know-how in a specific emergent technology that is a very hot topic in certain fields or industries. As another example, your company might own several patents having claims that solidly cover another company's leading money-making product. Or your company might be using a mark that stands firm in the middle of a particular target's brand extension strategy.

Each such revelation better prepares your company for developing marketing communications that will persuade your target to view your company's IP in a light that maximizes its perceived value.

Assign values to IP strengths

Each identified strength of your company's IP portfolio is strong precisely because it has a perceived value to one or more targets. Continuing with the previous examples, your company's deep know-how in a specific emergent technology that is a very hot topic in certain fields or industries might be worth $0.5 million to certain targets, and $7 million to others. Or your company's several patents having claims that solidly cover another company's leading money-making product might be worth $300,000 per year for the next 10 years to that company. Or your company's mark that stands firm in the middle of a particular target's obvious brand extension strategy might be worth a relatively easily estimated sum to that target.

Contemplating and approximating the monetary value of the strengths of your company's IP from your target's perspective will greatly enhance your company's ability to persuasively advocate for that IP when you approach that target to negotiate for your desired value extraction approach.

Weigh IP weaknesses

Of course, many approached targets will want to find a way to lower their cost of doing business with your company. In doing so, they might attack perceived weaknesses in your company's IP. Rather than being blind-sided by such attacks, the better approach is to prepare for them, and neutralize them as much as possible well beforehand.

This notion suggests carefully auditing any IP a potential target might find interesting, and honestly assessing its scope, limitations, and vulnerabilities, from both a technical, legal, and business perspective.

To be even better prepared to show how your company's IP is the best solution to fulfilling the target's needs, also consider the potential target's alternatives to doing business with your company, and the strengths and weaknesses of those alternatives.

Rank targets by value

When there are multiple potential targets and limited resources via which to approach them, it can make sense to try to identify which targets to approach first. One easy way to rank such targets is by the identified monetary value of your company's IP.

But this is not the only, or always the best approach. Consider a well-written and well-prosecuted patent, a non-exclusive license to which is worth $70,000 to a first target, $700,000 to a second, and $7 million to a third, all of whom clearly currently infringe several claims of that patent. Should the third target be approached first simply because the potential payout is much larger? Perhaps. But before making that decision, consider whether securing a license with the first target might help persuade the second target to also accept the license. And think about whether the funds earned from the first and second targets might help fund, or purchase insurance that will fund, litigation that likely will convince the third target to sign-up for that license.

Creating Persuasive Marketing

Even if your company has carefully researched the market, determined the market's needs, and innovated to fulfill those needs, it is unlikely the market will beat a path to your company's door. Instead, the market will need to be convinced that your innovation truly solves their problems, and does so better than the other available solutions. As hinted above, persuading the market of the value of your IP won't necessarily be easy. To successfully convince them, you can take any of probably a gazillion different approaches, but in general, you likely will need marketing communications that at least:

- interrupt,

- engage, and

- educate.

That is, your marketing materials need to reach your desired audience on both an emotional level and an intellectual level. Interrupting strikes at the emotions, getting prospects to pay attention to your message. Engaging and educating aim for your target's intellect, encouraging them to dig deeper into your message, advancing their understanding of the advantages provided by your intellectual assets and properties, and assuaging their concerns and hesitations.

Generally, the development of strong marketing communications starts by thoughtfully answering each of the following 7 questions:

1. Who is your target market?

2. Who are your primary competitors?

3. What would generally cause somebody to want/need to be involved with intellectual assets like those of your company in the first place? That is, under what general circumstances would your prospects start to think about intellectual assets and properties such as yours?

4. What particular problems, frustrations, annoyances, etc. do prospects experience that are solved by your particular intellectual assets and/or properties? Which of these "hot buttons" generate the most emotional response from your prospects?

5. What are the important and relevant issues and concerns buyers should be aware of when negotiating for your intellectual assets and/or properties, and how do you address them? How would you advise your best friend if they wanted to enter such a deal? That is, what do your prospects need to know so they can confidently, and wisely, enter a deal for your intellectual assets and/or properties?

6. What are the main advantages of doing business with your company versus its competitors? That is, how do you give prospects for your intellectual assets and/or properties what they really want?

7. What kind of evidence can you produce to prove your case? That is, what information do your prospects need to feel they are well-prepared to make the best decision possible? What will it take to assemble that information in an attractive, educational, and well-received format?

With carefully considered and detailed answers to each of these questions in hand, you will be well-positioned to begin drafting your marketing communications. As described above, your message should interrupt, engage, and educate. To interrupt and engage, your written materials will need strong headlines that paint a clear mental picture, hit your target's emotional hot buttons, and awaken their attention. Since you've already discovered what those hot buttons are, now you simply need to match them to the strengths of your intellectual assets and/or properties, and/or to how your company is willing to structure a deal involving them. Again, start with strong headlines.

Under each headline should be content that clarifies the headline, briefly educates the target how a deal involving your intellectual assets fulfills their hot button issues, and promises to provide more helpful information once they contact your company. If they find that content, they will become tightly engaged, will enthusiastically continue reading your presentation, and will likely contact your company to learn more.

As you draft that content, make sure your writing style is clear, quantified, and conversational.

Likewise, when presenting your marketing message in person, whether it be a sales pitch, product demonstration, investment opportunity, or licensing talks, you'll want to be concise, straightforward, and friendly.

Practice delivering your presentation, but try not to memorize it, and definitely don't just stand at a podium and read it. Don't be too dry, but don't go overboard with the enthusiasm. Good presenters are passionate and positive, but also balanced and professional.

Craft your presentations with your audience in mind and tailor the message to fit their needs. Anticipate the questions they'll ask and be prepared to answer them. Being overly prepared can't hurt. Doing your homework will not only make you more comfortable during a presentation, but will also show your audience that you care about their needs and are ready to fulfill those needs. Especially when presenting to potential licensees or investors, keep in mind that the most important things they'll likely want to know are: a) what you're offering and b) how much money they can make. At the same time, be ready to delve into the nitty-gritty details if requested.

Part of good preparation is also knowing ahead of time what terms are acceptable (and unacceptable). You need to know your company's bottom-line, deal-breaker scenario(s). That said, stay calm in the face of truly unreasonable offers and try to not take them personally. Asking questions in that kind of situation can help deflect confrontation and provide you with some valuable feedback. Arguing is unlikely to get you anywhere.

Often a great business partner brings more than money to the table. While knowing your bottom line is important, being open to suggestions and flexible enough to work out a win-win for all parties can bring opportunities for creative and profitable deals. Among other factors, take into consideration the networks and skills of your target audience as well as their speed and/or agility to grow your business before ruling out an offer that initially seems financially sub-optimal.

In-person presentations can be a highly effective way to get your message to those you most want to hear it. When paired with well-conceived marketing materials backed up with real evidence of your IP's value, your company can make a stronger case for itself in its efforts with prospects.

Preparing to Negotiate

Introduction

At this stage, your company has developed strongly-protected intellectual assets. Those assets clearly fulfill critical market needs. Your company's marketing materials persuasively communicate the value of those intellectual assets to well-chosen targets.

What else do you need to succeed? Plenty. And the following can help.

Carry a BIG Stick

Any intellectual asset that has real power is energized by 3 main prongs:

1.   robust market desire;

2. strong legal protection; and

3. plenty of financial muscle.

If the market does not care about your intellectual asset, then infringement of your rights to that asset are unlikely, and damages flowing from any such infringement probably will be minimal. Moreover, if the market does not want implementations of your intellectual asset, there will be little to no sales volume, revenues, or profits. Estimating the financial impact of the market's demand is the role of my RARE valuations. Growing the market's desire is the role of your marketing communications. But even huge market demand, by itself, is not enough to assure sustained profits.

When the rights to your intellectual asset are not strongly protected, you likely will not be able to successfully recover for infringement of those rights. On the other hand, if your company has developed strong IP rights, protected using my thoughtful, value-enhancing techniques, those rights often will speak for themselves, command healthy respect in the market, and discourage smart competitors from venturing too near.

But not all competitors are smart, and some feel they are large enough to roll-over smaller players. So even when your company holds strongly secured rights in a very desirable intellectual asset, you still must have sufficient financial ability to enforce your rights. And although it doesn't necessarily need to be, enforcing IP rights, such as via IP litigation, can be a very expensive endeavor.

IP litigators are unquestionably very expensive. For example, even when the damages sought are relatively modest, litigating a mark or copyright infringement suit can easily cost your company over $300,000, and patent infringement suits that don't settle beforehand typically cost between $700,000 and $7,000,000 to litigate to a final enforced judgment (and those costs exclude any damages awarded to compensate for the actual infringement!). A 2012 PricewaterhouseCoopers (PwC) study [34] of U.S.

patent litigations reported that from 2006-2011, the median damages award was about $4 million.

Nevertheless, most such suits do settle long before the legal costs become sky-high. The 2012 PwC study revealed that for the last twenty years, only about 2 percent of all issued patents get asserted in lawsuits, with an overall success rate of about 30 percent for those that are litigated to a non-appealable final judgment [35]. Still, fear of the legal costs associated with patent litigation can allow a small but reasonably well-funded company to drive poorly-funded competitors (such as those that do not hold a good IP defense insurance policy) from the market, or into paying a substantial, perhaps crushing, payment to settle the case.

That is, adequate funding can level the playing field by allowing a small company to successfully assert selected IP rights against a deep-pocketed competitor. A small company can obtain such funding in numerous ways, including: buying a good IP assertion insurance policy; recruiting investments targeted at IP enforcement; and requiring a deep-pocketed licensee to fund infringement litigation expenses, etc. For example, by purchasing adequate IP assertion assurance, a small company can be secure in the knowledge that, in exchange for the payment of relatively moderate premiums, it has the financial muscle it needs to endure sustained infringement litigation while exercising control over its litigation attorneys, strategies, and settlement terms.

Sometimes only (big!) money talks. But more times than not, substantial funding isn't needed to resolve a patent infringement concern. For example, in many pre-litigation scenarios, I have provided soothing strategic advice, successfully counseled for restraint, and even negotiated win-win situations where appropriate.

Similarly, although I have not scared away opponents with a roster of famous and amazingly expensive litigators on my firm's letterhead, I have been uniquely positioned to tap my extensive network and recommend a top quality attorney that's been truly right for my client's specific needs. That is, unlike many practicing patent attorneys, I've not been obligated to recommend a less-than-optimal litigator or other attorney simply because we shared office space in a mega-firm. Instead, I have relied on my network of best-in-class attorneys for their respective niches as strategic resources that can add value and power to my client's IP.

When a lawsuit is required to enforce patent rights, it surprisingly can be long after the patent issued. A recent study of patent lawsuits filed between September 16 2011 and September 15 2012 (represented in the chart below) suggests that when patent infringement lawsuits are filed, about 14% of their litigated patents are less than a year old. About 35% of their litigated patents are less than 5 years old, and nearly 63% are less than 10 years old at the time the suit begins. That suggests that the typical patent owner might be able to defer funding a budget for litigating a given patent until years after that patent issues.

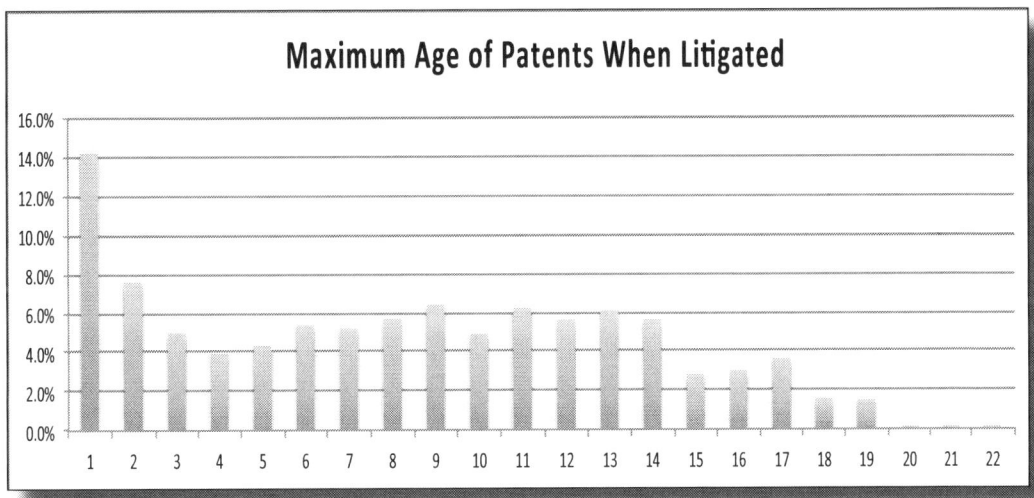

Stay Vigilant

Intellectual property protections, such as patents and registered marks, provide their owners with exclusive rights to the underlying intellectual assets. Those rights can include the legal power to exclude others from making, importing, using, offering for sale, and/or selling implementations of the intellectual asset.

Yet even before such rights have been secured for your company's intellectual assets, you can identify potential infringers, licensees, and business partners, and identify techniques for attracting them and keeping an eye on them. In *Step 3 – Survey*, you will find helpful explanations of how to survey the market and identify those prospects who are most likely to care about your intellectual assets. Many of these targets are also potential infringers, licensees, and/or acquirers.

By carefully tracking the activities of a likely target, you can stealthily gather evidence, build a strong case, and/or develop an appealing proposal, without necessarily prematurely tipping-off the target. In the meanwhile, you can investigate, analyze, and prepare strategies and tactics for enforcing your intellectual assets.

Thus, by silently performing such "discovery" and by thoughtfully strategizing, your company can take control of the enforcement process long before alerting the target, and can greatly reduce its costs if litigation is ultimately required.

So at the right time and on your preferred terms, after preparing to take whatever enforcement action is needed, you can persuasively present your case to the target, and thereby drive your desired outcome.

With that guidance in mind, let's finally turn to the myriad ways in which your company can profit from its well-protected intellectual assets.

United States Patent [19]

Warkuss et al.

[11] Patent Number: **Des. 385,220**

[45] Date of Patent: **∗∗Oct. 21, 1997**

[54] **AUTOMOBILE BODY**

[75] Inventors: **Hartmut Warkuss**, Ummern; **Gregory Guillaume**, Brauschweig, both of Germany

[73] Assignee: **Volkswagen AG**, Wolfsburg, Germany

[**] Term: **14 Years**

[21] Appl. No.: **54,271**

[22] Filed: **May 10, 1996**

[30]   **Foreign Application Priority Data**

Oct. 25, 1995 [DE] Germany M9508476.2

[51] LOC (6) Cl. **12-08**

[52] U.S. Cl. **D12/90**

[58] **Field of Search** D12/86, 90–92; 296/185

[56]   **References Cited**

U.S. PATENT DOCUMENTS

D. 352,482   11/1994   Cannara et al. D12/90

D. 367,440   2/1996   Mays D12/90

Primary Examiner—Melody N. Brown
Attorney, Agent, or Firm—Watson Cole Stevens Davis, P.L.L.C.

[57]   **CLAIM**

The ornamental design for an automobile body, as shown and described.

DESCRIPTION

FIG. 1 is a front perspective view of a new and ornamental design for an automobile body according to the present invention;

FIG. 2 is a left side view of the automobile body of FIG. 1 the right side view being identical;

FIG. 3 is a front view of the automobile body according to the invention;

FIG. 4 is a rear view of the automobile body according to the invention; and,

FIG. 5 is a top view of the automobile body according to the invention, the wheels, mirrors and spoiler shown in dotted lines form no part of the design.

1 Claim, 4 Drawing Sheets

R. H. GODDARD.

ROCKET APPARATUS.

APPLICATION FILED OCT. 1, 1913.

1,102,653.

Patented July 7, 1914.

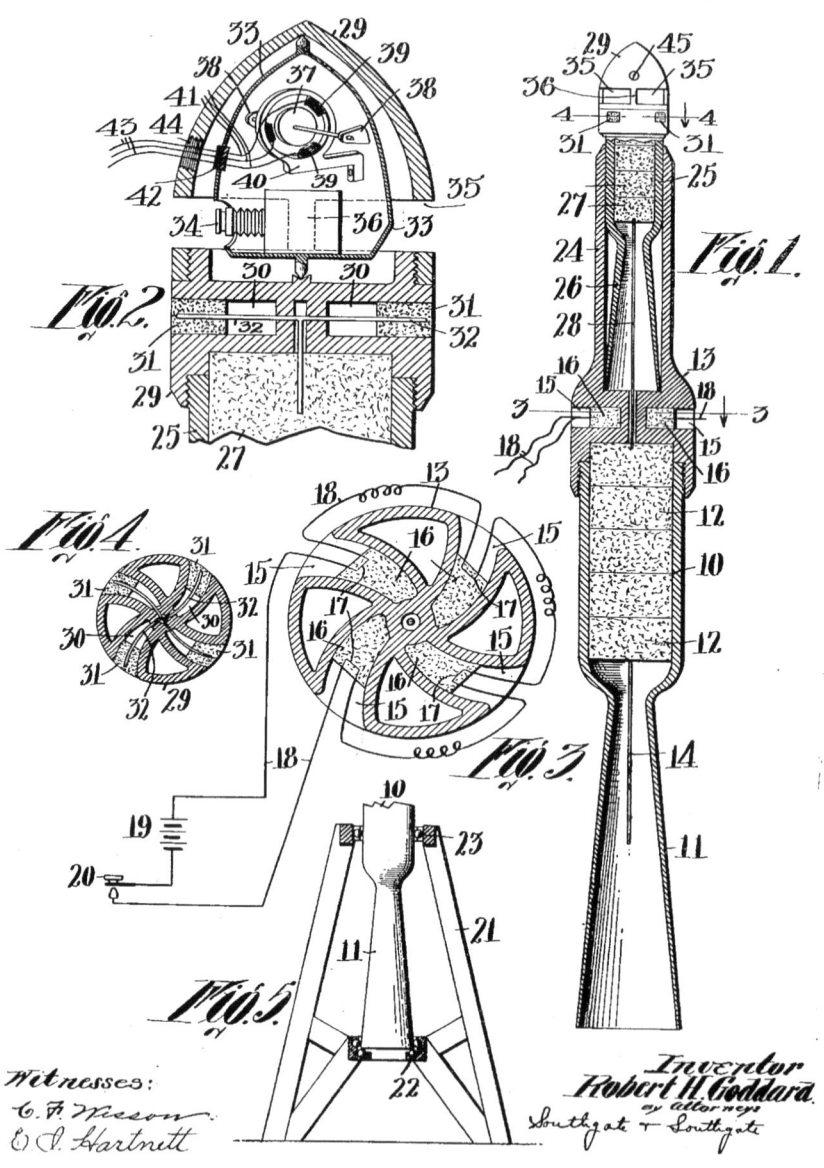

Fig.2.

Fig.1.

Fig.4.

Fig.3.

Fig.5.

Inventor
Robert H Goddard
by attorneys
Southgate & Southgate

STEP 7
HARNESS

If you really want to **harness** the value and power of your company's intellectual assets to optimize its returns, consider which of my 70+ tactics for exploiting those intellectual assets currently align best with your company's directions, and then vigorously pursue them.

What you'll learn

▸ How can a powerful IP portfolio attract the most desirable investors, employees, and customers?

▸ What are the best techniques for earning money with IP?

▸ When can an IP portfolio attract desired business relationships?

▸ How can IP discourage competitors from entering a market?

▸ How can a small company leverage its intellectual assets to out-maneuver much larger companies?

▸ What are the best ways to extract value from unwanted IP?

▸ How can your IP reduce risks from infringing other's IP?

Background

Harnessing the value and power of your company's IP portfolio (along with its intellectual assets not protected by property rights) can take many forms, such as earning enhanced profits or licensing revenues, discouraging infringers, and/or raising other's perception of your company's value.

Some harnessing opportunities might provide valuable market exclusivity, with the attendant extraordinary profits and the power to obtain injunctions, exclusion orders, seizures, and monetary damages against proven infringers.

Other opportunities might involve negotiating the license or sale of intellectual assets combined with lucrative supply agreements, technical consulting, and/or know-how sharing.

Less visible, but equally important possibilities can include divesting under-utilized assets, declining poor return on investment opportunities, and avoiding risks, such as preventing, mitigating, and resolving disputes, lawsuits, and related liabilities.

On occasion, it can be worthwhile for a company to harness the value and power of its IP portfolio by:

- using IP as collateral to fund other projects;

- donating IP to a charitable organization; or

- placing IP into the public domain to prevent others from obtaining exclusive control of simple improvements to it.

Beyond measurable financial returns, the growing strength of your company's IP portfolio can highlight your company's innovativeness and skills, encourage investors and early adopters, deter aggressive competitors, attract cooperative business relationships, and provide further leverage in licensing negotiations.

Your IP Team, relying on the expertise of competent counsel will vigorously pursue the most promising of the available opportunities while applying resources consistently with your company's mission, core values, and strategic directions.

70+ Tactics for Exploiting Your IP

To highlight some of the ways to harness, extract, and exploit the value and power of your company's intellectual properties, I have compiled the following 70+ tactics.

1.   *Capture intellectual properties.*

By inventorying your company's know-how and innovative concepts, and/or by describing how to implement them, such as via laboratory notebooks, innovation disclosure forms, and/or patent applications, your company can easily convert slippery or tacit thoughts into discrete, manageable, and marketable intellectual properties.

2.   *Manage knowledge and innovations.*

Once inventoried or described in writing, your company's know-how and innovative concepts can be much more easily tracked, protected, and developed, thereby preventing the loss, neglect, or mismanagement of your company's crown jewels – its valuable intellectual properties.

3.   *Get instant protection.*

By properly exploiting trade secrets, marks, and copyrights, your company can obtain enforceable rights immediately, inexpensively, and informally. When the potential risk-adjusted returns justify the costs, your company can seek to supplement and complement those rights via patenting, mark registration, and copyright registration.

4. *Slow idea leakage.*

By securing patent protection on at least some of its innovative concepts, your company can further discourage the theft or use of the trade secrets and know-how associated with those concepts, since any receiver of that information likely still will incur patent infringement liability if it attempts to implement those patented concepts.

5. *Highlight originality, cleverness, and skills.*

Through patent publications, your company can draw attention to its potentially patentable concepts, explain how to implement those concepts, and provide contact information for the company, thereby allowing others to discover your company's innovations, talents, and potential.

6. *Discover opportunities.*

When your company stays aware of other's innovations and technical developments, it can spot opportunities for improvement more easily, and then quickly move to fill those opportunities by creating valuable innovations of its own.

7. *Identify company's strengths.*

By searching closely related technologies, your company can discover which of its concepts are truly innovative, avoid re-inventing what is already known, and align future research and development efforts with the company's most unique and valuable skill sets.

8. *Avoid re-innovation.*

When your company stays aware of other's developments, it knows from whom to purchase or license existing solutions, thereby avoiding re-innovating what is known, freeing-up company resources for creating true innovations, and accelerating product development and time to market.

9.   Solve real problems.

Knowing that its efforts can be richly rewarded, your company can be inspired to keep a tight focus on the market's needs, how existing solutions don't fulfill those needs, and what it must do to discover and develop real and innovative solutions that generate substantial returns.

10.   Focus company's efforts.

Knowing the likely financial value of its most significant innovations, brands, and works, your company can elect to vigorously pursue those that will likely produce the highest risk-adjusted return on investment values for your company's IP portfolio.

11.   Rally the troops.

When a company's management can explain to its employees, in concrete, well-supported, financial terms, why the company has elected to pursue its chosen IP-related goals, those employees are more likely to understand their role in fulfilling those goals, to align their efforts with the company's objectives, and to go above and beyond in helping the company succeed.

12.   Improve time to market.

By identifying those innovations having the highest RARE values, your company will know which innovations deserve the most resources, thereby shortening their R&D timeline and accelerating their market introduction.

13.   Measure company's value.

Often, the intellectual assets of a company are its most valuable assets. By cataloging the intellectual assets of your company (or an acquisition or investment target), assigning reasonable RARE values to the most mission-critical intellectual assets, and analyzing those values, you can obtain a reasonable proxy for the valuation of the company as a whole.

14. Promote and increase company's value.

Perceptions of your company's value can be improved by drawing attention to its full palette of intellectual assets, emphasizing the protections being sought for your company's mission-critical innovations, and clearly explaining the significance, potential, and value of your company's most game-changing intellectual assets.

15. Advertise know-how availability.

Often, deals involving commercialization of patent protected concepts are absolutely dependent on the transfer of the associated know-how and/or trade secrets. Thus, the publication of your company's patent applications and patents can serve as advertisements that it holds relevant, yet secret know-how for implementing the patented concepts, and that it is potentially willing to sell and/or license both the patent rights and the know-how to others who want to commercialize them.

16. Inspire investments, mergers, and/or acquisitions.

The strength of your company's IP portfolio can help convince investors and potential collaborators that your company is managed and staffed appropriately to succeed in profitably commercializing its innovations, thereby encouraging favorable investments and business collaborations.

17. Secure financing.

Your company's IP can serve as collateral in the event the company is forced to default on repayment, can provide a lender a recordable security interest, and sometimes can be held in escrow pending repayment.

18. Negotiate better terms.

The more innovations that your company publicizes, the higher the quality of those publications, and the more IP protections the company is able to attain, the more likely that investors, lenders, and licensees will agree to terms that are favorable to your company.

19.   Immortalize inventors.

Each patent document that publishes one of your company's innovations serves as a permanent written commemoration of the contributions of the named inventors, enhancing both their reputation and your company's.

20.   Retain innovative employees.

By adopting an appropriate innovation incentive program, your company can timely and lucratively reward its innovative workers, thereby inspiring them to continue innovating, and to continue assisting the company as their innovations are commercialized.

21.   Pre-empt disputes.

Recognizing how innovations emerge, your company can put appropriate procedures and agreements in place requiring that innovations be promptly documented, disclosed, and assigned to the company, thereby largely avoiding future creation and ownership disputes.

22.   Extend competitive advantage indefinitely.

For each of its publicized innovations, your company can discover and develop dozens of related and extremely valuable implementation details after patent protection is timely sought.   If carefully managed, your company can **indefinitely maintain** that valuable know-how via trade secrecy, potentially even if patent protection is denied, or long after patent protection has expired.

23.   Supplement and complement other IP.

Although patent applications must enable others to implement their claimed concepts, and describe the best manner known to any of the named inventors at the time for doing so, as your company improves, replaces, and optimizes those implementation details, it has the opportunity to protect them as trade secrets for an indefinite period of time.   These vital trade secrets can add tremendous value to any license your company offers to others who seek to commercialize the patented concepts.

24. Deter inadvertent disclosure or use.

By identifying its know-how and labeling it appropriately, your company can remind its workforce of what to keep confidential, and, just in case something leaks, can remind the public and competitors what the company considers to be proprietary.

25. Benefit society.

In exchange for receiving exclusive patent rights to its innovations, your company will teach the world how to implement those innovations, thereby improving the world's knowledge base.   In addition, if your company's patented innovations are implemented and brought to market, society as a whole is likely to benefit from the improvements and advantages inherent in those innovations.

26. Educate market about innovative features.

By carefully using and enforcing its patents and copyrights, your company can publicize its innovations and works without fear of having them ripped-off with impunity by pirates or copycats.

27. Distinguish goods and services.

Via publicizing its innovations, your company can begin to teach its customers how its innovative concepts, as implemented in your company's goods and services, better solve the customer's problems when compared to the inferior solutions offered by your competitors.

28. Encourage early adopters.

Those potential customers that are most hungry for new solutions to their challenging problems will be the most willing, upon learning about your company's valuable innovations, to purchase your company's goods and services that embody those innovations.

29. *Foster industry standards.*

By offering non-exclusive, extremely affordable or royalty-free licenses to one or more of your company's innovations, your company can help establish those concepts as industry standards, which can very quickly build the reputation of the company. Also, because your company likely has a head-start on understanding and implementing those concepts, it can potentially lead the market in developing goods, services, and even other innovations based on the standards those concepts have fostered.

30. *Strengthen branding and/or positioning.*

Your company can use its marks to select a distinctive brand, build widespread awareness of that brand, extend the brand to related goods and/or services, and educate the market about the innovative features of the branded goods and services to further strengthen the brand and the company's desired market positioning.

31. *Diversify markets.*

As your company continues to educate its markets, it can gain the ability to expand, segregate, and precisely serve the needs of those markets based on specific innovative product features.

32. *Grow market share, revenues, and/or profits.*

The better your company's innovations solve substantial real-world problems, the better the company's ability to attract customers who are willing to pay more for those innovative solutions.

33. *Improve public relations.*

Because its innovations tend to solve problems better, faster, cheaper, etc. than previous solutions, or because its works tend to provide new aesthetic pleasures (paintings, music, literature, etc.), publicizing your company's innovations and works can lead to good press for your company.

34. Create loyal consumers.

With each newly publicized innovation, your company will build consumer trust that it is aware of customers' problems and needs that competitors ignore, and will clearly demonstrate its focus on and dedication to creatively solving those problems and fulfilling those needs.

35. Attract talented employees.

The more innovations and creative works your company publicizes, the more likely that innovatively and creatively talented prospects will seek out employment with the company.

36. Control exploitation.

By properly protecting its intellectual assets, your company will secure court-enforceable rights to exclude others from implementing the company's innovations, and can then license chosen others to practice those rights when, where, and how the company desires, or even completely refuse to license anyone if that better fits your strategic directions.

37. Finance assertion of IP rights.

Given the very costly nature of most IP litigation, the purchase of IP assertion insurance can level the playing field by allowing a small company to assert selected IP rights against a deep-pocketed competitor. In exchange for the payment of relatively moderate premiums, the small company will have the financial muscle to sustain the litigation while exercising control over their litigation attorneys, strategies, and settlement terms.

38. Design around other's IP.

The better your company knows how it has protected its own IP, the better it can determine the scope of a competitor's IP, investigate and implement commercially-feasible technical alternatives, and successfully avoid infringing on competitors' patent rights.

39. *Ensure prolonged market success.*

By performing clearance and non-infringement searches, your company can improve the odds that it does not infringe the patent or trademark rights of others, thus ensuring that any market success it achieves likely will not be cut short by infringement liability.

40. *Break competitors' strangleholds.*

Via carefully analyzing a competitor's patent, your company might be able to show that your planned implementations don't infringe that patent, or that the patent's claims are invalid. This knowledge can allow your company to comfortably enter the market, knowing that it can successfully defend against any infringement allegations raised by the competitor. In some cases, your company might even benefit from challenging the competitor's patent, such as by initiating re-examination seeking to convince the USPTO to cancel the patent.

41. *Pry open new markets.*

When your company's innovations are well-protected, the company has lined-up the financial muscle (e.g., via patent assertion insurance) to enforce those protections, and those innovations truly fill a pressing market need, your company will be well-positioned to carve out and grow a substantial market niche without fear of being excluded or trampled by the much larger competitors that previously dominated that market.

42. *Squash weak competitors.*

Although IP litigation can be very expensive to complete, most such suits settle long before the legal costs become sky-high. Nevertheless, fear of those costs can allow a reasonably well-funded company (such as one that has a good IP assertion insurance policy) to drive poorly-funded competitors (such as those that do not have a good IP defense insurance policy) from the market, or into paying a substantial, perhaps crushing, payment to settle the case.

43. Unnerve competitors' investors.

Investors who are considering making a substantial investment in a competitor can become discouraged when they discover that your company owns IP rights that could potentially ensnare that competitor in a costly infringement lawsuit. Such investors often will not be encouraged by arguments that the competitor might prevail in such a suit, for the simple fact that most investors don't want to buy into ANY litigation threat.

44. Thwart competitors' growth.

Careful study of a competitor's products and IP can identify the direction a competitor is headed and lead your company to create and secure a suite of innovative improvements, thereby fencing off the competitor and opening up opportunities for your company to exploit those improvements.

45. Hinder design-arounds.

When your company acquires patent protection for all technically feasible alternatives to its core innovative concepts, your company thereby forces its competitors to come to terms with your potentially insurmountable wall of patents or risk potentially devastating infringement liability.

46. Discourage attacks on your company's markets.

Those competitors who encounter a wall of patents surrounding your company's desirable innovations typically will be greatly discouraged from competing in your company's markets, or will be forced to deal with your company on its chosen terms.

47. Block competitors from entering potential future markets.

Upon carefully evaluating a formidable thicket of IP rights your company has developed around its innovations, many competitors will be dissuaded from considering even undeveloped markets that your company clearly plans to eventually enter to commercialize those innovations.

48.   *Dominate unprotected markets.*

Through careful selection of the countries in which it protects its intellectual assets, your company can leverage its enhanced profitability in those protected markets to subsidize, where legally allowed, competition busting prices in markets where it lacks intellectual property protection.

49.   *Conquer competitor's technologies.*

In some situations, your company might be able to convince a proven infringing competitor to license or trade-away some of its valuable core technologies to avoid being forced out of business while attempting to pay court-ordered damages for infringing your company's intellectual property rights.

50.   *Attract cooperative business relationships.*

An impressive IP portfolio will tend to strongly encourage others (e.g., investors, suppliers, customers, competitors) to seriously consider building a robust working relationship with your company.

51.   *Gain desired capabilities.*

By leveraging its IP, your company can secure needed research, manufacturing, distribution, marketing, and/or sales capabilities with little or no capital investment by the company. With an IP-based supply or purchase agreement, your company can rely on its exclusive intellectual property rights over goods and/or services to allow a chosen supplier to make specified goods and deliver them only to your company. Similarly, via a licensing arrangement, such as in exchange for receiving royalties and/or other compensation, your company can apply its exclusive intellectual property rights over goods and/or services by allowing chosen others to, per your terms: make implementations of your company's concepts; use the company's innovative concepts to research specific implementations and/or improvements; import goods made in an unprotected country into a protected country; and/or distribute, advertise, and sell authorized goods in particular markets.

52. *Earn licensing revenues.*

Using good licensing practices, your company can collect negotiated royalties on other's sales of products covered by your company's IP rights.

53. *Land favorable business deals.*

To attract a desired deal, your company can combine the license and/or sale of its IP rights or assets with lucrative supply agreements, technical consulting contracts, and/or know-how sharing arrangements. By packaging an attractive deal, you can convert a challenging relationship into a cooperative one.

54. *Win cross-licenses.*

Often, once it has secured market-respected IP, your company will be able to offer a competitor a license to that IP in exchange for receiving a license to the competitor's valuable IP.

55. *Pool patents among competitors.*

Your company might be legally permitted to persuade its competitors to pool their patents and cross-license each other to practice those patents, thereby cutting uncertainty and costs for all by avoiding messy, complex, and expensive infringement suits.

56. *Collateralize desired projects.*

By allowing a lender to hold and record a security interest in certain IP owned by your company, that IP can secure and ensure the availability of crucial funding for growth of your company.

57. *Inhibit raids on your employees.*

By applying well-drafted employment and confidentiality agreements and by properly protecting your company's trade secrets, your company can inhibit its competitors from attempting to hire-away your most innovative and/or knowledgeable personnel.

58. Dissuade key employee turnover.

Through the use of well-drafted employment agreements and via best practices for protecting your company's trade secrets, your company can dissuade its valuable innovators and most knowledgeable workers from considering your competitors' offers of employment.

59. Neutralize competitive threats.

Sometimes, it will be possible for your company to covertly and legally obtain rights to a competitor's IP via deals with the competitor's licensees. Those obtained rights thereby can shield your company from liability for infringing the competitor's rights in that IP.

60. Detect intruders rapidly.

By employing patent and trademark surveillance or "watch" services, your company can rapidly detect the emergence of competitive threats, including potentially infringing activities, before those competitors can firmly establish themselves in your hard-won markets.

61. Prevent, oppose, and resolve disputes, suits, and liabilities.

Leveraging its IP defensively, such as by counter-suing for infringement of its rights in that IP, your company can convince others to avoid or settle disputes regarding your company's allegedly infringing activities.

62. Force competitors into painful positions.

When your company exercises its rights to exclude (which are inherent in each intellectual property) against a competitor, your company can force that competitor to exit a desired market, re-design their product, drop market share, and/or absorb a substantial loss.

63. Halt thieves in their tracks.

When you timely learn that your company's trade secrets have been misappropriated, you can rapidly obtain a court-issued injunction that prevents the thief, and anyone who obtained your trade secrets as a result of the misappropriation, from disclosing or using your trade secrets until a court has had ample time to sort out the matter.

64. Obtain injunctions.

Your company can obtain a federal court-enforceable order that prevents others from making, using, promoting, and/or selling goods and/or services that have been proven to infringe your company's IP rights.

65. Exclude imports.

Federal court orders also can be obtained to prevent infringing goods from entering the country's ports and competing against your company's goods. Such orders allow the U.S. Customs Service to prevent importers from off-loading from trucks, ships, or airplanes any goods that have been shown to infringe your company's IP rights.

66. Seize infringing goods.

A court-issued seizure order allows federal law enforcement agencies to take possession of proven infringing goods. Such orders are typically implemented by the U.S. Marshals Service, and sometimes by the U.S. Customs Service, who use all necessary force to secure the goods and prevent anyone not authorized by the court from moving, handling, or even approaching them.

67. Impose substantial costs on competitors.

An injunction prohibiting a competitor from infringing your company's patent can force that competitor to stop manufacturing and selling an infringing product, thereby imposing serious costs on your competitor for legal fees, inventory loss, retooling, and/or advertising revisions.

68. Receive statutory damages.

When your company proves infringement of its registered copyrighted works via a federal lawsuit, the court is obligated to award statutorily defined monetary damages. The huge benefit of this approach is that you do not have to prove your actual damages. Instead you only need to prove that the infringer had access to your work (which is typically trivial assuming your work was published) and that their infringing work is substantially similar to yours, while deflecting any of the infringer's defenses, such as the fair use defense.

69. Win monetary damages.

Courts will typically force proven infringers of a company's IP rights to pay compensatory damages to that company. Depending on the type of IP and the facts of the infringement, your company can gain: the profits your company would have earned; the profits the competitor actually earned; a reasonable royalty assuming an arm's length licensing deal between your company and the competitor; and/or statutorily defined damages.

70. Collect enhanced damages.

Courts can order a competitor to pay your company up to 3 times the identified monetary damages when a competitors' infringement of your company's patent is proven to be willful.

71. Recoup litigation expenses.

Although an exception to the rule that each party must pay its own litigation costs, a court can force a proven infringer who engages in serious litigation misconduct to reimburse the winner (your company) for its reasonable attorneys' fees and other litigation expenses. Such litigation misconduct can include: frivolous lawsuits; overzealous advocacy; willful infringement of an asserted patent; and/or inequitable conduct in acquiring an asserted patent. The losing party must have acted in bad faith or at least with gross negligence in bringing or maintaining the suit. Conversely, by carefully analyzing its IP rights and the evidence of infringement, your company can avoid being on the wrong end of this painful court-ordered remedy.

72. Inflict criminal sanctions.

Although not available in every country, in some situations in the U.S., an infringing competitor can be held criminally liable for misappropriating your company's trade secrets, counterfeiting the company's trademarked goods, and/or infringing your company's copyrights.

73. Preclude blockades.

Promptly seeking protections for your company's innovative concepts can secure them before competitors do. Likewise, by acting timely, your company can purchase or obtain exclusive rights to other's pioneering concepts on which your company's innovative concepts build before competitors take advantage of the opportunity to lock-up those rights and thereby potentially block you from implementing your innovations.

74. Obtain tax deductions.

In certain situations, your company can donate an unwanted intellectual property to a U.S. charitable organization and earn a reasonable U.S. income tax deduction for the proven value of the actual revenues that charitable organization earns from the donated IP.

75. Earn assignment revenues.

At the appropriate time, your company can sell an under-utilized or unwanted intellectual property to extract at least a minimal return on what otherwise would be a wasting intellectual asset.

76. Reduce costs.

Your company can abandon the pursuit or maintenance of an intellectual property that is undesired and of insufficient value to donate or sell.

77. Prepare for re-launch.

When, due to dwindling funds, a company is on track to wind down (but not become insolvent), rather than disappear with no hope for revival, the company can relatively inexpensively retain and maintain some of its valuable IP rights until its successors can raise new financing with which to re-launch the company.

78. *Challenge slavish copiers*

Design patents can fill a vital role in the IP portfolio of certain companies. For example, because design patents tend to issue much more quickly than utility patents, design patents can be helpful for expediting your company's ability to challenge slavish copiers. Also, because infringement of a design patent tends to be simpler to analyze, pursuing an infringement action, and obtaining an infringement verdict against blatant pirates, can be much simpler, quicker, and cheaper than pursuing infringers of a utility patent.

79. *Unbundle your rights*

Licenses allow the IP owner to split the "bundle" of rights associated with owning a given intellectual property, in any of a wide variety of directions. An IP licensor can control which specific IP rights the licensee is permitted to implement, making licensing a very powerful and valuable tool for maximizing the return on the IP.

Implementing The Tactics – A Few Examples

As has probably become very apparent, optimizing your company's intellectual property power involves the exercise of thoughtful leverage, including the inter-related activities of appropriately generating, developing, securing, and utilizing that IP power. The following examples briefly illustrate not only some of these inter-relationships, but also how your company can implement some of the above-described tactics for optimally exploiting its IP power.

Acquire Intellectual Assets via Agreements

Whenever your company hires an employee or consultant, or collaborates with another company, there can be several relevant intellectual property concerns.

Of immediate concern is protecting your existing and future know-how, including your trade secrets, from theft and undesired disclosure. Also important is assuring that the other company does not taint your company with any information they are not permitted to disclose, such as the trade secrets of a third party.

Another significant concern is who will own and control any intellectual assets that are created as a result of the employment, consultation, or collaboration. This concern can become absolutely critical if the assets become highly valuable.

For employees, resolving this concern is rather simple. A well-drafted Employment Agreement will specify that all intellectual assets developed using company resources or within the company's field(s) of endeavor are automatically assigned upon their creation.

For consultants, the concern might be simple, assuming the company can convince the consultant to agree to similar terms as are contained in the company's Employment Agreements. Otherwise, whether the consultation arrangement should be entered should be carefully considered.

For collaborating companies, the concern is often much tougher to resolve. Sometimes, the other entity (including universities seeking research funding from your company) will have policies that prohibit them from assigning any intellectual asset created by their personnel (even when created jointly with your personnel) to your company. At other times, the other entity will simply smell money and want a piece of the action.

In any event, if you don't address this issue proactively, and a patentable innovation is created by joint inventors, the law defaults to joint ownership. That means that each inventor owns the entire innovation, and may exploit it as desired without accounting to any other owner. In other words, once the other entity's personnel assign their interest in the innovation to their employer, that entity is free to: bring implementations to market, license the innovative concept so that another party can bring it to market, or even sell their rights to your most hated competitor. This is obviously a sub-optimal situation!

Sometimes this issue can be resolved by setting-up a joint venture to which all joint innovations are assigned, and the profits from which are shared in some predetermined fashion.

At other times, you might be able to convince the other company to assign its interest in all joint innovations to your company, in exchange for you licensing those joint innovations to that other company under very favorable terms. Your company might be better able to persuade the other company to take this approach by offering to include in the deal a license to some of your other highly desired IP.

As you can see, if your company already has the leverage necessary to force its desired terms, such as when you are an employer utilizing a well-drafted Employment Agreement, there need be little concern over the ownership and control of any intellectual assets that arise. But when your leverage seems lacking, the power of your other IP sometimes can be harnessed to structure a deal favorably, and position your company for even greater long-term gains.

Integrate Protections for Intellectual Assets

Often, a company can and should secure a given intellectual asset using more than one type of intellectual property protection. For example, the basic functionality of a given innovative concept potentially can be protected via a utility patent. Yet certain implementation details for that concept often can and should be protected as trade secrets too. Moreover, if there are aesthetic features to the concept's commercialization, they might benefit from design patent protection. Of course, any mark or artistic work associated with the concept's commercialization should be considered for federal registration.

By taking an integrative approach to its intellectual asset strategy, your company can expand its intellectual property protections to cover more subject matter from more angles, thereby strengthening its abilities to exclude competitors, obtaining additional legal remedies for infringement, and/or securing backup legal rights and remedies if a primary form of intellectual property protection becomes invalid.

Make a Deal

So let's say you've really done it right. You've carefully followed the guidance presented in this book. Your company has brilliantly created, developed, and/or acquired a valuable intellectual property. Along the way, you've carefully avoided creating IP risks, mitigated all that you can, and followed best practices to add even more value to your company's IP. You've seriously considered the probable costs and returns associated with that IP, and know its likely RARE value. And you've even thoughtfully marketed your company's IP and found a strong prospect that sincerely wants to obtain rights to it.

Raking in fantastic returns on your IP investment should be a piece of cake from here on out, right? Well not necessarily.

Far too often, I have seen great IP deals unravel, simply due to poor deal-making practices. Hundreds of hours and thousands of dollars wasted. Promising relationships shattered and fantastic opportunities squandered. Buckets of blood, sweat, and tears down the drain. And yet all of this hardship could have been rather easily prevented, at comparatively low cost, and with relatively minimal hassle, frustration, and pain.

So let me share a few tips about how I believe you should approach striking a deal involving your IP. But before I do so, let's explore a few basics of how IP deals can be structured.

Sometimes, your company is willing to simply sell its IP, parting with it outright and completely. In that case, the deal-making process usually is very simple. Learn what IP the other party wants to buy. Determine that your company is willing to sell it. Negotiate the price (hopefully relying on your thoughtful market research, risk analysis, and RARE valuation for that IP). So long as the terms of the sale are no more complex than that (i.e., what is being sold, to whom, and at what price), I have been able to draft an assignment document to memorialize such a sale in very short order and at a rather low cost. Typically in these situations, it is a very easy process.

But far more often, your company will prefer to retain ownership of its intellectual property, only being willing to grant one or more licenses to certain rights in that IP in particular markets or fields of use that fit well with the company's IP strategy and tactics.

Licenses can be very powerful tools, for a number of reasons. First, they allow the IP owner to split the "bundle" of rights associated with owning a given intellectual property, in any of a wide variety of directions. Here are a few examples:

- The owner of a trade secret might be willing to grant to a "licensee" the right to *use* that trade secret, but not the right to *disclose* it to others. This situation is very common when purchasing custom equipment, and also in the contract manufacturing, custom programming, and franchising realms, among many others.

- A patent owner might grant a right to *make* (or possibly *have made*) implementations of the patented concept, but not the right to *use* those implementations, or to *sell* them to anyone other than the patent owner. This scenario is rather typical in contract manufacturing deals.

- The owner of a mark (the "licensor") might grant a licensee the right to apply the mark to certain products sold by the licensee, provided those products continually meet particular quality standards set by the licensor. How happy would Happy Meals® be without licensed cartoon characters to spice up the food?

- A copyright holder might grant a license to *publish*, *distribute*, or *perform* a work, but not to *create derivative* works from it. The Beatles might have licensed Apple to distribute their music via iTunes®, but not to create revised versions of, for example, "Hey Jude", "Let It Be", or "Strawberry Fields Forever".

As these examples illustrate, an IP licensor can control which specific IP rights the licensee is permitted to implement.

Moreover, the IP owner can decide whether there will be one licensee or many. Generally, when there is only a single licensee for a given right, the license is considered "exclusive", and when there are many licensees, the license is called "non-exclusive". Everything else being equal, an exclusive license is worth more than a non-exclusive, since the licensee has rights that its competitors can not acquire.

In addition, the IP owner can further control the who, what, where, when, and how of the IP rights, to nearly any desired degree of detail. For example, an IP license can specify permitted raw material suppliers, product features, sales territories, warranty periods, advertisement placement, and nearly anything else relevant to any implementation of the licensed IP rights.

The variety of possible terms that can be open to negotiation is effectively infinite, allowing a license to be precisely customized to the particular needs and desires of all its parties.

As you might imagine, the combination of all of these terms can effect and define the value of the license. Consistent with the flexible nature of licensing, that value can be monetized, realized, and captured by the IP owner in any of several ways. For example, a license can require payment by the licensee of:

- "up-front" fees;

- periodic minimum fees;

- "milestone" fees; and/or

- on-going "royalties".

Each of these types of payments has its own particular purposes, advantages, and disadvantages. For example, like "earnest money" in a real estate deal, the up-front fee can serve to signal to the licensor that the potential licensee is seriously interested in working out a deal. Depending on when the up-front fee is paid, it can serve to compensate the licensor for investing time negotiating with the potential licensee. Up-front fees also can guarantee the licensor some return regardless of whether the licensee fulfills all the objectives of the license, and/or can help the licensor build a "war chest" to fund enforcement of its intellectual property rights against infringers.

From the licensee's perspective, however, up-front fees can be undesired and risky, as they require a significant payout before the licensee has proven it can earn a significant return from implementing the licensed IP rights. Up-front fees are also undesired because they typically will not be returned if the IP rights turn out to be invalid.

The next fee to consider is the "minimum". Like up-front fees, periodically-paid minimum fees can signal to the licensor that the licensee remains interested in implementing the IP rights, and can prod the licensee into action, so that they are not paying for nothing. When required, minimum fees are often due on a quarterly or annual basis, but can be due according to any desired schedule.

Milestone fees differ from minimums in that milestone fees are tied to an event or occurrence rather than to a schedule. For example, a milestone fee could be paid upon delivery by the licensor of written documentation of certain know-how. Or a milestone could be paid upon issuance of a patent claiming a particular concept. Milestones also can be tied to licensee performance, such as landing regulatory approval for a product or service that implements certain licensed IP rights.

The fee most folks think of when they hear the word "license" is the royalty. From the licensor's perspective, on-going or "running" royalties can allow the licensor to share in the upside potential of the licensee's opportunity. Thus, if the licensee achieves fantastic sales revenues or profits, the licensor can benefit from that success. When negotiating the deal, if the likelihood of such success appears to be high, the licensor might be willing to take a lower percentage than if the odds of the licensee's success seem rather low.

From the licensee's perspective, royalties tend to preserve cash early-on, only requiring a payout if and after implementation of the IP rights proves successful. Yet when success arrives, on-going royalties can seem like somewhat of a "tax" or "drag" on that success. Thus, the more successful the licensee becomes, the more incentive they can have to try to invalidate the IP rights, thereby freeing the licensee from infringement liability and/or the royalty payment requirements of the license. On the other hand, if the licensee discovers that those IP rights are strong, and they hold those rights exclusively, they likely will be greatly motivated to help enforce those rights against their competitors, thereby preserving the market exclusively to themselves.

Like nearly any contract, a license can be revoked or cancelled if either party does not perform as the license requires, or can be designed to expire after a specified period of time or upon the occurrence of a particular event. Such expirations can be double-edged swords, potentially benefiting licensors by allowing them to re-negotiate more favorable terms if the licensee has earned substantial profits from implementing the IP rights, yet potentially allowing less-profitable licensees to escape from license terms that have become uncomfortably burdensome.

So far I have briefly discussed licensing terms such as the particular rights licensed, the exclusivity of the license, and licensing payments. Other substantial terms can involve any of:

- exclusive negotiation periods and/or rights of first refusal;

- restrictions on type of use (e.g., research, non-commercial, non-profit, etc.), fields of use, distribution channels, marketing, territories, etc.;

- ability to sub-license, assign, and/or transfer;

- cross-licensing of the licensee's IP to the licensor;

- prosecution of patent applications and/or mark registration applications;

- payment of patent maintenance and/or annuity fees;

- marking and/or quality control requirements;

- enforcement of the IP rights against past and/or present infringers;

- ownership and licensing of improvements and/or joint creations;

- encumbrances, escrow, and/or effects of bankruptcy;

- confidentiality, non-competition, and/or publicity;

- warranties, bonding, and/or indemnification;

- liquidated damages, dispute resolution, and/or survival of terms;

- and many, many more.

But rather than attempting to describe all of the potential terms of a license, I will now turn to how best to negotiate those terms, and most importantly, how to close the deal.

Often, soon after beginning to negotiate the terms of an IP license, a company will seek to heavily involve their IP attorney. This impulse is understandable, given that complex IP rights are involved, and that there can be a lot riding on the deal. But too easily, deals can turn sour once the attorneys get involved. And by sour, I mean the deal goes south, becomes overly complex, and falls apart. Why does that happen?

The answer is quite simple, as is the solution to the problem. Recognize foremost that good IP attorneys are skilled at spotting risks, designing contract language to avoid those risks, and arguing about why their proposed terms are better than those of the attorneys representing the other party(s) to the agreement. Yet this sort of extreme risk avoidance mentality quickly can become expensive, time-consuming, and adversarial. Any wonder deals so easily turn sour?

Unlike experienced entrepreneurs, managers, and investors, only relatively few IP attorneys truly understand that business is all about taking calculated risks. As skilled business folks instinctively know, the trick is to timely identify the extent of a risk, determine whether it can be easily mitigated, and if not, whether it is worth absorbing. Yet due to their training, most IP lawyers simply don't understand this way of thinking.

So what is the solution? Most often, it involves sticking to the following rather simple process, which I prefer for negotiating the terms of the typical intellectual property license, managing the distribution of its risks, and mostly importantly, closing the deal.

1. Businesspeople identify and negotiate basic terms.

Start by working out the terms of the deal before asking the lawyers to draft the licensing document. Then, there's little for the lawyers to fuss about, because you've already worked it all out with the other side.

But how do you know you've agreed to the right terms? Excellent question.

2. Attorney reviews and advises of potential risks.

The answer is to consult with your IP attorney while you are negotiating the terms of the deal, having him or her help you identify the nature and extent of the associated risks, and how best to minimize or avoid them.

But don't have your attorney draft those terms into a license agreement just yet.

3. Businesspeople identify and negotiate detailed terms.

Instead, write them in your own simplified language, and negotiate them, perhaps iteratively, with your business counter-part on the other side without a bunch of lawyers in the room or on the call. In that way, you should be able to arrive at a "term sheet" that lists, perhaps as bullet points and in plain English, the significant objectives and terms of the deal in 2 to 4 pages or so.

4. Attorney crafts legal provisions.

When both sides are comfortable with those term sheets, then choose one side to draft the license agreement, requiring that it not deviate from or add to, in any substantial degree, the agreed terms.

Although there will still be a few details to hammer out in the draft license agreement, this approach should minimize your attorney bills, and should prevent the "Chicken Little" or "Big Bad Wolf" situations of excess risk avoidance or unnecessarily adversarial stances that can devalue or kill the deal.

5. ***Businesspeople sign agreed-upon contractual document.***

Make it official by signing the finalized Agreement and successfully closing the deal.

The flowchart on the following page depicts the process laid out here and that I prefer for negotiating the terms and closing a licensing deal.

THE LICENSING PROCESS

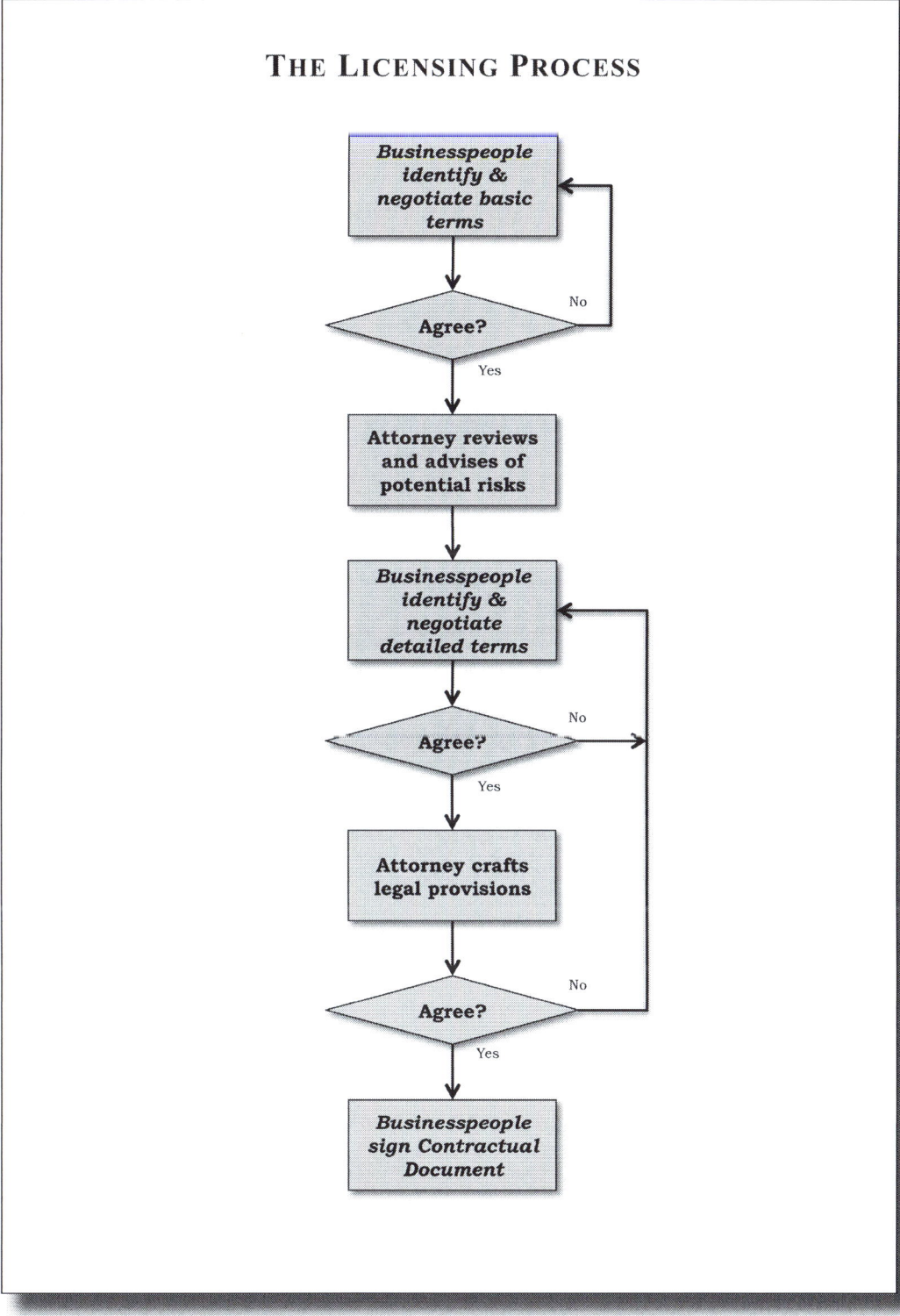

Exploit Complementary IP

Let's now take an even closer look at licensing intellectual assets and properties. In fact, the topic of licensing really makes apparent how the value of certain complementary intellectual assets, such as know-how and trade secrets, can reinforce, and be reinforced by, the value of related intellectual property, such as patents.

Earlier in this book (see page 163), I briefly discussed the constitutionally-based justification for the U.S. patent system. In a nutshell, inventors teach the world how to implement their innovation, and in exchange, are granted the rights to exclude the world from doing so for a limited period of time.

That "bundle" of granted rights includes the rights to exclude others from *making, importing, using, offering for sale,* and *selling* implementations of the claimed innovation of a valid, in-force U.S. patent. Interestingly, the owner of those bundled rights is permitted to unbundle them. That is, they can authorize another company to make, but not import, use, offer for sale, or sell, a claimed innovation. Likewise, a patent owner can authorize a different entity only to sell a claimed innovation.

And the ability to unbundle patent rights goes much further. As suggested in the previous section, a patent owner can authorize one company to sell east of the Mississippi, and another to sell west of the Mississippi, or one entity to make and import a red implementation, and another a blue one. The authorization can be exclusive or non-exclusive, transferable or not, and revocable or not. The owner can even limit an authorized party to implementing (making, using, selling, etc.) a claimed innovation only within specified technical or commercial boundaries, e.g., only within a particular industry, "field", market, or distribution channel.

The patent owner provides such authorization via a "license", which is typically documented and memorialized via a written "licensing agreement". Effectively, a license is an agreement not to exclude the other party from the specified activities, that is, a promise not to sue them for what would otherwise be an infringement of the patent.

A license need not be limited to simply authorizing the "licensee" to perform certain otherwise prohibited activities. The license can also require the licensee to take specified actions, such as making implementations according to rigid production specifications, or delivering implementations according to a strict timetable, or selling implementations at a particular price. Via a license, a patent owner, or "licensor", also can require a licensee to pay money for:

- discussing the license – this fee is similar to the "earnest money" paid in negotiations for purchasing a house, and effectively compensates the owner for taking the property off the market while trying to finalize the terms of the deal;

- granting the license – this payment is similar to a "security deposit" on a rented apartment or a "signing bonus" for a prized new employee;

- selling an implementation of the claimed innovation – this payment is often referred to as a "running royalty" and is often calculated as a percentage of the gross revenue earned on sales of licensed innovations; and/or

- keeping the license in force over time – this fee is akin to a monthly or yearly "lease" payment and is often referred to as a "minimum royalty", which need not be paid if the running royalties exceed its amount in a specified time period.

In essence, licensing offers nearly unlimited flexibility in crafting the terms of a deal. Almost always, terms can be worked out and documented that, from the perspective of each party to the agreement, appease that party's concerns and align with that party's interests. In a few relatively narrow situations, certain terms of a license might raise antitrust concerns, but nearly always such concerns can be alleviated by thoughtfully restructuring those terms.

So let's see how this incredible deal-making flexibility can play out in a real licensing situation.

I mentioned earlier in this book (see page 170) that each U.S. patent application is legally required to include a written description of the best way any of the inventors know of for implementing their claimed innovation, and in a manner that at least barely works for its intended purpose, as of the effective filing date of that application. But once the application is filed, there simply is no requirement (or ability) to update that description as those implementations are optimized. Thus, after a patent application is timely filed, lots of optimization and commercialization details can remain to be worked out, and each of those details can be maintained as a trade secret.

Yet because discovering and developing those trade secrets can require substantial experimentation and know-how, such trade secrets can be tremendously valuable. Therefore, even if a licensee acquires the rights to make and use (and possibly sell) implementations of a patented innovation, without the trade secrets, the value of those patent rights might be severely compromised, as the licensee just won't be able to implement the patented concept(s). Consequently, license agreements for patent rights very often also include a grant of rights to the associated know-how and trade secrets, for it is this vital information that will truly empower the licensee to obtain the full value of the licensed patent rights.

And just as with patent rights, the bundle of rights to know-how and trade secrets can be unbundled, divided, and limited to any desired degree. This ability includes limiting the authorization to particular times, places, fields, uses and requiring particular licensee behaviors. For example, a know-how/patent license can limit the licensee to making implementations using only a particular manufacturing process. As another example, such a license can require the licensee to share with and/or assign to the licensor (and disclose to no one else) all know-how and innovations derived from the licensed know-how.

Once again, the possibilities for harnessing the power of your intellectual assets are nearly unlimited.

Scare Investors Away from Your Competitors

Of course, your intellectual assets and properties also can be used to legally thwart, discourage, and undermine your competitors.

One interesting example of this is the ability to provoke fear, uncertainty, and doubt in your competitors' investors by patenting, or acquiring a patent to, a critical technology that each of those competitors will likely need in order to compete with your company.

A very interesting extension of this concept involves appearing to be on the path to patenting such technology. That is, merely by filing a patent application that appears to describe and claim a critical technology, even if those particular patent claims ultimately will not be granted (or eventually can be invalidated if they are granted), can potentially generate huge leverage. In particular, the fear that will arise in under-sophisticated investors who learn of such a patent application can play to your advantage if those investors are unwilling to fund your competitors, and can provide even more benefits if they instead flock to your side.

Generated properly, that fear will not be appeased by your competitors' arguments that your claims will not be granted, or if they have been granted, that they can be invalidated. For the reality is that most investors despise investing in the risks and costs inherent in potential lawsuits. Instead, they want to jump right on to a clear path to profits that is unencumbered by the risk of engaging in protracted and costly litigation.

Note that this tactic can be employed symmetrically, meaning that competitors can pull the same trick on you. Thus, if you take this path, you will need to think it through carefully, weighing the risks and benefits, and determining how to prepare and prosecute multiple patent applications that instill, and repeatedly re-instill, fear, uncertainty, and doubt in the relevant investment market.

Leverage Re-Exam to Strengthen or Destroy Patents

When your company is seriously threatened by a competitor-owned patent that claims a vital technology, or recently has even been sued for infringing such a patent, you can potentially undermine that patent while side-stepping or indefinitely deferring most of the costs of litigating over infringement, validity, and/or damages.

The USPTO offers a process via which an issued U.S. patent can be examined again, or re-examined, to verify the validity of its claims. This process can be initiated by a patent owner who desires to strengthen their patent against one or more particular pieces of prior art. It also can be initiated by anyone else, such as someone who desires to see the claims of the patent narrowed or extinguished. A re-examination request can be filed at any point during the period of enforceability of the patent.

Once a re-examination proceeding is underway, the degree to which a challenger of a patent is allowed to continue participating in that proceeding will depend on when the patent was issued. For patents that issued from applications filed on or after November 29, 1999, the challenger can participate throughout the re-examination proceeding. This participation can take the form of providing the patent examiner with strong arguments for rejecting the issued claims of the patent, pointed rebuttals to any arguments advanced by the patent owner, and solid evidence showing why even the patent owner's proposed amendments to the claims are themselves invalid and should be rejected by the examiner.

One huge benefit of re-examination is that if a company promptly initiates a re-examination proceeding after being served with a patent infringement suit, the court presiding over that suit is much more likely to be willing to postpone (or "stay") the litigation pending the outcome of the re-examination proceeding. Yet because re-examination proceedings occasionally can drag out for up to 10 or more years in the USPTO, such a stay can effectively kill the litigation, potentially permanently.

The primary downside of re-examination is that if a patent emerges from re-examination without narrowing its claims, those claims will be considered to be that much stronger, particularly with respect to prior art that was considered by the patent examiner during the re-examination.

Thus, a patent owner can leverage the re-examination process to bolster the validity of their claims, particularly when new and threatening prior art comes to light. Conversely, a patent opponent can leverage the re-examination process to destroy the validity of a patent's claims, forcing the patent owner to retreat to claims of less extensive, and potentially less valuable, scope.

Consequently, like many IP tactics, patent re-examination can be a double-edged sword that requires substantial experience and careful thought to apply profitably.

Hopefully, these examples give you plenty of food for thought about how you can better harness the power of your company's intellectual assets and properties.

T. A. EDISON.
Phonograph or Speaking Machine.

No. 200,521.   Patented Feb. 19, 1878.

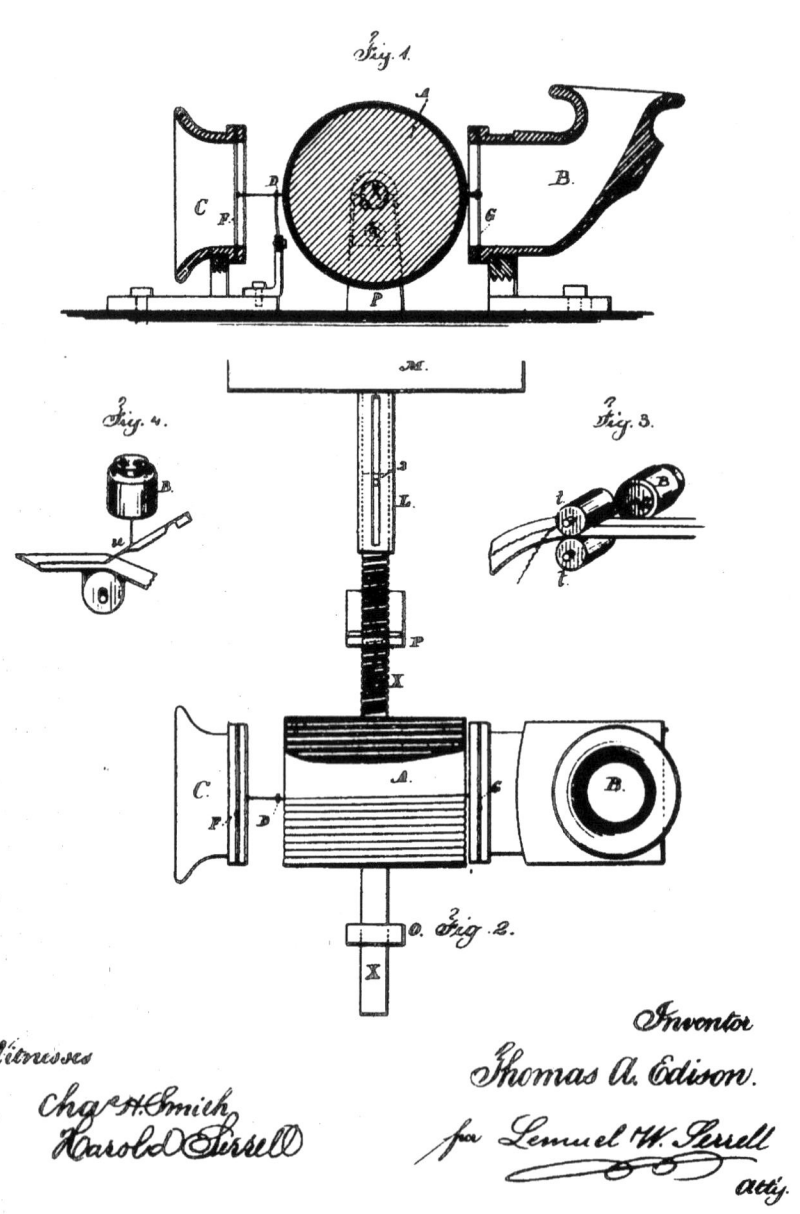

Fig. 1.

Fig. 4.   *Fig. 3.*

Fig. 2.

Witnesses   Inventor

Chas. H. Smith   Thomas A. Edison
Harold Serrell   per Lemuel W. Serrell
                                              atty.

SUMMARY

In this book, I have provided an overview of how you can strongly position your company to extract the maximum value from its intellectual property portfolio, avoid wasting thousands of dollars and hundreds of hours, and bypass unnecessary risks that can destroy that value.

In particular, I have shown how you can take these 7 steps to empower your company's intellectual property portfolio:

1. **Understand** why your company's sustained profitability almost inevitably depends on its successful exploitation of the intellectual properties that protect its most valuable innovations, know-how, and brands.

2. **Strategize** the best ways to align and manage your company's innovation process, intellectual assets, and IP, so that you can continually identify, enhance, and extract their full value.

3. **Survey** potential customer needs, market and technology trends, innovation opportunities, under-protected assets, threatening activities, infringements, and strategic relationships.

4. **Innovate** valuable solutions that can meaningfully differentiate your company from its competitors and lead to sustained profitability.

5. **Secure** your company's distinctive market position, such as by capturing and strongly protecting its intellectual assets, acquiring valuable intellectual properties, and avoiding infringements.

6. **Enhance** your company's intellectual assets, such as via careful analysis, valuation, and filtering, to optimize their value, and prepare your company to extract all of that value.

7. **Harness** the full value of each of your company's intellectual assets, applying any of my 70+ strategies and tactics.

Even if you read every word of this book, undoubtedly questions, concerns, or suggestions will remain, and others will arise from time to time. When they do, please feel free to contact me, such as via any of the mechanisms listed on my website, www.MichaelHaynes.com. While there, feel free to request any of my FREE Guides, which are updated relatively frequently.

Finally, and as always, I extend my very best wishes to you.

Here's to empowering your company's intellectual property!

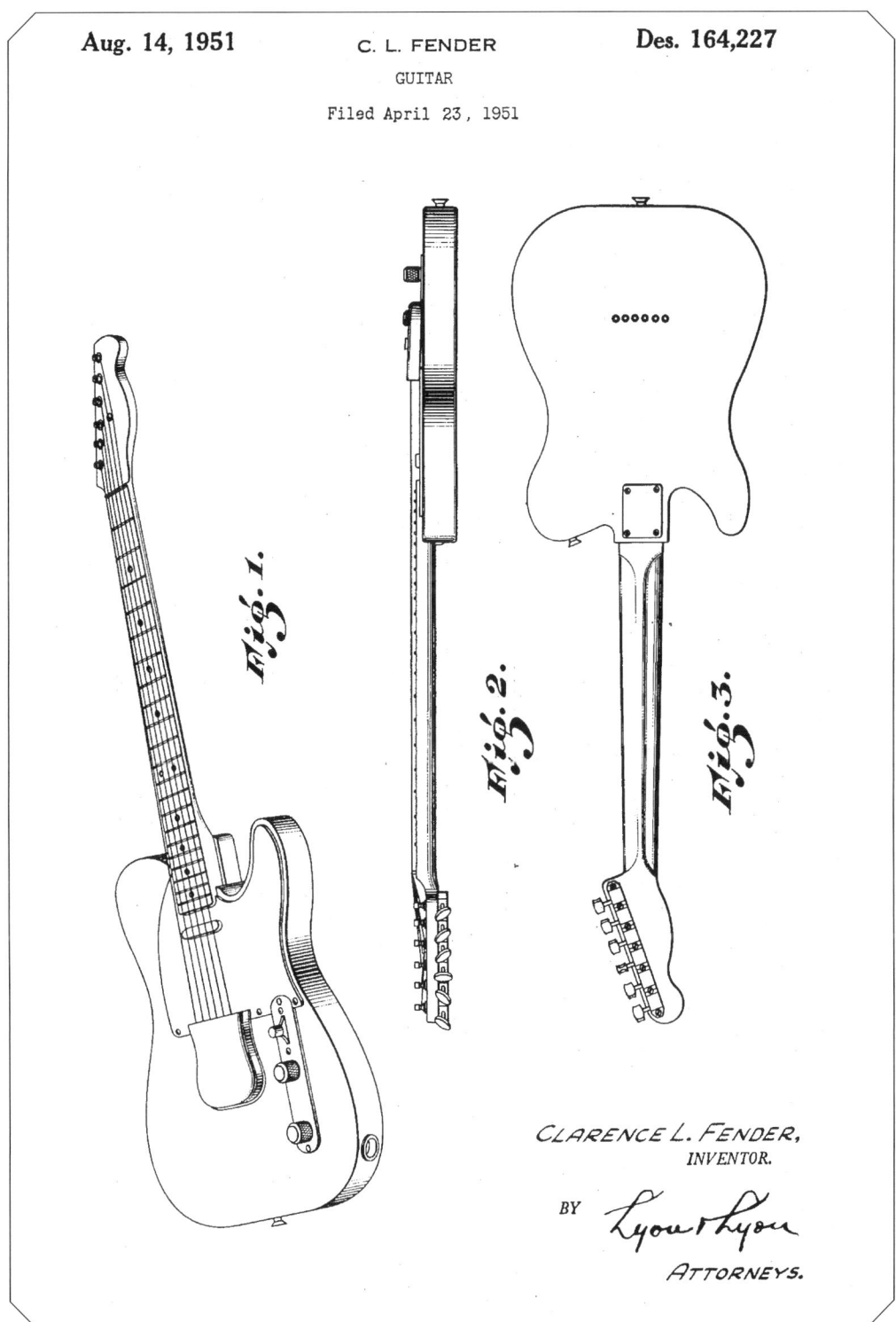

Aug. 14, 1951   C. L. FENDER   Des. 164,227

GUITAR

Filed April 23, 1951

Fig. 1.

Fig. 2.

Fig. 3.

CLARENCE L. FENDER,
INVENTOR.

BY

ATTORNEYS.

(12) **United States Design Patent**   (10) Patent No.:   **US D478,999 S**

Jobs et al.   (45) Date of Patent: ** **Aug. 26, 2003**

(54) **STAIRCASE**

(75) Inventors: **Steve Jobs**, Palo Alto, CA (US); **Karl Backus**, Emeryville, CA (US); **Rosa Sheng**, Emeryville, CA (US); **Ben McDonald**, San Francisco, CA (US); **Michael Waltner**, Berkeley, CA (US); **Colleen Caulliez**, San Francisco, CA (US); **James O'Callaghan**, New York, NY (US); **Graham Coult**, London (GB); **Damian Rogan**, New York, NY (US); **Scott Nelson**, Cirencester (GB)

(73) Assignee: **Apple Computer, Inc.**, Cupertino, CA (US)

(**) Term: **14 Years**

(21) Appl. No.: **29/164,077**

(22) Filed: **Jul. 15, 2002**

(51) LOC (7) Cl. **25-04**

(52) U.S. Cl. **D25/62**

(58) Field of Search D25/62, 69; 52/182, 52/184, 188, 190, 191

(56) **References Cited**

U.S. PATENT DOCUMENTS

5,022,197 A	*	6/1991	Aragona 52/184
D371,581 S		7/1996	Järnros
D389,588 S		1/1998	Dunk
D398,063 S		9/1998	Kline
D399,975 S	*	10/1998	Confer D25/62
D415,289 S		10/1999	Dalton
5,960,516 A		10/1999	Zoroufy et al.
D417,736 S		12/1999	Cavaness
D423,079 S		4/2000	Blount
6,059,269 A		5/2000	Ross
D428,629 S		7/2000	Cohen
D431,303 S		9/2000	Maiuccoro
6,176,027 B1		1/2001	Blount
6,205,722 B1		3/2001	Bromley et al.

* cited by examiner

Primary Examiner—Doris Clark
(74) Attorney, Agent, or Firm—Beyer Weaver & Thomas, LLP

(57) **CLAIM**

We claim the ornamental design for a staircase, substantially as shown and described.

DESCRIPTION

FIG. 1 is a perspective view of a staircase in accordance with the present design. The staircase has a transparent character.

FIG. 2 is a front view for the staircase shown in FIG. 1.

FIG. 3 is a rear view for the staircase shown in FIG. 1.

FIG. 4 is a left side view for the staircase shown in FIG. 1.

FIG. 5 is a right side view for the staircase shown in FIG. 1.

FIG. 6 is a top view for the staircase shown in FIG. 1; and,

FIG. 7 is a bottom view for the staircase shown in FIG. 1.

1 Claim, 7 Drawing Sheets

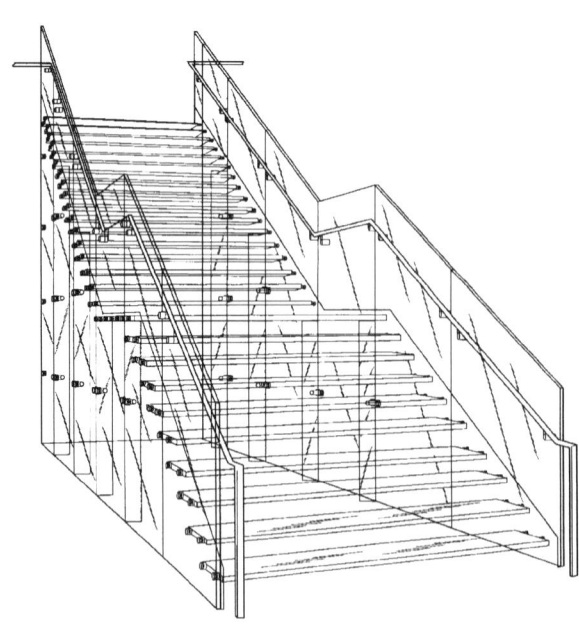

APPENDIX

INNOVATION DISCLOSURE FORM

1. General Instructions

Completion of this Innovation Disclosure Form should be considered upon conceiving a potentially valuable innovation.

1. This Form was designed to organize information about an innovation (i.e., an innovative concept, solution, idea, etc.) in a way that will greatly assist the Innovators, evaluators of the innovation, and associated patent attorneys.

2. If the timing is not urgent, consider deferring the completion of all except sections 4A, 8, and possibly 11 of this Form until after creating a Problem/Solution Statement for the innovation, and after performing an Innovation Search and/or Patentability Search.

3. To benefit those unfamiliar with the innovation, all requested information should be explained clearly.

4. Feel free to complete this Form manually or electronically.

5. If a question does not apply, write "N/A" or the like.

6. Add spaces, table rows, or sheets as needed.

7. If any unusual terms are used, or ordinary terms in an unusual way, explain those terms.

8. To protect the innovation, facts pertaining to it must be provable. Thus, all original drawings, notebooks, data, samples, records, etc., no matter how simple, should be dated, signed by the Innovator(s), properly witnessed, and carefully preserved.

9. To better describe the innovation, provide any helpful graphical information (drawings, sketches, flow charts, structural formulas, circuit diagrams, photographs, charts, or graphs, etc.). If in a computer format, please attach them in any of the standard electronic file formats (e.g., PDF, JPG, PPT, etc.).

2. This Innovator

Please complete this section of the Form *for each Innovator*, i.e., *anyone* who contributed to the conception of any innovation described via this Form.

Note that conception occurs when written evidence becomes available showing that an idea of a specific, complete, and operative implementation of the innovation was known to any Innovator, provided that, using that evidence, a person having ordinary skill in the technical field of that innovation could have constructed that implementation without extensive research or experimentation. If that implementation was actually constructed, one who only constructed that implementation and did not conceive it is not legally an Innovator.

Innovator number: _____ of _____ (total number of Innovators)

Innovator's full name:

Citizenship:

Company/Organization:

Work address:

Work Telephone/Fax:

Work E-mail:

Home mailing address:

Nature of this Innovator's contribution:

3. Conception

Conception occurs when written evidence becomes available showing that an idea of a specific, complete, and operative implementation of the innovation was known to any Innovator, provided that, using that evidence, a person having ordinary skill in the technical field of that innovation could have constructed that implementation without extensive research or experimentation.

1. When was work on the innovation begun? To avoid being locked in to a particular date, answer "At least as early as:" [a date you can easily prove].

2. When and where was the innovation conceived? At least as early as:

3. When was the innovation first described in writing in a lab notebook, computer record, or other document other than this Form? At least as early as:

4. Where is that description located?

5. When and how has the innovation been implemented (e.g., experiments, prototype, on paper only, etc.)? At least as early as:

6. What resources or facilities were used in conceiving of or implementing the innovation and by what organization were they owned or controlled?

4. The Innovation

This section of the Form is designed to capture the Innovator's current understanding of the innovation, including the best way currently known for making and for using it.

Yet before beginning to complete this section, to substantially reduce legal risks, very thoughtfully consider the dozen numbered suggestions presented in "*Step 5 – Secure*", under the heading "*How should an innovation be described?*".

A.   Overview

1.   Provide a short descriptive title for the innovation:

2.   What problem does the innovation solve?

3.   What does the innovation do? How does it do it?

4.   Consider providing a concise summary of the innovation that conveys a clear understanding, to the extent known, of the nature, purpose, operation, and the physical, chemical, biological, or electrical characteristics of the innovation. Such a summary can be provided, when required, to sources of funds, such as sponsoring governmental agencies, investors, etc.

B.   Details

1.   What makes the innovation different from known prior solutions?

2.   How is the innovation better than known prior solutions?

3.   Which parts or activities of the innovation are new?

4.   Has any aspect of the innovation been used before, even if for a different purpose? How has that aspect's function been accomplished in the past?

5. What parts or activities form the most preferred (if there is one) implementation of the innovation?

6. What function does each part or activity contribute to the innovation?

7. How do the parts or activities interact to make the innovation work?

8. If possible, use labeled sketches to detail the innovation. Be sure all essential parts or activities are shown on the sketch, and try not to include extraneous details. Measurements are not required, unless they are essential to the innovation.

9. For each part or activity, indicate if the part or activity (or, e.g., its form, supplier, dimensions, interconnection, or materials, etc.) seems to be important to the innovation. In other words, if the part or activity were eliminated, changed, or sourced differently, would the remaining device or process still be the innovation, and would it still work for its intended purpose?

10. Which parts or activities arc old or not part of the innovation?

11. Identify why the parts or activities are arranged the way they are, and not some other way. How else could the same end result be accomplished?

C. *Actual Reduction to Practice*

1. Does the innovation work? What proves it?

2. Has the innovation been tested experimentally? What experimental data is available?

3. What must be done before the innovation can be implemented?

4. What implementations of the innovation have been made & tested?

5. What innovation performance data is available?

6.   What is the nature of any continuing work on the innovation?

D.   *Limitations*

1.   What are possible problems with the innovation?

2.   Under what conditions will the innovation not work?

3.   What (if any) are the critical ranges of size, weight, pressure, etc., for each of the parts of the innovation (e.g., "the lining must be rubber with a durometer of 40 or more")?

4.   How can those critical ranges be overcome?

5. Alternatives

Describe the expected course of development of the innovation, and possible operable variations of the innovation. For a *machine or device*, describe alternative structures for performing the significant functions of the machine or device. For a *compound or biological material*, describe operable substitutions, modifications, breadth of substituents, derivatives, salts, etc.

Do not limit these answers to any particular prototype, or to the best way the innovation should be built. Instead, use imagination. How else could the innovation work? What are less desirable ways of making the innovation work?

1.   In what ways can any of the innovation's parts be eliminated, combined, changed, or equivalent parts substituted?

2.   In what ways can the function(s) of any parts be eliminated, combined, or changed?

3.   What is a generic description for each part (e.g., "fastener" instead of "Machine Screw", or "plastic" instead of "polypropylene")?

4. What other features or technologies might add value to the innovation?

5. What can be changed to make the innovation work better?

6. For what else can the innovation be used?

6. Software Implementations

Innovations that are implemented via software sometimes can raise some unique concerns. A few of those potential concerns are explored in this section.

1. Is the innovation implemented via software? ☐ Yes ☐ No *(skip this section)*

2. If yes, what are the inputs, basic functions, and outputs of the software?

3. On what particular hardware, O/S, etc. does the software run?

4. Has the software been built? If so, where was the software developed? Using whose hardware? Using whose software development tools?

5. Who were the developers of the software, if different from the Innovators?

6. What portions of the software were derived from existing software? What is that existing software? What aspects of that existing software were modified?

7. What third party content is included in the software?

7. Potential Prior Art

Determining whether to develop an innovation and/or pursue a patent for it can depend on the results of a patentability, non-infringement, and/or clearance search.

To access patentability, we start by identifying the known potential prior art, i.e., those compositions, devices, and methods that existed (whether physically or merely described on paper, and whether patented or not) before the innovation was conceived.

1. Who would be likely to purchase or use the innovation?

2. In what publications (e.g., documents, articles, patents, catalogs, databases, web pages, etc.), would they likely search to find something that provides the innovation's significant function(s)?

3. To what extent have those sources been searched for the innovation?

4. What publications describe some of the innovation's significant function(s)?

5. What publication (including any of the Innovators' own) comes closest to describing the innovation?

6. What other publications might be relevant to the innovation?

7. What do you believe to be the most relevant known prior art to the innovation?

8. How was each major function of the innovation provided by the known prior art?

9. How is the innovation different from the known prior art?

10. How is the innovation similar the known prior art?

8. Novelty and Grace Periods

Generally, to be patentable, an innovation must be novel (new) at the time of the innovation from the perspective of a person having ordinary skill in the associated technical field and having access to all relevant published information ("prior art"). Yet novelty can be destroyed by improper disclosure.

Fortunately, a non-confidential disclosure of the details of the innovation (verbally, in writing, via video, in a live demonstration, on a website, etc.) can trigger, for those U.S. patent applications having an effective filing date before 16 March 2013, a one-year "grace" period within which the application must be filed to preserve the right to seek U.S. patent rights.

For those U.S. patent applications having an effective date of 16 March 2013 or later, this grace period is eliminated, such that disclosures (particularly by anyone other than the inventor) at any time before filing a patent application can forfeit patent rights in the U.S. and in most foreign countries.

1. Is anyone believed to have filed with a patent office a Disclosure Document, Provisional Patent Application, or Foreign Patent Application describing the innovation?

If so:

    a. Type of Filing:

    b. Date of Filing:

    c. Where filed:

    d. Patent office reference number:

2. Describe each disclosure of the innovation (including confidential/secret disclosures) with any dates provided meaning "at least as early as":

How Disclosed?	Secret?	When?	To Who?	Where?
Discussion/Conversation		~		
Lecture/Talk/Presentation		~		
Demonstration		~		
Publicly visible use		~		
Internet/web posting		~		
E-mail		~		

How Disclosed?	Secret?	When?	To Who?	Where?
Abstract		~		
Poster		~		
Paper		~		
Thesis/Dissertation shelved		~		
News story		~		
Multi-media		~		
Video		~		
Provision of Sample or Material		~		
Other		~		
Other		~		
Other		~		

Provide details and copy of any above-listed disclosure. If made *under a written confidentiality agreement*, provide a copy of agreement.

3. Who outside of the Innovators' company(ies) has received any new materials (e.g., samples, compounds, DNA, cell lines, vectors, catalysts, alloys, etc.) related to the innovation? Where? When?

4. How has the innovation changed since it was publicly disclosed?

5. Has the innovation been used commercially, sold, offered for sale, or consumer-tested?

6. If so, where and when?

9. Non-Obviousness

Even if a concept is novel, to be patentable, it must be sufficiently "inventive" (non-obvious).

Obviousness challenges generally attempt to show that a person having ordinary skill in the art, facing the same problem as solved by the innovation, would have, at the time of the innovation, modified or combined prior art references to solve that problem, and therefore would have arrived at the entirety of the claimed subject matter.

Yet it sometimes can be difficult to show obviousness in the face of certain facts, evidence of which are requested here.

1. What new structural feature(s), new function(s), or unpredictable result(s) or benefit(s) does the innovation provide?

2. What currently available evidence tends to show that:

    a. the innovation recognizes a problem not recognized by others?

    b. the innovation solves a long-felt but unresolved problem?

    c. the innovation resulted from a very prolonged period of research?

    d. the innovation succeeds where others have failed?

    e. experts have expressed skepticism of the innovation?

    f. others actively discouraged taking the path the innovation follows?

    g. competitors or others have praised the innovation?

    h. the innovation produces unexpected results or benefits?

    i. the innovation produces synergistic benefits?

    j. others nearly simultaneously discovered the innovation?

    k. others have tried and failed to design around the innovation?

    l. others have copied the innovation?

    m. others have taken a license to the innovation?

    n. others have rapidly adopted the innovation?

10. Commercial Potential

Even if a concept is patentable, it typically also must be sufficiently valuable to justify the effort and expense of patenting. Determining value ("valuating") can start with assessing potential commercial demand for implementations of the concept.

1. What commercial products, processes, or improvements could reasonably result from the innovation?

2. What are the advantages, compared to existing solutions, of the innovation in terms of cost savings, speed, efficacy, safety, etc.?

3. What technical impact is the innovation likely to have on its field (e.g., marginal improvement, significant change, revolutionary upheaval, creation of new field, etc.) and why?

4. What is the degree of technical development of the innovation (e.g., theoretical design, prototype, complete product/process, ready for commercial testing/marketing, etc.)?

5. What development milestones must be achieved before the innovation can be commercialized?

6. What companies are now marketing competing solutions, or performing serious research in this area? Include contact information for individuals who would be good contacts at those companies.

7. What commercial firms might be interested in the innovation?

8. What is the likely economic potential of the innovation if successfully commercialized, in terms of annual revenues to all sellers?

☐ <$10,000 ☐ $10K - $100K ☐ $100 - $1M ☐ $1M - $10M ☐ >$10M

9. Is it likely worthwhile to spend at least $15,000 to $20,000 to obtain a U.S. Patent that protects the innovation?

☐ Yes☐ No (Please indicate the reason(s) for either response)

10. Indicate the kind of follow-up recommended for the innovation:

    ☐ Licensing to others in conjunction with sponsored research funding.

    ☐ Licensing to others in return for royalties and payments only.

    ☐ Dedication to the public domain without seeking royalties or funding.

    ☐ Other (please describe):

11. Please list individuals with technical or economic knowledge of the field of the innovation who reasonably could be asked (under confidentiality agreement) to review, assess, or evaluate the technical or commercial potential of the innovation.

Name	Address	Phone

11. Third Party Rights

Before beginning the patenting process, it often can be very worthwhile to determine who might hold any rights to the innovation.

A. *Employers*

1. Is the innovation within the scope of each Innovator's employment?

2. Was the innovation developed using any facilities of that employer?

3. Has each Innovator agreed in writing to assign innovations to that employer?

4. Does that agreement apply to this innovation?

B. *Sponsors*

1. Did any third party (government agency, school, etc.) fund development of the innovation?

2. Might that party reasonably claim rights in the innovation?

3. If so, list all sources (federal, state, corporate, foundation, etc.) of funds supporting the conception and/or reduction to practice of the innovation. This list should include funds used to support any Innovator during the period of innovative work as well as to purchase supplies and services. Attach a copy of the relevant innovation sections of each grant or agreement.

Funding Source	Grant/Agreement #	Contact Person & Info

4. Of those federal funding sources identified above (if any), indicate the federal funding source(s) that provided the *primary* source of funds for the innovation. A grant, contract, or cooperative agreement is a primary source of funds if the innovation was conceived or reduced to practice in the performance of work sponsored by the federal funding agreement. If more than one federal funding source is listed, indicate the source considered to be the lead funding source.

Funding Source	Grant/Agreement #	Contact Person & Info

5. Identify any projects and/or other innovations related to this innovation.

6. If funded by an external sponsor, has the sponsor been notified of the innovation, either directly, such as via a progress report, or indirectly, such as via an application for additional funds (date, sponsor, method of disclosure)?

C. *Other Organizations*

1. Is any Innovator under any obligation to assign any rights in the innovation to others?

2.   What agreement potentially grants a right of any sort in the innovation to any company or to any other non-governmental party (material transfer agreements, commercially sponsored research agreements, consortia agreements, consulting agreements, confidentiality agreements, etc.). If none check here _____.

3.   During any Innovator's work on the innovation, was any Innovator employed by any entity that might have a right to the innovation? If yes, please explain.

4.   Did any Innovator use proprietary materials owned by another organization to make the innovation? (Examples of proprietary materials: confidential information; biological materials such as cell lines, transgenic animals, vectors, or genetic sequences; chemical compounds; and software or source code).

5.   Was the innovation developed in the course of a consulting agreement with someone else? If so, did any Innovator agree that any innovations belong to that consultant?

6.   Were any materials, equipment, or software used in conceiving or implementing the innovation provided under a Special Agreement, such as Material Transfer agreements, purchase agreements, sponsored research agreements, or the like used?

7.   If yes, please provide the following information for each item and attach a copy of the Agreement.

Source of Materials	Materials	Copy Attached?

8.   Was any equipment or facilities used in the development of the innovation that was funded by, or belongs to any government agency?

12. Corroboration

In the event that evidence is needed to prove conception of the innovation, have a copy of this section signed by each Innovator and have the completed Innovation Disclosure Form witnessed at soon as possible by at least two people who are not co-Innovators and who are qualified to understand its contents.

A.   *Innovators*

I believe the contents of this Form to be accurate and complete:

Innovator 1 Signature: _____

Printed Name: _____

Date: _____

Innovator 2 Signature: _____

Printed Name: _____

Date: _____

B.   *Witnesses*

I have read and understand the contents of this confidential Form (including all attachments):

Witness 1 Signature: _____

Printed Name: _____

Date: _____

Witness 2 Signature: _____

Printed Name: _____

Date: _____

About Mike's Team

For over a decade, the top-notch team at my firm, Michael Haynes PLC, has included many very bright and hard-working patent attorneys, agents, and paralegals.

My team is deeply experienced with evaluating, securing, exploiting, and challenging intellectual property rights covering a very wide and continually growing range of technologies, including:

- **Electrical**: telecommunications, networking, electronics, sensors, actuators, power, controllers, micro-processors, computer hardware

- **Software**: operating systems, industrial control systems, embedded controls, database management systems, applications, user interfaces

- **Mechanical**: medical devices, automotive, aerospace, construction, machinery, micro-electro-mechanical systems, tools, consumer products, sporting goods, toys, manufacturing processes

- **Business**: finance, economics, e-commerce, insurance, statistics

- **Optics & Physics**: lasers, photonics, electro-optics, magneto-optics, lenses, cameras, radiography, thermometry

- **Materials**: properties, uses, processing, alloys, coatings

- **Chemical**: chelates, catalysts, polymers, inorganics, nano-tech, processing, water treatment, environmental clean-up

- **Biotechnology**: biochips, medical devices, medical treatments, bioinformatics, bioremediation

Our substantial expertise has presented Michael Haynes PLC with the opportunity to attract, competently serve, and successfully retain a wide range of local, national, and international clients.

Among our past and current clients are:

- Several Fortune Global 500 multi-national corporations,

- Many well-established businesses, and

- A few amazing start-ups.

Similarly, we frequently serve investors by assessing, valuating, and enhancing intellectual assets and properties, innovation management processes, and emerging companies.

Likewise, we often team with law firms who rely on our deep IP expertise to augment their own services, empower their client's IP, and strengthen their relationship with that client.

Finally, as needed to serve our client's needs, we recruit, guide, and collaborate with additional highly-skilled professionals, such as:

- Attorneys - IP, Corporate, Tax, Litigation, etc.;

- Subject Matter Experts - Technical, Financial, Business, etc.;

- Foreign Legal Counsel; and

- Advanced Searchers.

Given our substantial technical, business, and legal backgrounds, it should be no surprise that we have quickly absorbed the concepts and details of our client's innovations, business directions, and legal needs, so that we could seriously empower their intellectual property.

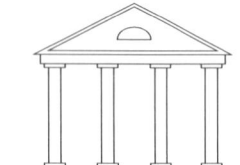

MICHAEL HAYNES

EMPOWERING INTELLECTUAL PROPERTY

®

About Mike

It's probably fair to say that Michael N. Haynes is very broadly experienced. Now in his 19th year in the intellectual property field, Mike has been degreed as a patent lawyer for over 16 years, a manager for over 22 years, and an engineer for nearly 30 years.

Mike started very young. He has been an entrepreneur for over 40 years, a computer programmer for over 35 years, and a systems architect and IT manager for at least 25 years.

Speaking of experience, as many companies eventually learn to their great dismay, some patent attorneys who prepare and prosecute patent applications have little to no experience with patent or trademark litigation. Yet Mike has deep and broad real-world experience and formal education in both patent and trademark litigation, including very heavy involvement in 12 patent litigations (8 U.S. and 4 foreign), along with lighter involvement in many more IP litigations.

Because of his solid patent litigation background, Mike knows and appreciates how patent law is developing. For example, above and beyond his formal legal education, Mike has read every Federal Circuit and Supreme Court patent decision issued within the past 10 years (roughly 2500 decisions). These are the courts that have the final say on U.S. patent law, and when they change directions, Mike Haynes knows it, and changes direction as needed, right away.

Mike also has extensive experience with agreements, licensing, and legal opinions. Mike has drafted and negotiated hundreds of employment, non-disclosure, assignment, and other agreements, including dozens of licensing agreements, some valued at 7 figures or higher. In his counseling practice, Mike has rendered numerous strategic, patentability, non-infringement, invalidity, and due diligence opinions.

Mike has integrated his vast experience into the preparation of over 950 patent applications, of which over 800 were U.S. patent applications. He also has prosecuted over 1450 patent applications, at least 1000 of which were U.S. patent applications. And his work has been fruitful. Over 1000 patents have issued based in some part on Mike's preparation and prosecution work, in over 45 countries, in a wide range of technologies.

And the bounty isn't limited to patents. Mike has filed over 125 U.S. trademark registration applications, and prosecuted an equal number. Currently, at least 70 registered trademarks are related to Mike's work.

Mike Haynes holds an MBA with course work in finance, marketing, strategy, accounting, information systems, human resources, economics, statistics, and management.

Mike also has deep and broad real-world experience in each of those areas, along with: product research, innovating, and product development; business development, marketing, and sales; capitalization, taxation, and accounting; manufacturing, operations, and administration; and finally, management information systems.

In addition, Mike has developed, produced, and/or marketed businesses based on legal services, software, plastic resins, specialized consumer products, rare coins, print media, food products, and more. He has created and run 3 profitable businesses on his own, and has a fourth currently incubating.

Mike gained his legal skills through assignments that have included:

- Michael Haynes PLC, Charlottesville, VA, Manager, 2002-Present

- LeClair Ryan, Charlottesville, VA, Officer, 2001-2002

- Kenyon & Kenyon, Washington, DC, Patent Associate, 1998-2001

- Howrey & Simon, Washington, DC, Patent Associate, 1996-1998

- U.S. District Court for New Hampshire, Concord, NH, Intern, 1995

- Pennie & Edmonds, New York, NY, Summer Associate, 1995

- William B. Ritchie, Concord, NH, Patent Intern, 1994-1995

Starting in 1994, during his initial year of law school, Mike learned to draft patent applications first-hand while working directly for a very bright, experienced, local patent attorney. Mike earned his patent registration number in 1995, and continued learning the details of patent drafting and prosecution from some of the best in the business while working for premier, world-renowned, patent and litigation firms.

Prior to embarking into the world of intellectual property, Mike spent over a decade gaining real-world technical experiences. For example, he spent 9 years serving The Dow Chemical Company in a variety of engineering and managerial roles. Also, Mike worked 2 years in technical roles in the electrical power generation industry starting in 1980. Moreover, Mike has assisted businesses in researching, assessing, and implementing computer technologies for well over 25 years.

Among patent attorneys, Mike has an unmatched formal education, including graduating in 1996 with a Juris Doctorate (JD) in the top 10% of his class at the Franklin Pierce Law Center, which continues to offer one of the highest-ranked intellectual property law programs in the country.

In addition to his law degree, Mike has earned a Master of Science in Electrical & Computer Engineering from The Johns Hopkins University, a Master of Business Administration from Central Michigan University, and a Bachelor of Science in Mechanical Engineering from Virginia Tech.

Since joining the legal profession, Mike has served many in the Fortune 1000, including such well known companies as AT&T, Siemens, Intel, Apple, Sony, Sun, Nokia, Samsung, Black & Decker, Procter & Gamble,

Tyson Foods, Boston Scientific, Wells Fargo, Lockheed Martin, Texaco, Tyco, Beckman, Monsanto, Mattel, Toyota, LucasArts, Daimler-Benz, Fisher-Price, and Huffy. His clients have also included many smaller businesses, start-ups, and even a major university.

To even better serve his clients, in 2002, Mike launched and continues to run his own law firm, Michael Haynes PLC. Mike and his entire team are deeply committed to providing peerless client service.

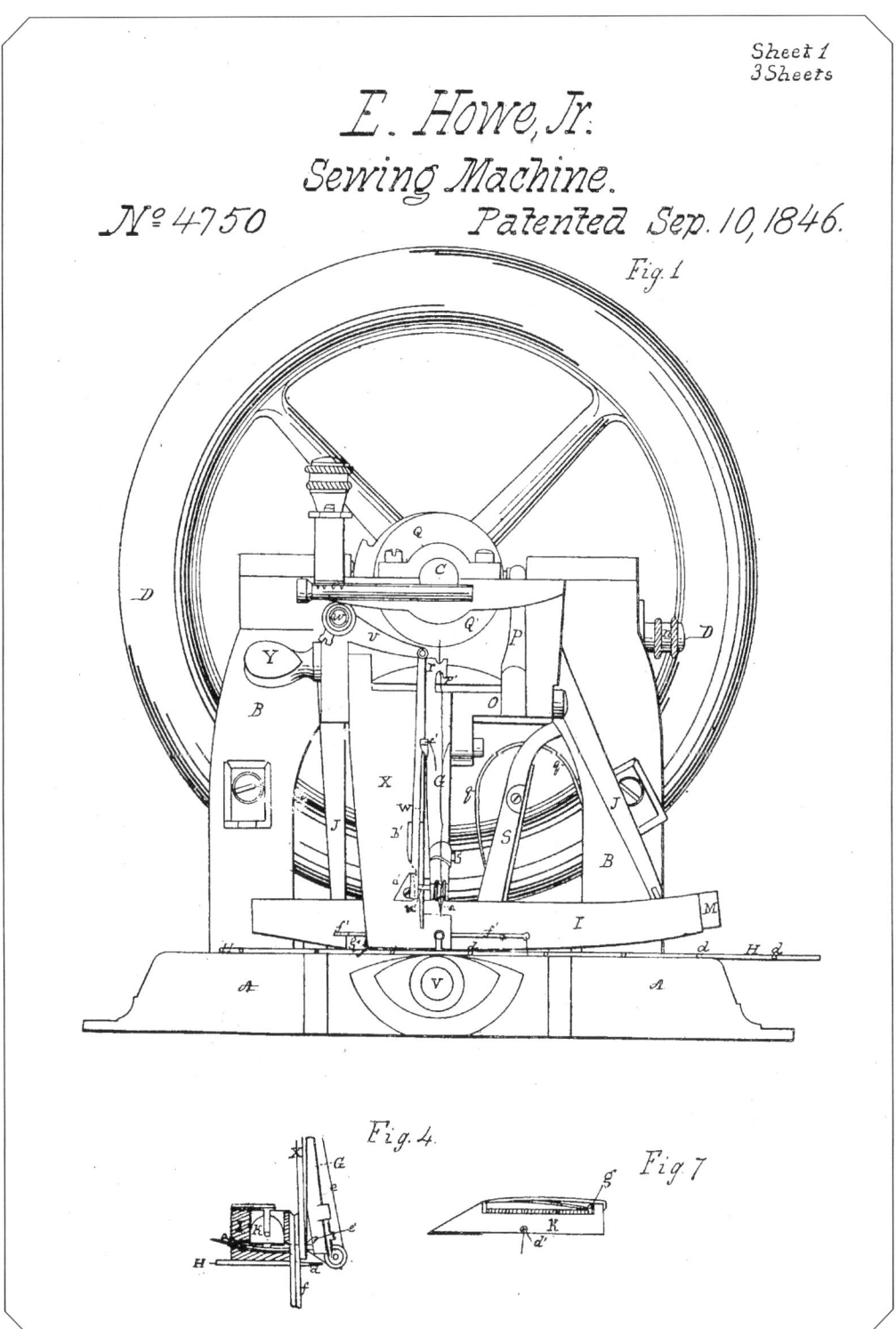

Sheet 1
3 Sheets

E. Howe, Jr.
Sewing Machine.
Nº 4750   Patented Sep. 10, 1846.

Fig. 1

Fig. 4

Fig. 7

W. S. BURROUGHS.
CALCULATING MACHINE.

No. 388,116. Patented Aug. 21, 1888.

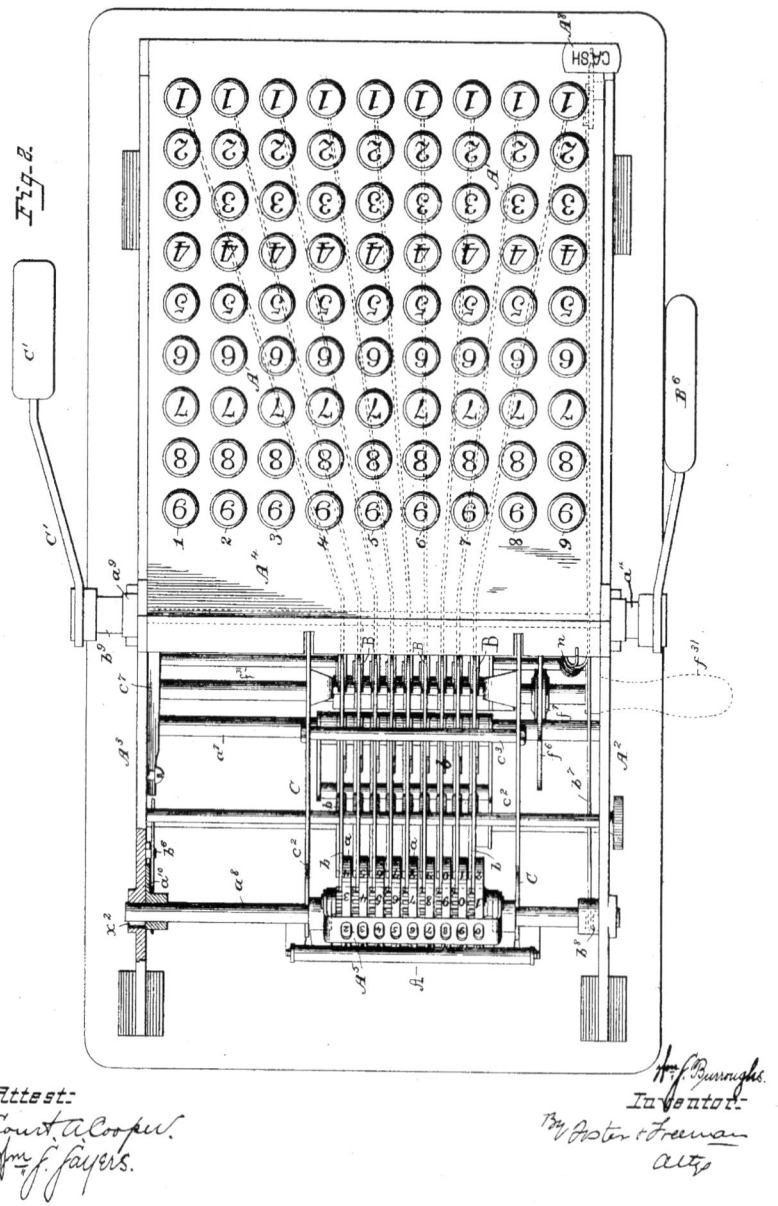

Fig. 2

ENDNOTES

1. *What is Strategy?*, Michael Porter, Harvard Business Review, November-December 1996, page 4 (emphasis added).

2. *Id.*, page 8 (emphasis added).

3. *How Competitive Forces Shape Strategy*, Michael Porter, Harvard Business Review, March-April 1979, page 145 (emphasis added).

4. *What is Strategy?*, Michael Porter, Harvard Business Review, November-December 1996, page 3.

5. *The Invisible Edge – Taking Your Strategy to the Next Level Using Intellectual Property*, Mark Blaxill and Ralph Eckardt, 2009, pages 10-11 (emphasis added).

6. *Id.*, page 44 (emphasis added).

7. *Id.*

8. *Id.*, page 10.

9. *Id.*, page 45.

10. *Id.*

11. *The Impact of Innovation and the Role of Intellectual Property Rights on U.S. Productivity, Competitiveness, Jobs, Wages, and Exports*, NDP Consulting, 2010

12. *Intellectual Property and the U.S. Economy: Industries in Focus*, Prepared by the Economic and Statistics Administration and the United States Patent and Trademark Office, March 2012.

13. *Ocean Tomo's Annual Study of Intangible Asset Market Value - 2010*, Press Release, 4 April 2011.

14. *The Economic Value Of Intellectual Property*, Robert J. Shapiro and Kevin A. Hassett, USA For Innovation, October 2005.

15. *Intellectual Property and the U.S. Economy: Industries in Focus*, Economic and Statistics Administration and the United States Patent and Trademark Office, March 2012.

16. *The Impact of Innovation and the Role of Intellectual Property Rights on U.S. Productivity, Competitiveness, Jobs, Wages, and Exports*, NDP Consulting, 2010.

17. *The Competitive Advantage of Nations*, Michael Porter, Harvard Business Review, March-April 1990, page 1.

18. *Re-engineering the Corporation: a Manifesto for Business Revolution*, Michael Hammer and James Champy, 1993.

19. Adapted from: *Measuring Innovation and Intangibles: A Business Perspective*, A. Stone, S. Rose, B. Lal, and S. Shipp, Institute for Defense Analysis, Science and Technology Policy Institute, Washington, D.C., 2008.

20. *Strategy and Structure: Chapters in the History of the American Industrial Enterprise*, Alfred D. Chandler, 1962, M.I.T. Press.

21. *What is Strategy?*, Michael Porter, Harvard Business Review, November-December 1996, page 1.

22. *360-Degree Feedback: Strategies, Tactics, and Techniques for Developing Leaders*, John E. Jones and William L. Bearley, Human Resource Development Press, 1996.

23. Adapted from: *The Customer-Centered Innovation Map*, Lance A. Bettencourt and Anthony W. Ulwick, Harvard Business Review, May 2008.

24. *Trends in Proprietary Information Loss: Survey Report.* ASIS International, sponsored by National Counterintelligence Executive & ASIS Foundation, August 2007.

25. *Intellectual Property Rights Violations: A Report on Threat to United States Interests at Home and Abroad.* National Intellectual Property Rights Coordination Center, November 2011.

26. *Id.*

27. *Patent Applications and the Performance of the U.S. Patent and Trademark Office*, Christopher A. Cotropia, Cecil D. Quillen, Jr., and Ogden H. Webster, Univesity of Richmond School of Law, February 26, 2013.

20. *Id.*

29. *The Timing of Patent Grants*, Dennis Crouch, Patently-O, January 11, 2013.

30. *Luck/Unluck of the Draw: An Empirical Study of Examiner Allowance Rates*, Shine Tu, Stanford Technology Law Review, Vol. 20, Forthcoming.

31. *The Future of Design in the United States*, David Gerk, The Future of Design Forum: Oxford, England, November 2-3, 2012

32. *Intellectual Property and the U.S. Economy: Industries in Focus*, Economic and Statistics Administration and the United States Patent and Trademark Office, March 2012.

33. *Jorda on Trade Secrets,* Professor Emeritus Karl Jorda, Franklin Pierce Law Center, 6 March 2008.

34. *2012 Patent Litigation Study: Litigation continues to rise amid growing awareness of patent value*, PricewaterhouseCoopers LLP, 2012.

35. *Id.*

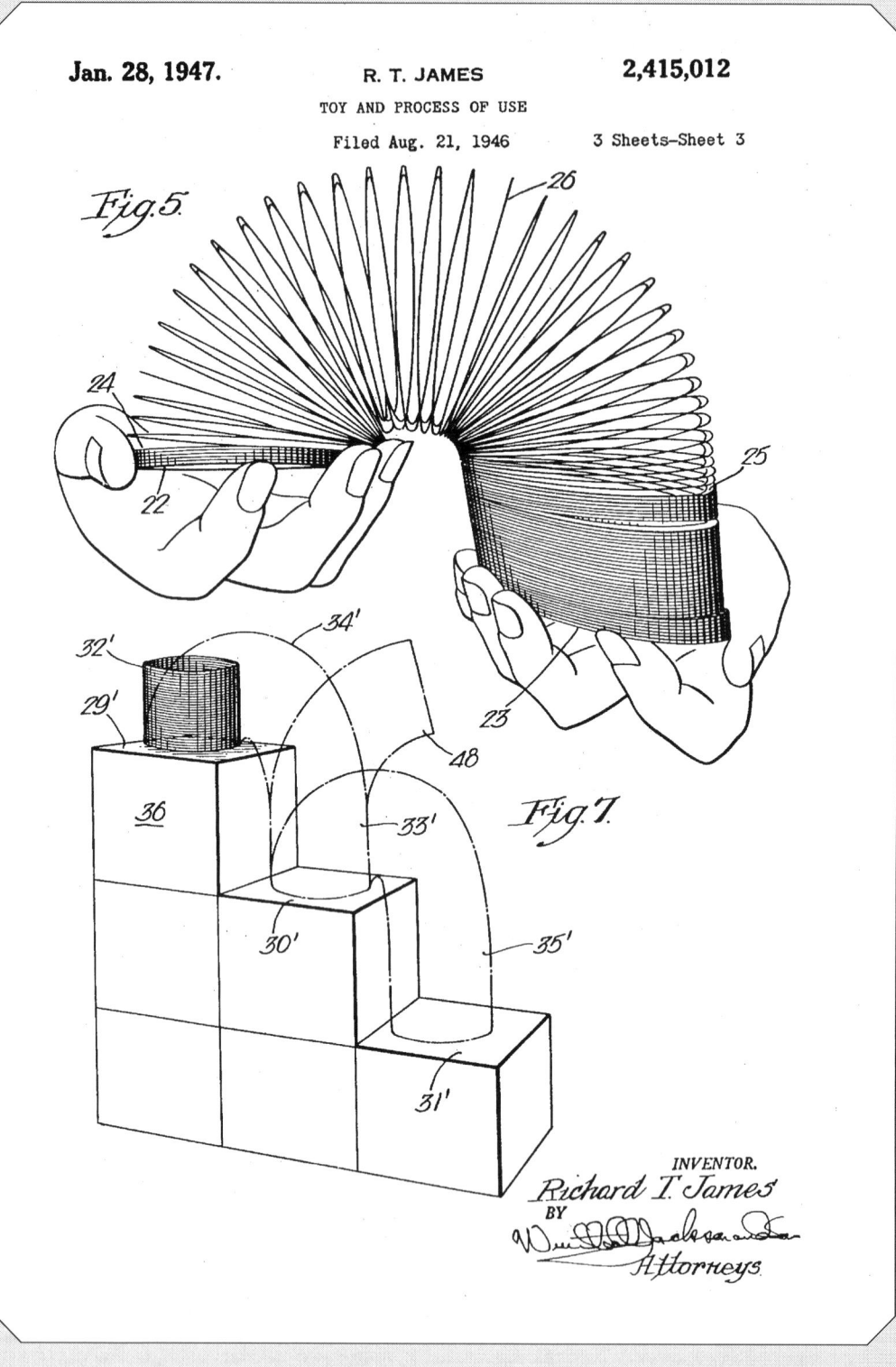

Fig.5.

Fig.7.

INVENTOR.

Richard T. James

BY

Attorneys

INDEX

Mapping Flowcharts

A

B

Performance A

Performance B

peripheral | core | peripheral

IPA1   IPA2

Scenario A1   Scenario A2

application cluster ⎫
                    ⎬ Externally
capability   ⎭ determined
groups

IP map   Ours IP

                Their IP

ML — claims to structure.
  "   "   tip/probe
              characteristics

16931470R00244